Holistic Aromatherapy
for Animals

A Comprehensive Guide to
Using Essential Oils and Hydrosols
with Dogs, Cats, Horses and other Animals

Kristen Leigh Bell

First published in 2002.

ISBN 978-1-899171-59-0

A CIP catalogue record for this title is available from the British Library.

Edited by Lynn Barton
Layout by Pam Bochel
Cover design by Damian Keenan

Printed and bound in the USA

6 7 8 9 10 11 12 13 12 11 10

Published by
Findhorn Press
305a The Park, Findhorn
Forres IV36 3TE
Scotland, UK
Tel +44-(0)1309-690582
Fax +44-(0)1309-690036
eMail info@findhornpress.com
www.findhornpress.com

TABLE OF CONTENTS

FOREWORD

By CJ Puotinen

For thousands of years, the world's dogs and cats ate a constantly changing variety of fresh, whole foods. Cats hunted rodents, birds and other small prey while dogs went after larger game and developed a more omnivorous diet. As they became part of the human family, these animals accepted anything tossed their way. Depending on where they lived, that might include fish, seafood, milk, eggs, poultry, raw meaty bones and anything left over from their human companions' food gathering, butchering, meal preparation and table scraps. Most of it was served raw, and all of it was produced locally and in season.

When pets needed medical attention, which wasn't often, they were treated with home remedies.

In the twentieth century, everything changed. Large-scale agriculture replaced small farms, chemicals became an industry, and storage methods such as freezing, refrigeration and canning made it possible to eat food grown thousands of miles away long after its harvest. Convenience foods replaced traditional cooking, and throughout Britain, the United States, Europe, Australia and other countries, pets began eating grain-based foods from cans, bags and boxes.

At the same time, home remedies gave way to modern Western medicine, and veterinarians rather than owners decided when and how pets would be treated. Annual vaccinations, antibiotics, steroids, anti-inflammatories and other pharmaceutical drugs became as routine as commercial pet food. Dogs, cats and other domestic animals received the best that modern medicine and scientific research had to offer.

One would expect this trend to improve health and lengthen life. Unfortunately, the opposite is true.

Statistics from veterinary organizations and dog and cat registries show that the life span of America's companion animals is now half what it was in the 1950s and 1960s. Forty years ago, the average Golden Retriever lived to be fifteen or sixteen, while house cats routinely lived into their twenties. Today the Golden Retriever's life expectancy is seven years. In fact, some American veterinarians consider a three-year-old Golden to be middle-aged. Similar statistics are given for Doberman Pinschers, German Shepherds, Great Danes, Rottweilers and other popular breeds, as well as for cats of every description. For centuries, dogs and cats were only reaching their peak at age seven to ten; now they're lucky to be alive.

And what kind of life is it? Our pets are plagued by allergies, skin and coat problems, tooth and gum infections, ear infections, urinary tract infections, parasites, chemical sensitivities, behavioral problems, arthritis, hip dysplasia and heart disease. Cancer, unheard of in animals a century ago, is now a leading cause of death.

The world's growing fascination with holistic pet care is a direct result of these problems.

The term "holistic" or "wholistic" refers to the entire patient. That's obvious, but what does it mean? We are so indoctrinated by Western medicine that it takes a moment to shift mental gears. If a dog has arthritis, hot spots (weeping eczema) and bad breath from infected gums, a conventional veterinarian will focus on each of these as though they are unrelated phenomena. Giving the dog anti-inflammatory drugs for his arthritis, steroids such as cortisone for the hot spots and antibiotics for his gum infection may suppress these symptoms and bring immediate relief. But suppressing symptoms doesn't make an illness go away. All three conditions are likely to recur and in fact grow worse, while the drugs used to treat them create new problems.

In contrast, a holistic veterinarian looks at the whole patient and explains to the owner how the arthritis, hot spots and gum infection are related. In addition to prescribing nutritional supplements, medicinal herbs or a homeopathic remedy, the holistic vet puts the dog on a fresh, raw, home-prepared diet. A few weeks later, his patient seems younger, happier and more lively. He sheds his coat and grows a gorgeous new one. His eyes are bright, he no longer limps, his breath smells sweet, he's calmer, and he stops stealing food from the kitchen counter.

Success stories like this are so common that holistic veterinarians take them for granted. The therapies that improve the health of dogs and cats are the same treatments that humans use, and they include everything from nutrition to chiropractic adjustments, massage, acupuncture, acupressure, homeopathy, flower essences, healing touch, herbs, magnets, sound, light, color, and more. Some of these are thousands of years old and others were developed in the twentieth century.

Aromatherapy, the healing use of essential oils and hydrosols, is a recent addition to holistic medicine's tool chest. No one is more qualified to write a guide to its use for pets than Kristen Leigh Bell. There are so many approaches to aromatherapy, so many products on the market, and so much conflicting advice in circulation that it's reassuring to have a guide who understands animals, has years of experience creating aromatherapy products for pets, and whose training includes a master's certification from the highly regarded Pacific Institute of Aromatherapy. Kristen's thesis topic was, appropriately, aromatherapy for pets.

Thanks to Kristen, I have learned where to obtain the highest quality essential oils and hydrosols and what to do with them. Pepper, my fourteen-year-old black cat, and Pumpkin, my husband's four-year-old red tabby, thrive on fresh, raw food and gentle hydrosols, which I add to their food, their drinking water and the air around them. Our Labrador Retriever, Samantha, is ten years old and runs circles around most dogs her age. Now that her friends have slowed down, her favorite playmate is a four- year-old Golden Retriever named Jack. Samantha's home-prepared diet and hydrosols have kept her in excellent health, free from the skin and the coat problems, gum disease and arthritis that plague most dogs her age. She has never used the systemic pesticides that are popular here in the United States for heartworm, flea, tick, mosquito and intestinal parasite prevention. Thanks in part to essential oils and hydrosols, Samantha's heartworm and parasite tests are always negative.

Aromatherapy is increasingly popular because it's versatile. It can be used alone or in combination with any other conventional, alternative, complementary or holistic treatments. Most importantly, it works.

But like other systems of medicine, aromatherapy can be dangerous if misused. This is why it's so important to buy the highest quality essential oils and hydrosols, to dilute them, and to use them appropriately. With Kristen Leigh Bell's excellent instructions, companion animals around the world can receive the best that aromatherapy has to offer without risk of injury.

For several years, I have enjoyed sharing Kristen Leigh Bell's insights with American pet lovers in seminars, books and magazine articles. It is now my great pleasure to introduce her to a worldwide audience in a book that will help veterinarians, groomers, breeders, trainers and all of us who love animals understand aromatherapy and appreciate its countless benefits.

CJ Puotinen
New York, 2002

Author of *The Encyclopedia of Natural Pet Care* and
Natural Remedies for Dogs and Cats

PREFACE

A Short History of Medicine:

"Doctor, I have an earache."

2000 B.C.: "Here, eat this root."
1000 B.C.: "That root is heathen. Say this prayer."
1850 A.D.: "That prayer is superstition. Drink this potion."
1940 A.D.: "That potion is snake oil. Swallow this pill."
1985 A.D.: "That pill is ineffective. Take this antibiotic."
2000 A.D.: "That antibiotic has side effects. Here, take this root!"

(Author unknown)

In our quest for good health, we have come full circle. At one time, our ancestors gathered medicinal plants and herbs to create home remedies for illness. Scientific advancement has led us to believe that we must now place our wellbeing into the hands of the medical establishment. There is a pill for ailments of every magnitude. As a result, we've lost touch with what is truly needed to maintain health and prevent illness and disease. What we've lost touch with is nature. We've only learned to repair ourselves when we are broken rather than to prevent ourselves from breaking in the first place.

This dilemma is not merely confined to the human population. As we began to domesticate various animals, we also started to subject them to the same process that we were putting ourselves through. We went to the doctor; we took our animals to the vet. We received antibiotics for minor illnesses, and so did our animals. We fed ourselves and families convenient processed food, and we did the same to our animals, feeding them dry kibble or an incomplete variation of what their natural diet should have been.

The consequences of our actions can be seen in the large percentage of humans and animals with illnesses ranging from allergies and digestive problems to cancer and immune disorders... and just about anything else you can imagine in between. One out of every four people in the United

States will develop cancer in their lifetime.[1] In the 52 years between 1935 and 1987, the number of Americans living with one or more chronic diseases doubled from 22% to 45%.[2] A 1932 study by Dr. Francis Pottenger proved that animals fed various cooked food diets in lieu of their natural raw food diets developed degenerative health conditions that were magnified in further generations.[3] While the specifics of this study have been questioned, it has nevertheless inspired both veterinarians and animal nutritionists to more carefully examine the benefits of natural raw food diets and supplementation instead of dry baked kibble.

Luckily, natural and holistic therapies are enjoying a rebirth in our present day and age. In July 2001, *Pet Age Magazine* reported that "More and more, owners are treating their pets as members of the family. With this in mind, it is not surprising that their interest in all-natural pet products is growing. 'Pet owners have become increasingly interested in maintaining the good health and wellbeing of their pets,' says Funda Alp, director of communications for the American Pet Products Manufacturers Association. 'They are using products containing natural ingredients and exploring alternative or nontraditional options in current health services.'"[4]

Modern medicine does not treat the entire animal or human. It directly addresses the problem, aiming to correct it as quickly as possible. In contrast, holistic therapies address the health of the entire organism by slowly and surely balancing the systems of the body, strengthening the immune system, and preventing disease.

In conventional veterinary practice, allergies may frequently be treated with antihistamines and steroids, with little emphasis given to assessing the cause of the allergies or managing the dog's diet or environment. A holistic veterinarian will ask, "Why is this animal exhibiting allergic reactions in the first place?" This vet will then begin to address various environmental influences in the animal's surroundings, such as diet, allergens, and cleaning and grooming supplies. Holistic treatments can take on many forms. Herbs, nutrition, homeopathy, acupuncture, flower essences, and energy healing are just a few of the various modalities that a holistic veterinarian might commonly use in their daily work.

It is only in recent years that aromatherapy, or essential oil therapy, has gained substantial acceptance; this is primarily due to French veterinarians who have begun using essential oils and hydrosols in their practices. Laypeople, of course, have been enjoying great success treating animals with the very same substances for many years; for it is not just the medical professionals who can safely and effectively administer these aromatic oils. Anyone enabled with quality essential oils or hydrosols and adequate knowledge can use a plant's most concentrated and energetic byproducts to improve the health of their animals, and treat and prevent various illnesses and common ailments.

The American Veterinary Medical Association has established guidelines on the use of complementary and alternative therapies with animals, but states no position on aromatherapy's results. "It's a very contentious issue and at this point, we don't have enough answers," says Craig Smith, a veterinarian and staff consultant for the Illinois-based organization. "We have a lot of anecdotal evidence, but not very much scientific evidence."[5] There exists very little specific scientific evidence in support of the vast majority of holistic modalities for humans, much less for animals. Aromatherapy is actually a science that has a much larger archive of supported scientific data than most other holistic care methods. However, most of these studies were originally published in French or German. Knowledge of these languages is required, because English translations are few and far between.

Aromatherapy was the first natural, holistic therapy I began using, and I rely on it as my primary form of healthcare to treat and balance all sorts of minor ailments and discomforts in the lives of my family and our pets. I have rarely needed to use any other sort of remedy to achieve the desired result. These powerful substances are the most fascinating, sensual and complex of all natural therapies – a combination that proves to be so enthralling it eventually develops into a grand passion for many.

It is my hope that you can also experience the enjoyment and empowerment that I have achieved through the use of aromatherapy with my pets. Through this book, it is my goal to provide you with the most reliable, safe and sound advice, recipes and resources to begin your aromatic journey.

Acknowledgements

I t is the culmination of many years of experiences and special people who have made it possible for me to bring this project to fruition.

First and foremost, this book is dedicated to my beloved Golden Retriever, Dublin, 3/5/87 – 9/5/00. It was only through Dublin's curiosity about my passion for essential oils that I began to even consider using aromatherapy with pets back in the early nineties. Many of my canine formulations were created specifically for Dublin's many health problems, which, of course, ceased to exist shortly after we began treatment with essential oils and a regimen of holistic care.

To all of my contributors, thank you for your willingness to share your knowledge, experiences and observations. Through your words, we will begin to make aromatherapy a respected form of holistic pet care.

This book would not have been possible without the help of CJ Puotinen, whose excellent advice and kind heart led to its growing from several pages of loose ideas into a completed manuscript.

Section 1

Aromatherapy Has Gone to the Dogs... and Cats... and Horses

Aromatherapy is not just for people anymore. In fact, it never was. Long before "aromatherapy" became prevalent in everyday life, essential oils were being tested on dogs and horses for their potential effects on humans. It began in 1912, when the father of modern aromatherapy, French chemist Rene Maurice Gattefossé, badly burned his hands while working and treated himself with Lavender essential oil. Gattefossé marveled at the speedy recovery of his burns and was inspired to immerse himself in an intense study of essential oils – the fragrant substances used by the perfume industry in France.[6]

Physiological similarities to humans made dogs and horses ideal test subjects for early essential oil research. Scientific study of the chemical constituents of essential oils in combination with case studies involving the application of essential oils for various veterinary treatments yielded positive results, leading Gattefossé to conclude that essential oils would have similar effects on human physiology. Thirty years later, Dr. Louis Sévelinge also used essential oils to treat animals, and the practice continued to become increasingly common amongst French veterinarians.[7] Today, it is no more unusual for a French veterinarian to prescribe a course of essential oils than it is for a French physician. Certain essential oil treatments are even covered by medical insurance in France.

And Exactly What Is Aromatherapy?

Now that you know how modern aromatherapy was born, you most certainly want to know exactly what it is. This is a topic often misunderstood. The mass commercialization of scented toiletries and bath products has led the general public to believe that anything that is scented is "aromatherapy". However, this type of mass-produced product has very little to do with what aromatherapy actually is, much less what it is capable of. "Aromatherapy" was the name given to the use of fragrant plant oils by Gattefossé, who also wrote the first book on the modality, *Gattefossé's Aromatherapy*. He defined aromatherapy as "A therapy or cure using aromas, aromatics and scents", noting that the most curative properties were found in plants.[8]

Today, aromatherapy is defined as the therapeutic use of pure, unadulterated essential oils, hydrosols, and other fragrant plant materials for holistic health treatments. You will see this basic definition in many variations, but the necessary elements of plant fragrance materials and wellbeing are always present.

In this book, when I refer to "aromatherapy", I am referring to the use of essential oils, absolutes and/or hydrosols. Essential oils, absolutes and hydrosols will be discussed in greater detail in Sections 2 and 3.

An essential oil is a volatile substance obtained from the leaves, flowers, roots, bark, seeds or fruit of a plant via steam distillation, carbon dioxide extraction, solvent extraction, or manual expression. Essential oils are non-oily, extremely concentrated and highly aromatic. They are usually highly diluted before use. Not all plants produce essential oil. In this book, I will often use the term "essential oil" to loosely encompass both essential oils and absolutes. (For an explanation of absolutes see Solvent Extraction, p. 24.)

A hydrosol is a water-based substance that is the byproduct of steam distillation of essential oils. Hydrosols contain water-soluble parts of the plant, and a very minute amount of certain essential oil components. They are extremely dilute, gentle and subtly aromatic. Not all essential oils produce a hydrosol, because not all essential oils are distilled with steam.

True or False Aromatherapy?

With the widespread availability of so many "aromatherapy" products on the market, it has become exceedingly difficult for the average person to understand what is and what is not true aromatherapy. A stroll through a pharmacy will reveal many products labeled as "aromatherapy"– everything from peach candles to grape lipstick, mango shampoo and coconut bath salts. And a pet store? You might see raspberry shampoo, banana coat conditioner and watermelon pet candles. While even an aromatherapy neophyte would be able to determine that these products are all synthetically fragranced, the average consumer could easily believe them to be natural because they are scented with something that sounds natural, such as fruit.

What the average consumer doesn't know is that natural fragrance materials do not exist for these scents, and many others. Fragrances such as these are synthetic chemical mixtures known in the toiletries and soap industry as "fragrance oils". These types of products are pseudo-natural, or false, aromatherapy products. In contrast, a true aromatherapy product is all natural, and contains only aromatic fragrance materials of direct botanical origin. However, even when real essential oils or hydrosols are used, there are still variations in quality that must be considered. These and many other aspects of essential oil and hydrosol quality and sourcing will be explored in detail in Section 2.

True aromatherapy is not limited to bath, body and grooming products, either. The term "holistic aromatherapy" refers to the use of therapeutic grade, pure essential oils or hydrosols in various formulations for a specific healing purpose, or as part of a daily aromatherapy regimen designed to influence the overall health of a human or animal. In this way, aromatherapy is used medicinally. This use of essential

Scents Commonly Perceived as "All Natural" Which Are Actually Laboratory-Synthesized Fragrances

Apple	Honeydew
Apricot	Kiwi
Banana	Lilac
Blackberry	Lily of the Valley
Blueberry	Mango
Cherry	Mulberry
Coconut	Papaya
Cranberry	Peach
Cucumber	Pear
Currant	Persimmon
Dewberry	Pineapple
Fig	Plumeria
Frangipani	Pomegranate
Freesia	Raspberry
Grape	Strawberry
Guava	Sweet Pea
Honeysuckle	Watermelon
Hyacinth	Wisteria

oils and hydrosols has very little to do with how they smell, but rather, whether or not they are needed by the body.

While it is always pleasant to use a blend that is aesthetically fragrant, this is not the primary goal of holistic aromatherapy. Many essential oils and hydrosols that are highly therapeutic, indispensable tools of the trade actually have rather curious scents. A perfect example of this is Everlasting, *Helichrysum italicum*, also known as Immortelle. The curative and restorative properties of this essential oil are so phenomenal that in recent years, eager aromatherapists have quickly bought out entire distillations. But to be truthful? This precious oil smells distinctly awful. Luckily, only a few drops are ever needed in blends, and the smell can be masked with other oils of therapeutic value. Many times we need to put aside the aesthetic aspects of essential oils and hydrosols and instead consider the valuable physiological effects of their use.

Personal Aromatic Inspirations

I am frequently asked how I became involved with aromatherapy – in particular, with aromatherapy for pets. When people ask what I do for a living, and I reply "I'm an aromatherapist", I get my share of pauses and strange looks. For some reason, saying you're an aromatherapist is more amusing than saying "I'm an herbalist" or "I'm an acupuncturist". This most likely has something to do with the new-age stigma unfortunately attached to aromatherapy. I was once consulting a client on the phone and suggested that she try aromatherapy to calm her dog, which was terrified of thunderstorms. She paused and remarked, "I don't really think it would be safe to light candles in a circle on the floor around my dog" (a certain percentage of the population believes that aromatherapy is merely the use of scented candles and potpourri). I have also heard aromatherapy referred to in a variety of derogatory ways, including "new-age fluff" and "silly smell pseudo-science". Actually, aromatherapy has had very little to do with new-age trends and beliefs – and everything to do with the tangible physical properties of the oils themselves.

I have suffered from various allergic reactions my entire life. A gnat bite on my eyelid swelled an eye shut for two days. A wasp sting caused my hand to grow to twice its normal size. My mother's perfume induced fits of sneezing and congestion. Certain bubble baths, lotions and laundry detergents caused tiny red bumps, or hives, on my arms, legs and torso. As a result, I avoided all perfumes and tried to use unscented products.

In 1992, I had neither heard of aromatherapy, nor was I terribly interested in holistic health. I was a 22-year-old graduate student, and my main priorities were writing my thesis and working various jobs to pay my expenses and tuition. I first heard of essential oils from a friend who was an esthetician working with Aveda products. Aveda was one of the first beauty companies in the United States to incorporate aromatherapy into their products. One sniff, and I was hooked. They smelled like nothing that I had ever experienced. The reason? The natural essential oils and hydrosols Aveda used as fragrance. Not only was I enamored by these scents, they did not aggravate my allergies.

Through Aveda, I was inspired to learn more about aromatherapy. I began buying books, learning as much as I could. I truly believe that it is the aromatic aspect of aromatherapy which captured my interest and has held it captive for so many years. The more I learned, the more essential oils I wanted. The more essential oils and hydrosols I had, the more potions I blended, and eventually I began making my own bath and body products using all natural ingredients. I used my stove for product formulation more than I did for cooking! With my new passion came the dissolution of my allergic tendencies. I could now enjoy natural, fragrant perfumes and body products without sniffing, sneezing and wheezing.

I also learned of the many special properties which essential oils and hydrosols have. Depending on the material, some of these properties include: antibacterial, antifungal, antipruritic (stops itching), regenerative, anti-inflammatory, tonic and balancing, and calming or stimulating the central nervous system (these, and many other aspects of essential oils and hydrosols will be discussed in Sections 2 and 3). With my newfound knowledge, aromatherapy became a form of medicine for me. When I had a cold, I used essential oils to lessen the symptoms. A headache was easily thwarted with Peppermint and Eucalyptus. A cut or burn healed quickly with an application of essential oils and hydrosols. My home also smelled wonderful, and essential oils became my natural perfume – that everyone wanted to know the brand name of.

And the Dog?

Aromatherapy had such a positive influence on me that I saw no reason why it couldn't do the same for my Golden Retriever, Dublin. He too was plagued by allergies, which manifested themselves as skin and ear infections. He also seemed to have a strong interest in the essential oils and hydrosols I was using, and would lay at my feet, or nudge my leg when I was working. When I let him smell certain things, he would show keen interest, often trying to lick or eat the bottle. He showed a similar interest in the herbs that I grew, frequently ingesting parts of the plants. However, I could find no available information about the use of essential oils or hydrosols with pets. At that time, no aromatherapy books mentioned any veterinary applications. I was on my own, with only my own knowledge, common sense and high quality aromatics to guide me.

The perfect opportunity to introduce Dublin to aromatherapy arose when he had surgery to remove a softball-sized fatty tumor from underneath his front leg. He was left with a large, angry incision that had two drains. The vet was concerned that Dublin would have difficulty healing because his immune system was compromised from earlier illnesses. She gave me an antibiotic ointment to apply to the incision every day.

I never opened the tube of ointment. Instead, I formulated a blend of essential oils that had antibacterial, antipruritic and regenerative properties. I carefully chose oils that I knew to be gentle, but still strong enough to achieve the desired effect. I would continue to formulate blends along this principle well into the future.

Since dogs have such sensitive noses, I knew that I had to dilute the blend more than I would for a human, so I decided to try $1/4$ of the human dilution and see how it worked. Several books I owned recommended that blends for children be 25% of the adult dose. Because of this, I felt 25% was a very safe dilution to start with. I diluted the essential oils in hazelnut oil – a lightweight, quickly absorbed, fatty base oil. I applied the blend twice daily and in ten days, returned to the vet to have the drains and stitches removed. The vet was amazed at how well it had healed and was impressed with her decision to prescribe the antibiotic ointment. Then I showed her the unopened ointment and told her what I had used in its place. After a brief pause, she laughed. She had never heard of essential oils and actually recommended that I not use them in the future!

I wasn't so easily influenced, because I had seen the results that essential oils had – first in myself and then, my dog. I began to formulate other blends for Dublin. An ear cleanser, a spray for itchy skin, a massage oil for sore joints and a shampoo to soothe his flaky skin. The results were extraordinary. Within a year of beginning aromatherapy treatments with Dublin, he was practically a new dog. His allergies had subsided, and his ears were pink and healthy. His coat had re-grown and was healthy and luxurious. Our trips to the vet were now few and far between.

I attribute his recovery to multiple variables. Aromatherapy helped to soothe his ailments and clear them up, making him more comfortable. Continued use of the essential oils prevented recurrences and allowed me to make another major change in Dublin's life – his diet. I began to feed him a high quality, human grade dog food instead of the store-bought food he was used to. Also, our home was no longer cleaned and deodorized with harsh and synthetic cleaning products or detergents. Essential oils and natural soaps were used to clean dishes, floors, surfaces and laundry.

My success with Dublin inspired me to try out my blends on other dogs, and family and friends happily volunteered their pets (after a very thorough explanation, of course). I began creating customized blends for various dogs, and was successfully treating many common canine ailments with essential oils. Calming hyperactivity, repelling fleas and ticks, clearing up allergies and skin infections and reducing fatigue in sick and older dogs were just a few of the many ailments that essential oils helped. Many of my original recipes for these blends can be found in Section 4, which covers aromatherapy for dogs.

Not long after I began using essential oils and hydrosols with Dublin, a book on veterinary aromatherapy was published. It was 1994, and the book was *Veterinary Aromatherapy*, by French naturopath Nelly Grosjean. I immediately bought the book and quickly finished it. I was pleased to see that others were also using aromatherapy with pets, but I was surprised at some of the essential oils that Grosjean recommended for animals, as well as the strength of some of the recipes. They were much stronger than I would consider using on myself, or on my dog. My very low dilutions (using as little essential oil as possible to achieve an effect) had proven to be very successful for me. Despite Grosjean's groundbreaking work, I decided to continue with what I had already established to work for many of the dogs I blended oils for. I continued to refer to *Veterinary Aromatherapy* as a guide, but I used it mainly as an inspiration from which to continue my own work and my safety-conscious blending style.

The Aromatic Lifestyle

As a result of my introduction to aromatherapy, I had gone from never using a holistic remedy to becoming totally immersed in one and I had immersed Dublin, my canine companion as well. I used essential oils and hydrosols every day, in as many ways as I possibly could. Through aromatherapy courses and conferences, I began to meet other people who found that aromatherapy had the same effect on them – an aromatic awakening. I could only attribute this to the sense of smell, a human's most powerful and primitive sense. Something very powerful had gripped me. Through using essential oils for my dog and myself, I had become empowered. I had regained my ability to care for my own health. Instead of relying on medical doctors, veterinarians or Western medications, aromatherapy had given me the ability to treat a vast number of everyday ailments in a completely natural, effective manner.

Aromatherapy puts the healing power of nature into the hands of the people – exactly where it was before the scientific revolution and technological advancement made natural remedies practically extinct. Modern pharmaceuticals may have started with natural substances, but they were quickly synthesized into mass produced, powerful medications, such as antibiotics. By making it possible for us to treat ourselves naturally, essential oils and hydrosols help us to be more in tune with our bodies. Caring for our bodies holistically has many great advantages.

Similarly, the use of aromatherapy with pets puts the ability to bestow and maintain good health into the hands of us, the pet owners, potentially minimizing the need for acute and crisis care. Essential oils and hydrosols are well suited to treat a variety of common animal ailments. However, responsible pet ownership is a must. There is a fine line between caring for your pet holistically with aromatherapy and knowing when it is time to consult a vet for intervention. Aromatherapy is not meant to take the place of conventional veterinary treatment. If an animal needs to be taken to the vet for more immediate care, then this should definitely be done.

I am consulted by many pet owners who are aware of the ailments their pets are suffering from because of a veterinarian's diagnosis. In these cases, pet owners will frequently wish to turn to holistic remedies to treat their animals instead of using the vet-recommended medications. These pet owners choose the holistic remedy with the knowledge that if it does not work or if the pet's condition is too severe for it to be cleared up quickly, they may need to go back to the vet and receive the medications originally recommended. On the other hand, if a pet owner contacts me and says, "I think my dog has condition A, but I'm not sure", I will always

Animal Ailments That Can Be Treated With Aromatherapy

Allergies	Incisions
Anxiety	Infected ears
Bad breath	Insect bites
Burns	Insomnia
Congestion	Itchy skin
Cracked paw pads	Joint and muscle pain
Cuts and scrapes	Loss of appetite
Deodorizing	Mange
Dirty ears	Motion sickness
Fatigue	Skin infections
Fear	Skin irritations, hot spots
Flatulence	Teeth cleaning
Flea and tick infestations	Teething pain
General detoxification	Unhealthy fur and coat
Grief	Weak immune system
Hyperactivity	
Hypersexuality	

recommend that the animal be taken to the vet and examined for a diagnosis.

Once you begin caring for your animal holistically, you will most definitely find that the frequency of trips to the vet diminishes. This is because you are addressing the various needs of your pet's health as an entire organism. Nutrition, exercise, environment, grooming and limiting exposure to synthetic chemicals can go far towards greatly improving the health of your pet. There are many holistic modalities that can be used alongside aromatherapy with your pets. This book primarily focuses on aromatherapy, but a recommended reading list can be found in Appendix 3.

How Do Essential Oils and Hydrosols Work with Animals?

Since essential oils and hydrosols are often seen solely as aromatic substances, it can be rather difficult to understand how they are capable of having such an impact on an animal's health. The mystery is easily unlocked when one realizes that while these materials' most dominant feature is their scent, their true capabilities are determined by their chemical composition. Plants produce essential oils for a variety of reasons: attracting insects, repelling pests and fighting off bacteria, molds, viruses and fungi. A variety of tasks yield a a vast spectrum of chemical compounds within any given essential oil. The complexity of essential oils also makes it possible to use them in a variety of ways.

Aromatherapy works with animals on multiple levels: physically, emotionally, conditionally, evolutionarily and spiritually. These same levels also apply to our own use of natural aromatics, but overall the experience is somewhat different due to our documented emotional responses to various smells. Scents are processed by the human brain's limbic system, which is the most primitive part of the brain. The limbic system also has a strong connection to our recall of certain emotions. This is why the scent of lavender might bring back strong memories of one's grandmother, or the smell of baking bread might instantly unearth memories of a certain time or place. We have no scientific proof that animals have this type of reaction to aromatics, nor do we even know if their brains process smells in this manner. Last year, I read a short blurb in *Pets Part of the Family* magazine about a dog who was calmed when his owner spritzed Victoria's Secret Green Apple perfume, a synthetic fragrance, on him. One of my clients recently sent me an e-mail about how her greyhound was calmed down during thunderstorms when she burned synthetic gingerbread-scented candles. These two examples are not aromatherapy because they are dealing with synthetic fragrances. Nevertheless, they are very interesting examples which show that even synthetic fragrance oils with no therapeutic value (i.e. potential to affect an animal's physiology based on the chemical makeup) can have a marked effect on an animal's emotional state. I personally believe that this points towards these dogs having an emotional reaction, or preference, to these synthetic fragrances that in turn were soothing to them psychologically.

While it is obvious that animals prefer certain scents and that they are even capable of appearing to like certain aromas, we cannot link this to any center of emotional activity in their brains. While my Golden Retriever, Dublin, liked to smell essential oils, flowers and herbs and would eat herbs and even try to roll in them, there was no way that I could link this to any type of stored emotional memory that he may have had. Although the lack of complex emotional factors simplifies aromatherapy use with animals to some extent, other factors such as which oils or hydrosols to use, their quality and purity, and how they should be diluted, influence the safety and effectiveness of using aromatherapy with animals. An animal's size and keen sense of smell must be taken into account. For instance, dogs have a much larger nasal cavity than humans do, and as a result their sense of smell is 50–100 times stronger than ours. While humans have approximately 45–50 million scent receptors, dogs average 200 million!

While most aromatherapy treatments are the result of humans selecting certain essential oils or hydrosols and blending them for use with animals, there is a method which allows animals to be more actively involved in the choice of the essential oils given. Kinesiology aromatherapy is a method by which aromatic substances are chosen based on a subject's preference for them. In simplest terms, if subjects like the scent of an oil or hydrosol, then they must have a physiological or emotional need for it. With humans, this preferential method of choosing is quite obvious. Some kinesiologists refer not only to a human's smell preference, but also to the body's reaction to a certain aroma. They may determine whether your smell preference is learned or actual with a resistance test by having you hold your arm out to the side, while they push down on it, as you smell the oil. It is a bit trickier with animals, however. They can't exactly tell you, "I love the Rose, but the Peppermint isn't doing it for me". You can closely monitor their reactions to see whether or not they want the oil. Animals will show varying reactions when presented with essential oils or hydrosols. The greatest level of interest is when they lick the bottle or your hand when a drop of the oil is applied. In other instances, they may sniff intently, but not lick. They may sniff and turn their head away. Or they may sniff and walk away. Or they may not even need to directly sniff, but know instinctively to move away. These reactions are the basis for whether or not an animal needs an oil. The kinesiologist will then take her observations and establish an essential oil/hydrosol protocol for the animal, testing at varying periods of time to establish whether or not the animal still needs the oil/hydrosol. Most kinesiology aromatherapists administer small amounts of oils/hydrosols via ingestion.

Regardless of the application or method used, aromatherapy primarily works on the physical level with animals. Essential oils and hydrosols will have varying effects on an animal's physiology. The antibacterial, antiviral, antifungal, anti-inflammatory, antipruritic, sedative, stimulating and regenerative properties of certain essential oils and hydrosols have been proven and discussed time and time again in scientific studies and aromatherapy books during the last 20 years. These plant materials exhibit similar physiological effects on all mammals. To achieve a desired physiological effect, they can be applied in several ways. They can be applied topically, diffused and inhaled, or taken internally. Hydrosols are most often applied topically and taken internally, since their water-base does not make them suitable for diffusion. This also clears up one of the most common questions I hear – "If my dog has an ear infection, then how will smelling something help him?" If only aromatherapy weren't so misunderstood...

Topical application is the most common method, and has the greatest benefit because the substances are applied directly to the area in which they are needed. If an animal suffers from an ear infection, a diluted blend of essential oils and other botanicals would be applied to the inside of the ear. If the animal has an insect bite or a skin irritation, they could be applied directly to the affected area. Once applied, aromatics chosen for their various physiological effects can begin to get to work. Topical application includes essential oils or hydrosols in formulations that are applied with the fingers or an instrument, via massage, via spritzers and sprays and even in shampoos or conditioners. Common mediums for essential oils or hydrosols used topically are ointment and balms, liquid vegetable or nut oils, water-based sprays and various grooming preparations.

The act of topically applying a formulation to an animal leads directly to the level of affect – the emotional level. Most companion animals react to human touch in a positive manner, especially dogs and cats. Horses and small mammals, such as tame rabbits or rodents, appear to enjoy it as well, although to not so great an extent. Topical application has an increased benefit because not only are essential oils (or hydrosols) being applied directly to the area where they are needed, they are being applied to the animal by a human. If this is a human with whom the animal has a bond (or the potential to form a bond), then that bond can be strengthened through touch, massage and the application of natural essential oils in appropriate dilutions. One of the most profound examples of this would be the use of calming, sedative essential oils with fearful, skittish animals that have been abused. I have found aromatherapy to have a profound effect on dogs in shelters and on recently adopted or "rescued" dogs.

Nigel's story

I have experienced the transformation that aromatherapy can have on an abused, abandoned animal first-hand through humane society volunteer work and also with my own rescue dog. Nigel, a Standard Poodle and Labrador Retriever cross, was adopted from the Humane Society of Lackawanna County, Pennsylvania. He had been at the shelter for four months, having been previously rescued from an abandoned house with many other animals, including his littermates. He was extremely thin, skittish and timid and would urinate submissively with human contact. Nigel would cower when spoken to and run and hide underneath the table if voices were raised. I knew that earning his trust would be a lengthy process, not to mention a challenging one. Most challenging was trying to teach Nigel some of our basic household rules without sounding harsh or raising my voice. Quietly saying the word "No" had no effect on Nigel, while saying it loudly frightened him and sent him running for cover or submissively urinating on the floor. Aromatherapy massage was instrumental in Nigel becoming a more trusting, less fearful dog and eventually a loving, affectionate and well-behaved member of our household.

I formulated a calming blend of essential oils, diluted in a base of sunflower oil (recipes for canine calming blends can be found starting in Section 4). I introduced Nigel to his essential oil blend one afternoon when he was calmly resting on the floor next to me, basking in a spot of sunlight. He was most content and not showing any signs of fearfulness or mistrust, so I brought the bottle out and put a drop on my hand, letting him smell it. He sat up, cocked his ears forward, and began to intently sniff my hand, and then to lick it. There was no doubt that he was interested in the blend that had been created for him. With his obvious approval, I sat on the floor next to him and began to massage several drops of the diluted blend into the fur of his neck, chest and belly, while talking to him in a soothing and quiet voice. He didn't flinch, move away or begin to urinate submissively. After a few minutes he was resting peacefully, belly-up.

I continued my massage sessions with Nigel, gradually forging a strong bond with him and earning his trust. He began to become more affectionate with me, more open to receiving affection and less timid when spoken to or corrected. He also very quickly reacted to the calming essential oils even when they were applied to him without a lengthy massage. Nigel had learned to associate the smell of the essential oils with the experience of being massaged, soothed and reassured. In this manner, he was conditioned to associate their use with a positive experience. This form of training is very effective due to the pairing of human touch, which dogs essentially crave, and essential oils, which appeal to both their curiosity and their powerful sense of smell. While the essential oils had an obvious physiological effect on Nigel via the inhalation of evaporating aromatic molecules with sedative effects on the central nervous system, this effect might not have been so pronounced without the oils being applied via massage and with conditioning in mind.

Essential oils function also on a conditioning level in the same way that Pavlov's dog was taught to exhibit a certain physiological response at the sound of a bell. Pavlov initially rang the bell and the dog showed no measured response. Pavlov then would ring the bell and feed the dog. Pavlov found that the dog eventually learned to associate the sound of the bell with food, and would begin salivating whenever the bell tone was heard. This is called classical, or Pavlovian conditioning. It is based on the experiments of Ivan Pavlov, a Russian physiologist.[9] In this manner, the structure of Pavlovian conditioning can influence dogs (and other animals) to exhibit certain behavioral and physiological responses to the scent of essential oils and hydrosols, just as they would to the sound of a bell or other stimulus. Imagine if Pavlov had associated the sound of the ringing bell with something negative, such as being yelled at, crated or hit. The dog would have been conditioned to react to the bell tone in a very different way if this had been the case! For this reason, it is of utmost importance to associate all applications of essential oils with as positive an experience as possible. This is not always possible, but in the use of essential oils and hydrosols for common animal ailments (as opposed to acute or crisis care situations) a certain amount of control can be practiced in order to obtain the most positive results. The scent of aromatherapy oils or hydrosols is a powerful stimulus that can eventually trigger a learned reaction, be it behavioral or physiological.

Here are some examples of situations where essential oils should not be initially introduced (Please note that while sometimes it is impossible to adhere to behavioral conditioning, it does help in yielding the most positive results):

■ If an animal is fearful of loud noises, fireworks, storms or crowds, avoid introducing essential oils at these times.

■ If an animal is fearful of other animals, people or things, introduce essential oils only when the animal is alone, and in a calm state of mind.

■ If an animal is in great pain or in shock, wait until the animal has stabilized and is calmer before treating it with essential oils.

■ If an animal dislikes grooming, use aromatherapy to calm the animal and introduce various grooming procedures to it gradually – for instance, with ear cleaning, nail, hoof and paw care, teeth cleaning, brushing and coat care, and other maintenance.

These are just some examples of situations to avoid; there are many more that a pet or animal owner will encounter. Temper your strong desire to use essential oils or hydrosols immediately with a sense of timing for the best results, now and in the future.

As with humans, some animals may dislike certain essential oils or may exhibit certain strong reactions if you use too much or too strong of a dilution with them. Some of these reactions are mild precursors to the more serious symptoms of toxicity that will be explored in depth for each animal in that animal's specific section of this book. Here are some distinctive signs to watch for which indicate a strong distaste or reaction to too much of a good thing:

- Pacing
- Panting
- Drooling, excessive salivation
- Turning head away from treatment
- Showing no interest in sniffing treatment when offered
- Whining, whimpering
- Frantically rolling or rubbing against the ground or objects
- Sneezing, snorting and respiratory distress

The use of aromatherapy with animals is a complex, varied and highly individualized process that works on multiple levels. So far, we have examined three of the major levels: physical, emotional and conditional.

These are the most obvious and easiest to understand. The evolutionary and spiritual manner in which essential oils work is decidedly more abstract.

The evolutionary level obviously refers to the theory of evolution and supposes that one of the reasons that essential oils, hydrosols and botanical ingredients work so well with mammals is because the plant metabolism was a precursor to our own existence. Certain chemical substances produced by the secondary metabolism of plants are also produced by insects, animals and humans as the building blocks of higher metabolic processes. According to the theory of evolution, all life on earth descended from single-celled organisms which gradually evolved into multi-celled organisms, algae, fungi, plants, coniferous trees, insects, animals and eventually, human beings. Kurt Schnaubelt, author of *Medical Aromatherapy*, refers to this as the "biosynthetic blueprint… (that) existed long before there were humans. It is an archaic chemical pathway that has, like the other biochemical pathways of life, existed since the dawn of life on planet earth."[10]

The biosynthetic pathway that Schnaubelt refers to is the mevalogenic pathway. This theory asserts that monoterpenes, the dominant group of chemical constituents comprising the majority of essential oils are the basis for more advanced molecules. Beginning with monoterpenes, a series of more complex molecules are metabolized. Squalen (found in plants), steroids and heart glucosides (both found in humans and animals) are all triterpenes that are products of the same biosynthetic pathway that produces monoterpenes.[11] Simply, plants, insects and mammals are chemically interrelated. The use of natural, plant-based therapies with animals and humans represents a homogenous way of using substances which are already the stepping stones of our metabolisms to aid in balancing and healing the body, be it animal or human. It is on this basis that synthesized fragrances have little, if any therapeutic value. They lack the very basis, structure and complex patterning that essential oils and hydrosols so closely share with us, and, of course, with our animals.

The theory of biosynthetic pathways can be used to explain and support a variety of other holistic modalities, but the basis is always quite simple. Organic matches up with organic. Fresh, raw food is healthier than processed, chemically treated food. When synthetic or non-organic elements are introduced into a natural system such as that of a plant, animal or human, an imbalance occurs. This can all be very simply summed up in three words: *natural is better*. Essential oils and hydrosols have an affinity for mammalian systems due to our shared biosynthetic pathways. They work efficiently and effectively, with few, if any side effects. This biochemical compatibility is for the most part unheard of in modern medicine.

Evolutionarily, we – meaning animals, humans, and plants – are intertwined, and essential oils are highly expressive of that union.

The last level on which essential oils work with animals is the most abstract and controversial of all – the spiritual level. In this case, "spiritual" refers to that which cannot be seen, explained or scientifically proven. This is certainly the most new-age aspect of aromatherapy, but undeniably, one that many people are innately drawn to – not only by their own intense personal belief in the spiritual, or the unseen, but by hundreds of years of folklore, which colorfully embellishes and lends credence to the unseen power of plant substances. This is often described as the vibrational energy, or vibration, of a plant substance.

Essential oils are often referred to as the very soul, or essence, of a plant. They are byproducts of the secondary plant metabolism, meaning that they are not essential to the life of the plant. This does not mean that they are not highly instrumental, however. Why do essential oils exist, and how did they come about? It is believed that monoterpenes, the chemical component present in almost 100% of all plant essential oils, began to be produced by plants as a form of communication. This is most interesting, due to the fact that many insects use terpenes to communicate with one another, often to attract other insects for reproduction, to mark their territories or to lure prey. The first group of plants to produce essential oil was the conifers, or needle trees. The large amount of essential oil produced by these trees is highly evident when one walks through a forest or purchases a Christmas tree at the holidays. The aroma of pine needles fills the air for days. Why did the conifers begin to produce essential oils? It was critical to their survival. Essential oils are the key defenses that a plant has to protect itself from invaders, such as bacteria, molds, viruses, fungi and pests, such as insects and animals. Some plants even repel humans with their scent. Other plants use essential oils to attract insects and animals, for the purpose of reproduction. The vast number of tasks which essential oils perform for plants is what makes their existence so fundamentally important.[12] Without them, plants would have no evolutionary advantage – or, as many believe, no soul.

Does a plant have a soul? Do essential oils possess distinct vibrational energies? Why do essential oils have such a profound impact on new users? Maybe it is how they smell, or maybe it is something far greater than that. For many, essential oils are seen as energetic, powerful substances capable of influencing, changing or balancing the vibrational energy and aura of animals and humans for the purpose of holistic healing. It is believed that blocked energy, or even "holes in the aura", are solely responsible for the entire spectrum of physical and psychological illness and suffering.

This may sound far-fetched, but it has a basis that is not only well documented, but also the cornerstone of many religions. What is *chi*, or *prana* or *kundalini*? It is the life force, or universal energy. Buddhists, Hindus and yogis all refer to these powerful universal energy systems which must be kept open and in balance for optimal health and, in turn, for spiritual enlightenment. Acupuncture and acupressure seek to unblock the flow of *chi* through various meridians of the body with fine needles and firm touch. Reiki unblocks these energy meridians and restores the balanced flow of *chi* through the body, without an animal or person even needing to be touched by the practitioner. The *asanas* of yoga unlock *samskaras* in the body, balance *prana* and awaken the *kundalini* through continuous movement and breathing to restore balance and good health.

Both humans and animals possess these energy systems and can be influenced by vibrational healing. Ironically, at the time I am writing this book, flower essence therapies are more commonly used in holistic veterinary practice than essential oils, which have a tangible, proven scientific basis. The sheer number of vets who are using energy therapies with animals is astounding. I recently visited www.ahvma.org, the official website of the American Holistic Veterinary Medical Association. The site lists names and contact information for holistic vets along with the modalities that they use in their practices. Flower essences, Reiki, crystals and gemstone essences were practiced by more than half of the approximately 400 vets listed (Chinese herbs, nutrition, chiropractics and acupuncture or acupressure being found in most every listing). Fewer than ten of the listings offered aromatherapy or essential oil therapy, and aromatherapy is not even listed as an accepted modality. I am in no way questioning the use of generally accepted remedies such as flower and gemstone essences, crystals or Reiki. However, I am definitely wondering why aromatherapy is practiced in such a limited fashion – in spite of its great potential to treat humans and animals at both the physical and the energetic levels.

French naturopath and aromatherapist Nelly Grosjean refers to essential oils as "small showers of energy". Patricia Davis, author of *Subtle Aromatherapy*, has devoted an entire book to exploring and unlocking the mysteries of the subtle, or vibrational, nature and uses of essential oils. Davis refers to subtle aromatherapy as "the use of oils to affect the subtle body, the psyche and, indeed, the soul. In doing so, the user draws on the subtle, energetic and vibrational qualities of essential oils, rather than their physical properties."[13] In this manner, essential oils can be used in a way no different than a holistic practitioner or vet would use certain flower or gemstone essences, crystals or other forms of vibrational treatment. Indeed, the use of vibrational aromatherapy with animals is a topic so rich and varied that an entire book could be devoted to it. For the purposes of this book, however, we will explore the wonders of this mysterious branch of aromatherapy in conjunction with the more common uses of aromatherapy, the spiritual, or vibrational, aspect of a certain essential oil or hydrosol being mentioned in various recipes and case studies, if applicable.

Still doubtful? Then consider the wonders of Kirlian or AuraVision™ photography. These methods of photography capture the energy field, or aura, of a subject – be it a plant, animal or human. The Kirlian method involves the application of very low volt energy to a subject to measure its magnetic field. Kirlian photographs show marked changes in the coronas, or energy fields, of subjects, depending on thoughts, moods, health and various alternative treatments.

A similar type of photography, which is often marketed as Kirlian photography but in actuality is quite different, is AuraVision™. This method involves attaching a sensor that reads changes in skin temperature and skin moisture to the subject's finger. The readings are translated on the film into varying shapes and colors around the subject's head. Before and after readings will show different colors and patterns in the energy field, due to how the subject is affected by the treatment being given. Numerous examples involving the use of essential oils with AuraVision™ photography exist.

Although this type of photography is not considered to be true Kirlian photography, it is nevertheless a very interesting vehicle through which to capture the energetic effects of essential oils on a physical body. Vibrational aromatherapist Ixchel Susan Leigh and artist Sharon Starr Walker photograph subjects before and after they have been exposed to essential oils.[14] The intense color changes in the captured aura surrounding the subject are phenomenal. I have never seen an AuraVision™ photograph done of an animal before and after essential oil exposure, nor do I know if any exist. The thought of what the process would reveal is definitely very exciting.

With a basic knowledge of the history of aromatherapy and its uses with animals in place, we can now move forward to contemplate the most important aspect of using essential oils and hydrosols with animals – the quality and purity of the substances themselves.

There is no point in using aromatherapy with animals if the tools you are using are inferior. Not only will you get poor results, but you may also cause harm to the animal you are trying to care for.

Section 2

The Tools of the Trade and the Perilous Quest for Purity and Quality

(Essential Oils, Absolutes, Hydrosols and Other Botanical Ingredients...)

Beware. You are now going to consider one of the most hotly debated topics of modern aromatherapy – purity. A quick flip through *Gattefossé's Aromatherapy*, the first aromatherapy book, written in the first half of the twentieth century by aromatherapy pioneer Rene Maurice Gattéfosse, will tell you next to nothing about essential oil purity, adulteration and testing. If you are wondering why, the answer is quite simple. Back when aromatherapy was born, plants were not grown for use in the production of essential oil with synthetic fertilizers or dangerous pesticides. Most plants used were "wildcrafted," a term now given to essential oil derived from a plant growing wild in nature. Also, essential oils and fragrance materials were extracted primarily for use by the perfume industry, and thus the demand for such materials was very low in comparison to what it is today. As demand increased with the growth of the perfume industry, so did adulteration. Distillers began to cut essential oils with cheaper oils, and with the advent of scientific technology, even to cut them with nature-identical chemicals of no therapeutic value.

The number one enemy of the extraction and production of quality aromatic fragrance materials is supply versus demand. With the growing popularity of aromatherapy and the use of essential oils by the commercial toiletries industry, the demand for essential oils has grown at an exorbitant rate, far overshadowing the rapid growth of the French perfume industry in the 1930s. What this means is that the vast majority of commercially available essential oils have been tampered with in some way or another. This practice, unfortunately, negates the therapeutic capabilities of the oil and also destroys much of the powerful life force which pure essential oils possess.

The aromatherapy trend has experienced expansive growth resulting in distillers increasing their yields in the most unethical of ways. Luckily, a small percentage of pure, high quality essential oils do exist from reputable suppliers and distillers. These oils are often referred to as genuine, authentic, therapeutic-grade, aromatherapy-grade or wildcrafted and/or organic. The key is finding these suppliers, which can often prove to be a daunting task. You are in luck, however, because this book includes a list of tried and true, trusted, reputable suppliers so that much of the guesswork can be avoided.

So Exactly What is an Aromatherapy-Grade Essential Oil?

Oils that are produced specifically for the aromatherapy industry are typically made with the same care and attention that goes into a fine bottle of wine. Artisan distillers produce these premium quality essential oils from plants available in the wild or grown organically specifically for the distillation. Often, the distillers are small family-owned businesses, who take great pride in their work. They are paid top dollar for their product, and the therapeutic value and purity of their oils is unparalleled. Many of the oils end up being used in medical aromatherapy applications where oils are ingested. When oils are administered internally, quality could not be more important.

Essential oils produced for holistic and medical aromatherapy uses are carefully monitored through all aspects of the process – from the growth of the plants to the distillation process itself. Distillation is treated scientifically, with utmost care being given to the temperature and timing of the procedure to ensure a complete oil is extracted from the plant material, which in turn yields the greatest therapeutic value.

The majority of precious chemotypes used exclusively in aromatherapy are grown by artisan distillers. Some of these valuable chemotypes include Hyssop decumbens; Thyme linalol, thujanol or geraniol; Rosemary verbenon and Basil linalol. Wondering what a chemotype is? A chemotype is a variation of a plant species that is a result of growing conditions. It's amazing to think that where a plant grew, how much sunlight and water it received and the altitude at which it grew could have such a radical effect on the essential oil content of the plant, but it does.

Thyme is an herb that yields a variety of chemotypes when grown in different areas. All of the thyme chemotypes are the same species, *Thymus vulgaris*, but radical differences can be found in the essential oil produced by plants from different growing conditions. Thyme grown at sea level in hot, sunny conditions yields your typical *Thymus vulgaris*, a hot essential oil characterized by high amounts of phenol, a strong antibacterial, medicinal and very irritating essential oil component. In contrast, Thyme grown at higher altitudes with less sunlight, less oxygen and more water yields a much softer essential oil, characterized by various chemical components and almost none of the harsh phenols! These various thymes are labeled as "linalol", "thujanol" or "geraniol" based on the dominant constituent that composes their chemical makeup. Chemotypes are valuable for achieving powerful effects with certain essential oils that typically would be too harsh to use. For this reason, you will see many chemotypes listed in the recipes featured in this book. They are wonderful, highly therapeutic variations of essential oils. These chemotypes and the other essential oils recommended throughout this book will be discussed in detail in Section 3.

Food-Grade and Industrial-Grade Oils

Most of the essential oil produced in the world is "food-grade or industrial-grade", meaning that its intended use is for food, flavoring, pharmaceuticals, cigarettes, cleaning supplies and chemicals. Most Peppermint oil produced ends up in menthol cigarettes. Same for most of the Clove oil produced in the world. Citrus oils are typically employed in cleaning supplies and Anise oil finds its way into candies, baking flavorings and cough syrups. Oil produced for uses such as these is distilled for quantity, not quality. In the United States food-grade or industrial-grade oils are added to items based on strict guidelines established by the Food and Drug Administration (FDA) and the Research Institute for Fragrance Materials (RIFM). In contrast, food-grade, industrial-grade or aromatherapy-grade oils used in aromatherapy applications have no definite established guidelines for safety, which leads us to a mantra which you must commit to memory: *100% natural does not mean 100% safe.*

Some Essential Oils Should Be Avoided

There is a common misconception that all natural ingredients are always safe, always gentle and never cause reactions. In reality, this couldn't be further from the truth. Many natural substances are highly toxic and irritating despite being of botanical origin. Certain plants throughout history have been used to end pregnancies (pennyroyal), to end lives (hemlock), to awaken higher states of consciousness (marijuana, psylocybin mushrooms, opium), to revitalize (cocaine, once found in Coca Cola™), and some plants can be a real pain when rubbed up against (rue, poison ivy, poison oak). Some plants are safe in small doses and fatal in others, as in the case of digitalis, a drug prepared from the seeds of the foxglove plant, which in minute amounts is used as a cardiac stimulant. In larger amounts, it is deadly.

Essential oils, due to their highly concentrated nature, are especially prone to misuse. Wormwood essential oil, *Artemesia absinthum*, which is high in neurotoxic ketones, is a key ingredient in the once popular French alcoholic aperitif, Absinthe. It is suggested that Vincent Van Gogh may have cut off his ear under the influence of the drink. Contemporary references can be found in movies such as 2001's *Moulin Rouge*, where characters all were mesmerized by the "green fairy" after imbibing the chartreuse-green liquid. Absinthe is now banned in many countries, and where it is available, it contains a minute amount of wormwood in comparison to what it once contained. I repeat – "100% *natural does not mean 100% safe*"!

Certain essential oils which are commercially available should be avoided altogether in pet care and in my opinion, most human aromatherapy uses as well. While the vast majority of aromatherapy books will discourage the use of these essential oils, there is no doubt a curious newcomer who unknowingly purchases these oils for their own use would suffer a range of mild to serious consequences.

Essential Oils That I Recommend Avoiding With Animals	
Anise	Juniper (use
Birch	j.berry only)
Bitter Almond	Mugwort
Boldo	Mustard
Calamus	Oregano
Camphor	Pennyroyal
Cassia	Red or White
Chenopodium	Thyme
Clove Leaf and	Rue
Bud	Santalina
Crested	Sassafras
Lavender	Savory
Garlic	Tansy
Goosefoot	Terebinth
Horseradish	Thuja
Hyssop (use	Wintergreen
decumbens	Wormwood
variety only)	Yarrow

When we are using aromatherapy with animals, we must adopt a "less is more" stance, as well as one of common sense. In other words, there is absolutely no point in using a harsh, irritating, toxic or sensitizing essential oil when a gentler option exists. I frequently see flea-repelling products for both cats and dogs which contain Pennyroyal essential oil. This oil is very high in ketones, a chemical constituent that is both neurotoxic and nephrotoxic (toxic to the kidneys). In addition, it is a known abortifacient. While it is a wonderful flea repellent, the risks associated with its use are simply not worth it. Especially not when a blend of other safe and well-tolerated oils would be equally effective.

It is crucial to stress that essential oils are highly concentrated substances, and large amounts of plant matter are required to produce even a small amount. It is estimated that the yield of essential oil from different plant materials is between 0.005% and 10% of the plant. This small percentage of actual yields varies from plant to plant, but here are some estimates:

- 50 lbs. (22.7 kg) of eucalyptus produces 1 lb. (450g) of Eucalyptus essential oil.
- 150 lbs. (68 kg) of lavender produces 1 lb. (450g) of Lavender essential oil.
- 500 lbs. (226.8 kg) of sage produces 1 lb. (450g) of Sage essential oil.
- 2,000 lbs. (907.2 kg) of rose petals produces 1 lb. (450g) of Rose essential oil.

(Marcel Lavabre, *Aromatherapy Workbook* [15])

As previously discussed in Section 1, an essential oil is a volatile substance obtained from the leaves, flowers, roots, bark, seeds or fruit of a plant via steam distillation, carbon dioxide extraction, solvent extraction or manual expression. Essential oils are non-oily, extremely concentrated and highly aromatic. They are usually highly diluted before use. Not all plants produce essential oil. In this book, I will often use the term "essential oil" to loosely encompass both essential oils and absolutes.

A hydrosol is a water-based substance that is the byproduct of steam distillation of essential oils. Hydrosols contain water-soluble parts of the plant, and a very minute amount of certain essential oil components. They are extremely dilute, gentle and subtly aromatic. Not all essential oils produce a hydrosol, because not all essential oils are distilled with steam.

Since the use of high quality, pure and unadulterated essential oils and hydrosols is of the utmost importance with animals, I have spared no details in this section, as many aromatherapy books do. In contrast, in-depth information is provided, for it is only through knowledge that you will be able to make the best decisions for the animals in your care.

How Aromatic Materials Are Extracted from Plant Material

Aromatics are extracted from plant material in a variety of ways. Essential oil can be produced in various parts of the plant, from the flowers, leaves and stems, the fruit, berries, bark, seeds or roots.

■ **Steam Distillation:** This is the most commonly used method of essential oil extraction, which also typically produces the greatest yield. Historians date the first known instance of steam distillation of plant oils back to Dioscorides in the first century A.D. With steam distillation, plant matter is placed into a large cylindrical vat on top of a mesh screen. The bottom of the vat is filled with water that is brought to boiling. As steam rises through the plant matter, the plant's essential oil is released from storage and carried to the top of the still with the steam, where it condenses. A special lid equipped with a cooling coil delivers the essential oil to another vat, where the distilled water separates naturally from the essential oil. Essential oils and water do not mix. Whereas essential oils are lipophilic (fat loving), water is hydrophilic. These polar opposites repel each other, allowing the water to be easily removed from the condensate. The water left over from the steam distillation of essential oils is known as the "hydrosol", and is widely used in aromatherapy applications. While essential oils are concentrated, lipophilic and highly aromatic, hydrosols are dilute, gentle, hydrophilic and subtly aromatic. They are well suited for use with cats and other small animals because of this. Hydrosols will be explored in depth later in this section.

■ **Solvent Extraction:** This method of extraction is reserved for delicate plants and flowers that cannot be extracted in any other way. Sometimes it is also used to result in a higher yield with certain flowering plants, such as roses. With solvent extraction, the plant matter is immersed in a solvent, such as acetone. The lipophilic nature of the essential oil in the plant is such that it is dissolved into solvents, but repels water, or hydrophilic substances. Plant matter is kept in the solvent for varying amounts of time, until the greatest amount of essential oil has been leeched from the petals. The solvent is then evaporated, leaving behind a thick, creamy substance called the "concrete", which contains essential oils and plant waxes. Next, the concrete is treated with alcohol and filtered, removing the plant waxes and residual solvents. The alcohol is then evaporated, and the resulting liquid is called the "absolute". Solvent extraction is widely used for jasmine, rose, neroli, tuberose and other precious fragrance materials such as broom, osmanthus, tobacco, oakmoss and carnation. Absolutes are most commonly used in perfumery and cosmetics. Some controversy exists over the actual amount of solvent left in a completed absolute. Technological advancement and the use of less toxic solvents have much alleviated this worry in recent years, however.

- **Expression:** This simple method is used for citrus fruits such as orange, lemon, lime, mandarin, tangerine, bergamot and grapefruit. It is the only way for the pockets of essential oil in the fruit rind to be released. No heat is used, and the fruit rinds are placed under pressure, which causes the essential oil to squeeze out of the rinds. Most fruits do not produce essential oil in their rind or skin. This is essentially why the only fruits you will find essential oils available for are citrus fruits.

- **Enfleurage:** This is the oldest method of obtaining essential oil from a plant. Plant matter – usually flower petals – are placed on sheets of glass coated with a thin layer of lard. Daily, the petals are removed and replaced with new ones until the lard has absorbed the scent of the flower petals. Once again, this method relies on the lipophilic qualities of the essential oils in the petals. When put in contact with a fatty substance, the oils are drawn into, or attracted to, that substance. The aromatic lard can then be used in creams or balms. It can also be treated with a solvent to dissolve the lard and yield the concrete, and thus, an absolute. This fascinating method of extraction is well detailed in the book, *Perfume: A Story of a Murderer* by Patrick Süskind. This murder mystery vividly portrays enfleurage and the perfume industry in France. While it is not for those who are easily made queasy, it is a recommended read![16]

- **Carbon Dioxide Extraction:** This relatively new method involves the extraction of essential oil from plant material with carbon dioxide gas. The procedure, which takes place at room temperature and under tremendous amounts of pressure, must be conducted within heavy, stainless steel equipment, which is considerably more expensive than traditional steam distillation stills. Due to the absence of heat, water and solvent, carbon dioxide extraction yields a final result that is as close as you can possibly get to the plant's actual aromatic substances. Very few distillers are using this method due to cost prohibitions, but the extracts produced by this method are of the highest quality, unmarred by adulteration and, of course, quite costly. Some oils commonly extracted with this method are German Chamomile, Sea Buckthorn, Vanilla, Calendula and Rosehips.

- **Florasol Extraction** (also known as phytols): This is the newest method of essential oil extraction, and it involves the use of a low-temperature tetrafluoroethane gas, which is fully removed at the end of the process. This method was devised in the U.K. and is being used there to produce "florasols" of superior quality. The advantage? The resulting extracts are more concentrated than essential oils from steam distillation or carbon dioxide extraction – so less is needed in blends and formulations.

Methods of Essential Oil Adulteration

Understanding the ways in which essential oils are made impure or adulterated helps us to realize the importance of using pure oils. Here are several examples that show you different ways in which oils are tampered with and how you can avoid the use of such oils.

- **Citrus Oils and Pesticides.** Citrus oils are extracted from the rind of the fruit via expression. In this method, the fruit rinds are mechanically pressed and the oils run out, resulting in essential oil. While this all sounds clean and simple, it isn't. In the United States citrus groves are routinely sprayed with all types of toxic pesticides. When the fruit rinds are expressed, guess where the pesticides go? Right into the essential oil yield. Most citrus oils are ultimately used in cleaning supplies, but many are purchased and sold by essential oil suppliers for aromatherapy and toiletry use. What this means is that most citrus oils contain varying amounts of unknown, potentially toxic and irritating pesticides. There are a few things that you can do to avoid this. The easiest way to avoid the pesticides is to purchase only organic citrus oils. Organically grown plants are not treated with pesticides or synthetic fertilizers. If you cannot find an organic version of the oil, try to purchase citrus oils distilled in a country other than the United States The incidence of pesticide use is much higher in the United States than it is in other countries. Your safest option is to opt for organic only citrus oils.

- **Base Oil Dilution.** Some unethical companies will purchase essential oils and then dilute them into fatty base oils to yield more oil. This is typically done with high cost oils such as Rose, Jasmine and Neroli, but I have seen it done even with Lavender, Peppermint and Rosemary. The practice of dilution is only unethical if it is not indicated on the bottle. Aromatherapist Suzanne Catty describes her experience with this practice in her book, *Hydrosols: The Next Aromatherapy*.[17]

When a well-known natural body care company opened its first store in Toronto, I visited this beautiful boutique with a colleague. We explored the store, sniffing merrily away until we came to the essential oils. There were testers, so, of course, a drop instantly went on the hand, and... lo and behold, it contained carrier oil, a vegetable oil used to dilute essential oil. When we asked the salesperson about this, we were told that these were the purest oils available, and no, they were not diluted in any way. Even when we pointed out that although they certainly were good quality, they were actually 'oily' or greasy to the touch, and not completely volatile, as true essential oils should be, the salesperson referred to the label copy, which said they were pure and did not mention any dilution. Unconvinced, we asked the salesperson to make a call, just to check. Four phone calls later she finally found someone who could tell her that, indeed, these oils were diluted, in fractionated coconut oil, to be precise, and that they were at 30% concentration. That was in 1996. Since then the labeling has changed, and all this company's essential oils now state very clearly that they are diluted in coconut oil.

Catty goes on to query the reader, "If a reputable 'natural health' company can do this, what is being done by companies that have no interest in the bigger picture but just want to make a profit using the most effective marketing tag?" A very pressing question, indeed. The easiest way to test for base oil dilution in your oils is to place a drop of the oil on a white sheet of paper. If an oily stain is left behind, then in most cases the oil is cut with base oil. This test works best for oils that are clear and watery in appearance before dilution. The other sure test is the one that Catty used. Essential oils are not oily or greasy to the touch unless diluted in a base, or carrier, oil. If the oil straight out of a bottle labeled as 100% pure essential oil is greasy, then you can bet that it is cut with base oil.

■ **Dilution With Synthetic Fragrance Oils.** This method of adulteration involves taking natural essential oils and adding, or cutting them with, synthetic fragrance oils of the same scent. This practice is most common with pricey floral absolutes, such as Rose, Gardenia, Jasmine and Neroli. Synthetic fragrance oils have no therapeutic value and can cause skin irritations. In addition, they typically have a cloying, sweet smell that will be immediately noticeable to a trained nose and most likely produce a quick headache. For the untrained nose, this practice often goes undetected.

■ **Dilution With Less Costly Essential Oils.** In this method of adulteration, a more costly and precious essential oil will be diluted with a less expensive oil with similar scent qualities. The essential oil most commonly diluted in this manner is Rose essential oil, often referred to as Rose Otto. Since you can estimate that one rose flower produces only a single drop of essential oil, it is easy to imagine how many roses it takes to produce any notable quantity of the oil, and how expensive this must be. For this very reason, unethical distillers and distributors will often resort to cutting pure Rose Otto with Rosewood essential oil, to increase yield.

Often, only the most experienced nose can detect this adulteration, and sometimes, only a chemical analysis of the adulterated oil will reveal the crime. Sometimes, price is the best indicator. If you see a bottle of Rose essential oil advertised at a price that seems too good to be true, it probably is. Look elsewhere, and never sacrifice quality just to get a deal. Anatolian Treasures, a highly reputable essential oil supplier based in Turkey and owned by Butch Owen, sells pure Anatolian Turkish Rose Otto for $94 for 10 ml. In contrast, I have seen inferior suppliers selling "pure Rose Otto" for as little as $20 for the same amount. This practice is also commonly seen with Neroli, where the oil is diluted with Petitgrain to stretch yield. Both Petitgrain and Neroli come from the orange tree, but the flowers yield Neroli and the leaves and immature fruits yield Petitgrain. Any Neroli with a suspiciously low price is most definitely "Neroli sur Petitgrain", although sometimes you may find a supplier who has the ethics to advertise it as such and thus sell it at an appropriate price.

■ **Dilution With Nature-identical Chemicals.** This is the most insidious method of adulteration of all, because it is often impossible for even the trained nose to detect. Technological advancements have also made this the most common method of adulteration. Not only do we now have the scientific know-how to detect hundreds of trace components in essential oils to verify purity, but unethical distillers and distributors can also use this technology to take an inferior distillation and add nature-identical chemicals to bring it up to par, or take a good distillation and increase certain components to stretch the yield. This practice reduces or negates the therapeutic value of an oil and also increases the chances that adverse reactions may occur through the use of the oil.

One of the most classic examples of this type of adulteration is one that is openly advertised by many suppliers. Have you ever seen Lavender advertised as Lavender 40/42? Many people assume that this is a highly desirable oil, but in fact, it is anything but. Lavender 40/42 is Lavender to which synthetic linalyl acetate has been added in order to boost the overall linalyl acetate percentage to 40%–42%, an amount which is found naturally in a small percentage of premium lavender distillations, and is considered to be highly desirable – but not when it's done synthetically!

Why the discrepancy in the first place? It's all in the distillation. The highest quality oils with the most therapeutic value are distilled at the lowest temperatures and for the longest period of time, to ensure that all volatile essential oil components are removed from the plant matter – in effect, to make sure that the "whole oil" has been distilled. In contrast, inferior distillers go for quantity over quality. They distill the oils at higher temperatures for shorter periods of time, so that they can produce more quickly. This yields an incomplete oil, which they then attempt to rectify with nature-identical chemicals to match what the chemical composition should have been in the first place! This practice is also seen with Tea Tree, where synthetic cineole is added to create a more desirable oil. In many cases, the practice goes undetected, or is found only when an experienced essential oil chemist detects anomalies during various types of testing.

■ **Alchemy.** Much like the ancient alchemist, who could supposedly turn lead into gold, the experienced nose can actually alchemically combine certain essential oils to mimic more expensive scents! Carnation absolute is incredibly costly, but a substitute can be created with proper amounts of Black Pepper and Ylang Ylang, which is then sold as Carnation absolute for a high price. Other combinations for alchemical blending also exist, and an excellent resource book for this practice is *Essence and Alchemy: A Book of Perfume*, by Mandy Aftel (see Recommended Reading, Appendix 3). This type of adulteration is only unethical when it is being used to misrepresent a blend of essential oils as something other than what it truly is.

Essential Oil Testing

As you can see, the essential oil business can be downright tricky at times. Often, there seems to be no way to guarantee that you are getting the real thing. To further the confusion, many people believe that if an essential oil is labeled as pure and natural then it legally has to be. While this is somewhat true, most people believe this because they think that the Food and Drug Administration (FDA) regulates essential oils. This is hardly the case. In fact, there is currently no governing body that tests or dictates benchmarks for essential oil quality. What this means is that huge variations in quality exist, adulteration runs rampant, and buying essential oils is a very risky business.

Although finding the highest quality oils is difficult, companies often provide many valuable indicators that point towards (or away from) their producing a high quality oil. Bear in mind that every single company will claim that their oils have been "tested". Very few of these companies actually have tested their oils, which is a very expensive process. Essential oils can be tested in a variety of ways, some of which are more commonly used than others.

■ **Gas Chromatography Testing** (GC Testing): This is the most common method used to test essential oils. This method of separating the volatile compounds that make up essential oils results in an analysis which is referred to as a chromatogram. It is an intimidating chart full of jagged lines, with numerous peaks and valleys. The cost of GC testing has gone down considerably in the last five years, and a reputable test can now be performed and interpreted for around $200–$300. The complexity of a GC test is such that only a highly

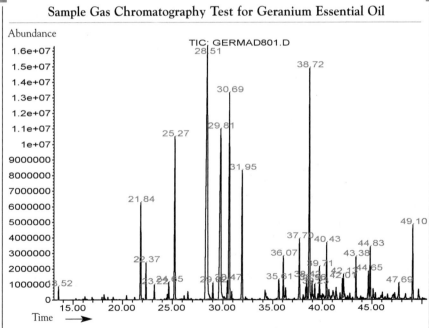

Sample Gas Chromatography Test for Geranium Essential Oil

"The composition of the sample corresponds to that expected for natural Geranium essential oil from Madagascar. This sample had the highest content of furopelargone A ever observed by this laboratory. No adulteration or contamination was detected. Odor quality is excellent."[18]

—*Dr. Robert S. Pappas, Applied Essential Oil Research*

trained individual can interpret the tests accurately. Many companies that say they have all of their oils GC tested may have done so at one point, or they may just have obtained copies of GC tests done on other oils. Since very few people can decode a GC chromatogram, even if a company provides you with one, it is quite worthless unless you know that you are dealing with a highly reputable company already. Essential oil crops and distillations vary from year to year, so what was reaped and tested one year may very well differ from what is produced the next, rendering previous GC tests useless. Who knows that adulterants weren't added from one year to another? GC tests are valuable, but a certain amount of trust must be present in order for them to be valid indicators of reputation.

■ **Mass Spectrometry:** This is a more detailed method of testing an essential oil that combines a GC chromatogram with a mass spectrometer. Even greater detail is revealed about the chemical makeup of an essential oil, and all constituents are identified and analyzed against databases to verify exact identification of all elements present. Mass spectrometry is of particular value in identifying the difference between natural and nature-identical synthetic adulterants, making it an indispensable tool for thwarting unethical standardization methods.

Top 30 Components: Geranium Essential Oil

RT Library/ID	Area%	RT Library/ID	Area%
13.52 alpha-pinene	0.31	38.33 citronellyl propionate	0.44
21.84 linalool	3.53	38.72 guaia-6,9-diene	9.61
22.37 cis-rose oxide	1.02	39.71 geranyl propionate	1.05
23.22 trans-rose oxide	0.43	40.43 germacrene D	1.92
24.65 menthone	0.52	41.08 bicyclogermacrene	0.72
25.27 isomenthone	6.63	41.39 geranyl isobutyrate	0.52
26.55 alpha-terpineol	0.27	42.01 citronellyl butyrate	0.69
28.51 citronellol	21.34	42.12 delta-cadinene	1.01
29.02 neral	0.53	43.38 geranyl butyrate	1.30
29.82 geraniol	11.88	44.65 2-phenylethyl tiglate	1.08
30.47 geranial	0.76	44.83 furopelargone A	1.83
30.69 citronellyl formate	9.33	45.13 geranyl isovalerate	0.40
31.96 geranyl formate	4.96	49.10 geranyl tiglate	2.42
36.08 beta-bourbonene	1.40	49.67 geranyl 3-methylpentanoate	0.44
37.69 beta-caryophyllene	2.20		

This GC test and its accompanying chart of the top 30 essential oil components in the analyzed sample reveals just how complicated essential oils and their chemistry are. I've never seen an aromatherapy book which shows an actual GC test, so I knew that I wanted to include one here to portray the complex nature of the substances we are studying.

The chart on the previous page details the top 30 components in the sample tested. If you think it looks complicated or intimidating at first glance, recall that any one essential oil can have up to 100 or more individual and trace components!

Things to Take into Account When Looking for a Good Essential Oil Supplier

There are many things that can ultimately influence whether or not the oil you are purchasing is of excellent, mediocre or inferior quality. These various aspects should be approached quantitatively, because the presence of even a few of these points does not guarantee that an oil is of superior quality. In contrast, the lack of some of these items also does not necessarily mean that the oil is of inferior quality. For example, I have purchased plenty of wonderful essential oils that did not come with tamper-proof caps, from smaller suppliers. Use your judgement, and your intuition!

- All oils should be packaged in amber, cobalt or violet glass bottles, unless they are sample sizes or sample vials.
- All bottles should have tamper-proof caps and/or orifice reducers.
- All bottles should be labeled with the following information, or the following information should be readily available on the company's website, catalog or brochure:
  - Common name (i.e. "Thyme")
  - Scientific, or Latin name (i.e. "Thymus vulgaris")
  - Chemotype, if applicable (i.e. "Thymus vulgaris ch linalol")
  - How oil was extracted (i.e. "Steam distillation")
  - Part of plant oil was extracted from (i.e. "Flowering tops")
  - Country of origin ("i.e. "France")
  - Date of extraction (usually used for distillation only)
  - Lot number (usually corresponds to a GC/MS test for that oil)
  - Amount of oil in bottle (i.e. "10 ml")
  - Contact information for company offering product
  - Growing method: Wildcrafted, organic, certified organic, ethically farmed, conventionally farmed

- The words "100% pure essential oil" or ingredients, if a blend or carrier-diluted single oil

■ Price – it should always be more than you want to pay. If it is a cheap deal then be ready for a cheap oil. For instance, if you see $^1/_2$ oz. (15 ml) of Neroli being sold for $14 at one supplier and for $100 at another, you should know that "something is up" with the $14 price tag. That "something" is most likely adulteration.

■ Avoid large commercial brands in pharmacies, supermarkets or health food stores. These oils will always be of a lower quality with a higher price tag to account for the series of middlemen they pass through before hitting the shelves.

■ The best oils are obtained via mail order.

■ The best suppliers are usually small companies.

■ The best companies usually do not sell essential oils *and* fragrance oils (synthetics). There are of course, exceptions to any rule...

■ The best suppliers can answer all of your questions in an educated and professional manner

■ The best suppliers have appropriately priced oils that show a large variation in price. Oils should never be similarly priced or priced the same per bottle.

■ The best suppliers will most often have formal aromatherapy education and may even be aromatherapy educators, authors or chemists.

■ The best suppliers offer a large variety of oils and show a great interest in distillations, offering rare and hard-to-find oils, such as Basil, Thyme, Hyssop or Rosemary chemotypes.

■ The best suppliers will stress how the plant the oil came from was grown and will often have a wide selection of organic, certified organic, genuine or authentic oils.

■ The best suppliers often travel far and wide to source their oils and develop relationships with growers and distillers. They may freely share their travel stories with you or even detail them in sales materials or websites.

■ The best suppliers often run out of things! Only a certain amount of an essential oil is distilled each year, seasonally. My best suppliers are frequently out of things that I need, and I have to wait until the next distillation to order.

- The best suppliers know what is going on in contemporary aromatherapy and are well read in topics such as current issues and trends in aromatherapy.

- The best suppliers often are partnered, with or recommended by, aromatherapy organizations or schools.

- The best suppliers go to great lengths to provide customer service and an excellent product, because in the end, their oils represent them and how they do business. Bad news travels quickly in this world!

- The best suppliers will always make samples available at a reduced price and often for free.

- The best suppliers /distillers will have each distillation tested and be able to provide you with the results of the tests as well as an interpretation of the test. The test results will match the lot number on the oil itself.

- Glossy brochures and full-color materials do not a good supplier make! Most small companies put their money into their oils. Some of the best companies I have ever purchased from offer black and white photocopied catalogs.

- Avoid pyramids and multi-level-marketing companies. While some of these companies may provide good quality oils, they are always overpriced, and they are most often sold via distributors who usually lack the knowledge and training necessary to help you make an educated and appropriate purchase. They also often recommend the use of exorbitant amounts of oils in their suggested treatments, for obvious profit reasons. Not only is this practice unsafe, but it is unethical. Safety should never be put second so that someone at the top of a pyramid scheme can make more money.

- Fancy labels are not always synonymous with quality. Fancy labels are just that – fancy labels. You can't judge a book by its cover with an essential oil. If you have a plain label with the proper information and you have forged a personal relationship with a person who seems trustworthy, that means a lot more than a pretty label. If you can find all that and a fancy label on the bottle, then you're lucky!

In Section 8 of this book you will find lists of reputable essential oil and hydrosol suppliers.

Hydrosols

HYDROSOL PURITY AND QUALITY – AN ENTIRELY NEW SET OF RULES

Hydrosols truly are aromatherapy's new kids on the block, for it is only in the last five years that any real intensive research has gone into their use. Many people have no idea what they even are, and those who have heard of them are basically unsure. The all-important aspects of quality and purity remain, but there are some vast differences between essential oils and hydrosols, and in turn, alternate concerns. When it comes to sourcing a high quality hydrosol, you'll need to put aside some of what you've learned about essential oils and see things in a new light.

Since hydrosols are water-based, they are more fragile and easily affected by storage aspects such as sterility, packaging, heat, light and age. Some essential oils last indefinitely, and many improve with age. The fact is that very few essential oils go bad and those that do have actually just oxidized, making them unsuitable for topical use. Oxidation is common in citrus and pine oils and can be avoided by refrigerating the oils and bottling them with minimal headspace, or air, in the bottle. Essential oils don't spoil, and they certainly don't become homes to colonies of bacteria. Unfortunately, hydrosols often do. And, just as with essential oils, various forms of adulteration do exist.

I have yet to have the pleasure of meeting anyone as well versed in hydrosols as Suzanne Catty. Catty has pioneered the use of hydrosols and her book, *Hydrosols: The Next Aromatherapy*, should be a staple of any aromatherapist's library. Through Catty's work, many of the mysteries of hydrosols have been solved, standards for quality and purity have been assessed, the tendency for hydrosols to have highly variable shelf life debunked, and various research efforts instated.

We will first discuss the sourcing of high quality hydrosols, then move on to storage. Finding a good hydrosol supplier is harder than finding a good essential oil supplier, and there are increased demands on you even after you purchase, to store your hydrosols correctly and use them within their shelf life.

Most hydrosol suppliers also carry essential oils. Hence, if you have found a trusted and reliable source for essential oils, it is highly likely that this supplier will ascribe their high standards and ethical business practices to the hydrosols that they carry, as well. A certain amount of trust is key, as there are never any guarantees, due to the obvious variability which mother nature introduces to keep things interesting…

Here are some questions you might want to ask your supplier. As with essential oils, a quality hydrosol does not have to adhere to each and every one of these guidelines. Think qualitatively, and take personal relations into account.

- **Authenticity:** Is this a true hydrosol, from the steam distillation of essential oils, or is it just water with essential oils added? Sometimes the "rose water", "lavender water" or my personal favorite, "violet water" that you see in stores is water with added essential oils or even fragrance oils. This is not a true hydrosol.

- **Storage:** How does the supplier store the hydrosols? Hydrosols should be refrigerated and kept in sterilized dark glass containers, usually amber. They are sometimes shipped in plastic, but should be transferred to glass upon receipt.

- **Handling:** Does the supplier sterilize the bottles and equipment that she uses to package hydrosols for resale? What does she sterilize with? Since hydrosols are water-based, sterile containers and minimal handling is important.

- **Age:** How old is the hydrosol? When was it distilled? When does it expire?

- **Distillation details:** Does the supplier have pertinent information about the distillation of this hydrosol? Where was it distilled? When? What was the method of farming the plants? What part of the plant was the hydrosol distilled from? Is it from the first or later distillations? (Many of these aspects also apply to essential oils as well as hydrosols.)

- **Preservatives:** Does the supplier add any preservatives, such as ethyl alcohol, grapefruit seed extract or synthetic chemicals? Hydrosols should be preservative-free when purchased from a supplier. Whether or not you want to add preservatives after purchasing is up to you. If you do, ethyl alcohol is best (less than 5% total).

- **Samples:** Does the supplier offer sample sizes of hydrosols? Any good hydrosol supplier will offer you free or low priced samples of hydrosols so that you can test them, just like you would essential oils.

- **Labeling:** What information is provided on the labels? Are the details of the distillation on the label? Is a "best used before" date listed on the label?

Once you've gone through the entire process of selecting and purchasing samples from a variety of suppliers, you will no doubt select your favorite distillations and purchase larger bottles. What you do with them after you receive them is as important as how you selected them in the first place. Here's a checklist:

1. Immediately upon receipt of the hydrosol, wash your hands thoroughly with soap and water, and pour a small amount of hydrosol into a clean, clear glass. Inspect for particulate matter or a milky appearance. While hydrosols vary in color, they are all primarily clear and should contain only minute particulate matter. Large chunks or strings of matter most certainly point towards a bacterial bloom. In the original container, there may be a "skin" growing on the surface, as well. Call your supplier for information on returning the hydrosol if this is suspected.

2. Smell the hydrosol! How does it smell? Usually quite different from the essential oil. If a hydrosol smells spoiled or rancid, it has most likely "bloomed" and contains bacterial growth. In most cases, you would have identified this based on your initial visual inspection. Sniff carefully for any signs that alcohol has been added to the hydrosol.

3. Once you've assessed that the hydrosol has not bloomed and everything smells up to par, you'll want to repackage it into dark glass if it was shipped in plastic. Sterilize a dark glass bottle with ethyl alcohol and allow it to dry completely, then dispense your hydrosol into the new container.

4. You've gotten this far, now watch where you put it. Your hydrosol should ideally be kept refrigerated for optimum shelf life. If you don't have access to refrigeration, then opt for a cool, dark place. If you don't have this, then by all means keep it away from heat sources or direct sunlight.

5. Hydrosols should last anywhere from six months to a little over two years if treated carefully and properly stored.

These are merely the basics of hydrosol inspection and storage. Many more advanced processes do exist, such as filtration and preservative methods. I highly recommend *Hydrosols: The Next Aromatherapy* by Suzanne Catty for serious hydrosol students. Unlike essential oils, which can be tested for purity via GC or MS tests, these methods do not work so well for water-based hydrosols. There is a simple test that you can conduct on your own which will reveal whether or not a hydrosol falls within "base values".

Enter Suzanne Catty, once again. Catty noticed that each hydrosol had a different shelf life. Investigation into this concluded that all hydrosols have different pH levels, or general ranges of pH values that they fall into. Water has a pH of 7. While hydrosols are watery, they certainly are not water! The presence of a myriad of water-soluble plant components makes their pH highly variable. To refresh your chemistry-tired minds, pH is a quantitative measurement of the acidity or alkalinity of a substance. It is valuable in verifying the freshness and stability of hydrosols, because changes in pH indicate the growth of bacteria. The initial pH of a hydrosol is also a general indicator of how long of a shelf life it will have. For instance, the more acidic (lower pH) a hydrosol is, the longer its shelf life will be. The more basic, or alkaline (higher pH) the pH, the shorter its shelf life will be. It is hydrosols with short shelf lives for which pH testing is so valuable.

Catty has established baseline pH ranges for hydrosols, and uses these values to test any suspicious changes. If the pH value changes by 0.5, this indicates the presence of bacterial growth. This test is easily done with pH strips, available through a scientific or medical supply store or catalog. When in contact with the hydrosol, the strips will change color. To determine the pH, you simply match the strip to the color chart included with the strips. It is worthwhile to note that any added preservatives will affect the pH of a hydrosol, so take this into account when using this as a method of testing and comparison![19]

Suzanne Catty's pH Ranges for Some Commonly Used Hydrosols (Preservative-free) (from Hydrosols: The Next Aromatherapy)

Cornflower	Centaurea cyanus	4.7–5.0
Geranium	Pelargonium graveolens	4.9–5.2
German Chamomile	Matricaria recutita	4.0–4.1
Lavender	Lavandula angustifolia	5.6–5.9
Lemon Verbena	Lippia citriadora	5.2–5.5
Neroli	Citrus aurantium	3.8–4.5
Peppermint	Mentha piperita	6.1–6.3
Roman Chamomile	Anthemis nobilis	3.0–3.3
Rose	Rosa damascena	4.1–4.4
Rosemary (cineole)	Rosmarinus officinalis	4.2–4.5
Witch Hazel	Hamamaelis virginiana	4.0–4.2

Purity, Quality and a Host of Other Botanical Materials

If you are dealing with essential oils and hydrosols, then it is most likely that in the course of your journey, you will be needing a variety of other botanical materials to use in the creation of your blends and other formulas. The quality of these ingredients is important too! You've spent so much time in making sure that your aromatic materials are of the highest quality that you certainly don't want to ruin it all by adding them to inferior blending mediums or formulations. Base oils, herbs, clays, soaps, waxes and butters are some of the ingredients you may end up using.

Regardless of which exact ingredients you choose, you'll certainly want to make sure that they are all natural. Remember "natural is better" and all that evolutionary talk about the biosynthetic pathways in Section 1? It couldn't be more applicable here. We have established that natural is better because it is biochemically compatible with our bodies and our pets' bodies, and we've learned that the introduction of synthetic ingredients in an organic system leads to an imbalance. This couldn't be more applicable to the principles of blending essential oils and creating products with them.

It is a total waste of time to take carefully sourced, high quality oils and then add them to a synthetic soup of ingredients. What's even worse is when this "soup" is used on you or your animals. Unfortunately, most commercially available products contain a vast number of synthetic chemicals, many of them petrochemicals, most of them not biodegradable. But lucky you – you're not only taking the time to learn about how to safely use aromatherapy with your pets, but to learn about the importance of natural grooming preparations as well. After all, this is holistic aromatherapy. We are addressing the health of the entire organism. We are in turn addressing the purity, quality and origin of every ingredient and treatment we use with our animals. A holistic, true aromatherapy product will always be 100% natural.

Carrier, or Base, Oils

Fatty nut or vegetable oils are a primary dilutent for essential oil use. A variety of base oils are available and they are extracted in various methods. The most common methods are solvent extraction and cold pressing. Solvent extraction is similar to the solvent extraction used with essential oils, but there is a greater chance of trace amounts of solvent remaining in the base oil. For this reason, cold pressed oils are preferred. Oils extracted in this manner are mechanically pressed from nuts, seeds and plant matter with the absence of heat. Heat is used to refine base oils, most often to remove undesirable natural smells that characterize the oils pressed from nuts such as sesame, rosehip, and shea and cocoa butters. This type of refining may produce an end-product that is more desirable to the cosmetics and toiletries industry (which usually wants to add its own synthetic scents and sees natural scents as a major problem), but it actually produces an oil that has less therapeutic value because heat destroys valuable components of the oil. The highest quality, most therapeutic base oils are always cold pressed, unrefined oils.

There are many base oils available for use in aromatherapy with both animals and humans. Different plants yield base oils of varying chemical composition, producing a range of textures, colors, therapeutic value and shelf life. Certain base oils are more prone to rancidity, and it helps to add vitamin E, a natural antioxidant, to blends made with oils such as these to extend shelf life.

I frequently receive comments from people who are wary of putting "oil" on their animal's coats. They don't want their fur to be greasy, or to attract dirt. Oil has a bad rap, that's for sure. When most people hear "oil", they think of a greasy, fatty substance that sticks, attracts dirt and can only be rinsed off with soap and water. This is the case with mineral oil and petroleum jellies, but not with natural vegetable and nut base oils. Rest assured that a light application of a natural base oil will be absorbed by the skin and fur of the animal and will not contribute to a greasy or dirty appearance.

Base Oils Suitable for Animal Aromatherapy:

- **Apricot Kernel Oil,** *Prunus armenica:* This is a highly moisturizing, penetrative base oil high in essential fatty acids. It is revitalizing for dry or irritated skin. Shelf life: 6–12 months

- **Avocado Oil,** *Persea americana:* This pale-green fatty oil pressed from avocado pits is high in proteins and Vitamins A, D and E. Its characteristic aroma usually means that it is blended in with other base oils rather than being used on its own. Shelf life: 12 months

- **Castor Oil,** *Ricinus communis:* The thick, viscous oil pressed from castor seeds is an excellent emollient. It is believed that the oil has strong penetrative and therapeutic properties, thus anything added to it will be quickly absorbed by the skin. However, it is so thick that it needs to be blended with lightweight oils for ease of use. Shelf life: 12 months

- **Coconut Oil,** *Cocos nuciferas:* Coconut oil is solid at room temperature, but melts at 76° F. This smooth, lightweight and quickly absorbed oil is highly suitable for massage and bodycare. Shelf life: Indefinite

- **Hazelnut Oil,** *Corylus avellana:* This pale-gold fatty oil expeller pressed from hazelnuts is lightweight and has excellent skin absorption properties. Shelf life: 6–12 months

- **Jojoba Oil,** *Simmondsia chinensis:* Jojoba oil is actually not an oil but a liquid plant wax. It is an excellent moisturizer that resembles human sebum. Jojoba oil has a very long shelf life, so is excellent to use in blends or added to other oil blends to extend shelf life. Shelf life: Indefinite

- **Olive Oil,** *Olivea europaea:* This medium-green, nutty-scented oil is pressed from the pits of olives. The first pressing is most desirable and is referred to as "Extra Virgin". Olive oil is a staple moisturizer that is full of nutrients. Shelf life: 12 months

- **Rosehip Seed Oil,** *Rosa rubignosa:* Added to other base oils for skin regenerating blends and to prevent scarring and ease inflammation, rosehip seed oil is high in fatty acids and antioxidants. Shelf life: 12 months

- **Sesame Oil,** *Sesamum indicum:* This is a golden, nutty-scented base oil pressed from sesame seeds. Its heavier weight and lingering scent usually dictate blending it with other lighter oils. It has anti-inflammatory properties. Shelf life: 6–12 months

- **Sweet Almond Oil,** *Prunus dulcis:* This is a lightweight, odorless base oil high in Vitamins A and E, an excellent moisturizer and skin penetrator. Shelf life: 6–12 months

- **Sunflower Seed Oil,** *Helianthus annus:* This is a lightweight, quickly-absorbed base oil pressed from sunflower seeds; it is high in vitamins A and E and is even more desirable due to its low price. Shelf life: 3–9 months

In the course of creating aromatic products for your pets, you will undoubtedly need a variety of other botanical ingredients in addition to base oils. You may begin to create balms or ointments and explore using beeswax or solid butters such as mango, cocoa, shea or kokum butter. The opportunities are endless! While we won't go into great detail about these auxiliary ingredients, I have included some helpful advice to aid you in making educated and knowledgeable purchases.

- **Herbs:** So many herbs are commercially grown and treated with pesticides, that it is extremely important to purchase organically grown herbs whenever possible. You may find that you use herbs to create herbal rinses to use in grooming or to infuse base oils with to increase the range of their therapeutic value. I think one of the most enjoyable ways to incorporate herbs into products is to grow your own. A yard isn't necessary for a nice herb garden, because a variety of herbs can be easily grown on a windowsill in clay pots. Just don't put them on too low a windowsill, because you may find that your dogs (or cats) may do a little grazing of their own! For further information on herbs and pets, consult *All You Ever Wanted to Know About Herbs for Pets* by Mary Wulff-Tilford and Gregory Tilford (See Recommended Reading, Appendix 3).

- **Butters:** Chocolatey-scented cocoa butter, shea butter, mango butter and kokum butter are all wonderful ways to increase the therapeutic value and moisturizing capabilities of home-made balms and ointments. Purchase only unrefined butters for the best results.

- **Waxes:** Waxes are necessary in the creation of balms or ointments as emulsifiers. Beeswax is most commonly used, but vegetable emulsifying wax and floral waxes, such as jasmine wax can also be used. Once again, unrefined, unbleached waxes are best.

- **Clays:** There are a variety of clays that you can use in poultices, which can be created with herbs and essential oils. I prefer French clays, such as French green, red or white clay. White clay is the gentlest and least absorbent, red is moderately absorbent, and green clay is the most powerful of the three, with strong properties of absorption.

- **Aloe Vera:** Aloe vera is an excellent ingredient for soothing the skin and aiding in skin regeneration. The ideal way to use aloe is to keep a plant on hand and use the leaves as needed, but most of us instead rely on aloe vera gel or juice. Commercially available aloe vera is frequently preserved with synthetics, so check to make sure of what you are buying. Small bottles of preservative-free aloe vera can be purchased from reliable sources and kept refrigerated for a longer shelf life.

- **Alcohols:** Natural alcohols are important ingredients in water-based spritzers or misters, for they not only act as natural preservatives, but also as astringents and emulsifiers. Remember, essential oils and water don't mix. Alcohol helps. But not the alcohol you might be thinking of. "Rubbing", or isopropyl, alcohol is not suitable for use in natural products because it's not natural. It is a harsh and drying synthetic alcohol. You should preferably use grain alcohol, or ethanol. If you are unable to obtain grain alcohol, then vodka will do quite nicely.

■ **Flower Essences:** Flower essences are a form of vibrational, or energy healing, frequently used by holistic veterinarians. Over 100 essences currently exist, and new ones are being introduced every day. The most popular line of flower essences is the 38 traditional English Bach Flower Remedies™, and the famous Bach Rescue Remedy formulated by Dr. Edward Bach. Other practitioners have introduced flower essences based on the native flora of their own countries, as seen in the variety of essences offered by Flower Essence Services, which features North American Flower Essences. Some companies are presently even creating flower essence blends specifically for animals. Many people mistake flower essences for aromatherapy. They are entirely different forms of treatment, and flower essences have no detectable floral or herbal fragrances. There are several excellent sourcebooks on flower essences for animals. I suggest *Bach Flower Remedies for Animals,* by Helen Graham and Gregory Vlamis or *Bach Flower Remedies for Animals* by Stefan Ball and Judy Howard (See Recommended Reading, Appendix 3). Flower essences can be safely added to a variety of aromatherapy treatments to increase the synergistic effects of the formulation.

■ **Gemstone Essences:** These essences are relatively new, but are enjoying popularity amongst those who are familiar with flower essences. Like the flower essences, gemstone essences are also a form of energy healing, which aims to balance the energy fields, energy flow and aura of a body. Crystals and gems have long been used to accomplish this, often simply by being carried, worn or used in treatments. Gemstone essences can be added to aromatherapy formulations and also used with flower essences as well. They are entirely safe and have no side effects.

■ **Soaps/Shampoos:** Many pet owners who learn about making their own soaps find that they can create wonderful soaps for their pets with the addition of herbs, teas, hydrosols or essential oils. There are two different types of soap – cold process and glycerin soap. Most beginners opt for glycerin, or "melt and pour" soap because it is very simple and fun to use. You just melt the block of soap, add your ingredients, and pour. The main drawback of glycerin soap is that varying amounts of petrochemicals are added to glycerin soap. While it is practically impossible to find a 100% natural glycerin soap, there are suppliers who try their best to limit the use of synthetics.

Cold process soap is the traditional soap making process, which is preferred by purists, The cold process involves the use of fatty oils (base oils or butters) combined with lye to create, fatty acids or, you guessed it, soap. This process creates a hard, smooth bar with creamy lather. Different base oils and butters will produce varying amounts of lather and moisturizing effects. Herbs and essential oils are often added. This process takes a considerable amount of time, as it often takes the soap several weeks to "cure", but it is the only way that a truly 100% natural bar of soap can be created.

Avoid washing your pet with commercially available soaps from the supermarket. Most of these soaps are not truly "soap", but rather, chunks of harsh chemical detergents. These synthetic ingredients can be harsh, drying and irritating to an animal's skin.

You may be tempted to add some essential oils to your favorite liquid soap or dish detergent to make a quick shampoo for your pet. Here are a few things to consider before you do this. Most commercially available liquid soaps are synthetic soaps. The only liquid soap I would recommend that you add essential oils to is Dr. Bronner's Liquid Castile Soap, which is made from olive oil. They offer a baby formula that is unscented and is wonderful to add essential oils to. This soap does not work so well for long-coated animals, though, because it strips a good deal of moisture from the coat and leaves behind a residue.

A much better choice in the creation of a liquid shampoo is to make your own shampoo using an ingredient called "decyl polyglucose". This is an extraordinarily gentle soap that is commercially sold under the name "Plantaren". Decyl polyglucose (also known as decyl polyglucoside) is created by combining a cornstarch glucose with fatty alcohol. The end result is a superbly gentle non-irritating cleanser, which can be safely and ethically used for grooming. Recipes for making your own shampoos are included in each animal's section of this book.

Decyl polyglucose is a revolutionary ingredient that is being incorporated in foaming products more and more each passing day. Whether the products are for pets, babies or humans, the results are all the same – a gentle and natural way to cleanse and avoid synthetic ingredients and preservatives such as sodium laurel sulfate, coco betaine, ammonium laurel sulfate, DEA, urea, parabens and others.

Section 3

A Closer Look at the Aromatics Used in This Book...

This is where you can read more about the aromatics used in the recipe section of this book. The essential oils and hydrosols listed here are chosen specifically for use with animals based on their gentleness, chemical constituents, safety, and physiological/psychological effects. I've also attempted to include a broad price range of oils, because I realize that not everyone who wishes to use aromatherapy with their pets has a full wallet with which to buy copious amounts of Helichrysum or Thyme chemotypes!

I haven't even bothered to list stronger, more powerful and readily available essential oils such as Pennyroyal or Oregano because there are gentler, equally effective essential oils available that are more suitable for use with animals and it is these essential oils that will be focused on.

Basic Essential Oil Chemistry

The thought of organic chemistry can be daunting, but some knowledge of the basic chemical groups of which essential oils are composed is necessary in order to understand which oils are safe and gentle, and which are stronger or irritating. Since the chemistry of essential oils is a more advanced topic, I am keeping this as simple as possible. Further reading on the subject can be found in the books of Kurt Schnaubelt and Marcel Lavabre (See Recommended Reading, Appendix 3).

Every essential oil is represented by dominant chemical groups that determine its effects. I will refer frequently to these groups when discussing essential oils and their wondrous capabilities.

- **Monoterpene Alcohols:** One of the most prevalent chemical groups, monoterpene alcohols has tonifying, antibacterial, antiviral and immune boosting effects. Some oils that are high in this chemical group include: Eucalyptus, Peppermint, Rose, Rosewood, Tea Tree, Hyssop decumbens, Thyme linalol, Thyme thujanol, Ravensare aromatica and Lavandin. You might see some specific monoterpene alcohols referred to as linalol, terpinol or terpinen-4-ol. Essential oils belonging to this group are very gentle and tolerable due to their hydrophilic nature. They are easily metabolized and not irritating to the kidneys.

- **Monoterpene Hydrocarbons:** The citrus and pine oils make up this group, which have a dominant antiviral and stimulating effect. Essential oils such as Pine, Spruce, Fir, Orange, Lemon, Lime, Mandarin and Grapefruit all contain monoterpene hydrocarbons. Toxicology reports have revealed that cats are extremely sensitive to this chemical group. Citrus and pine oils can be irritating to the skin and can also cause photosensitization. Essential oils from this group should be kept in bottles with little headspace and also refrigerated to prevent oxidation, which increases irritation. Some monoterpene hydrocarbons include pinene and limonene.

- **Esters:** Esters are the calming components of certain essential oils. They are also balancing and have powerful antifungal effects. Lavender, Clary Sage, Petitgrain, Geranium, Ylang Ylang, Roman Chamomile, Cardamom and Marjoram all contain esters. Essential oils from this group are gentle and tolerable and can be used with little risk of irritation. Some esters include linalyl acetate and geranyl acetate.

- **Phenols:** If you see phenols mentioned in this book, it is because they should be avoided with animals. Phenols are powerful, hot and stimulating oils, due to the presence of a benzene ring in their chemical structure. They have powerful antibacterial properties and a strong medicinal smell. Oils high in phenols include Oregano, Savory, Thyme vulgaris (often called Red or White Thyme), Phenols are highly irritating to the skin. Cats are particularly sensitive to phenols. I avoid the use of any phenol-containing oils with animals. Thymol and carvacrol are both phenols found in essential oils.

- **Ketones:** Essential oils such as Thuja, Yarrow, Pennyroyal, Rue, Hyssop, Wormwood and Mugwort all contain ketones. These powerful chemical constituents are stimulating and aid in tissue regeneration; they have mucolytic effects (meaning that they aid in the production and elimination of mucous) and the potential to be neurotoxic and abortive. Not all ketones are equally "guilty". There are various types of ketones, and some very gentle and tolerable essential oils contain small amounts of highly beneficial ketones, such as Helichrysum, Rosemary verbenon, Peppermint, Atlas Cedarwood, Vetiver, Eucalyptus and Sage. These oils can safely be used in small amounts with animals with no ill effects. Oils with high ketone content that should be avoided due to neurotoxic and abortive effects are Rue, Santolina, Mugwort, Thuja, Wormwood, Hyssop and Pennyroyal. Frighteningly, Pennyroyal is a very common ingredient in numerous commercially available flea-repellent products for both dogs and cats.

- **Lactones:** A small number of essential oils contain lactones, which are mucolytic.

- **Phenylpropanes:** Essential oils from this group are stimulating, antibacterial and potentially irritating, similar to the phenol group. Cinnamon, Clove, Anise, Tarragon and Basil all have phenylpropanes in their chemical makeup. Certain phenylpropanes are more powerful than others. For instance, eugenol, found in Clove can actually burn the skin, whereas methyl chavicol, found in Basil is much gentler and has a stabilizing effect on the central nervous system.

- **Sesquiterpene Alcohols:** This group is vast and varied, exhibiting a wide range of effects, from anti-inflammatory to anti-allergenic, liver and gland-stimulating, tonifying and antibacterial. Essential oils containing sesquiterpene alcohols are generally well tolerated with no ill effects when used in dilution. Ginger, Niaouli, Sandalwood, Carrot Seed, Spikenarde, Patchouli, Vetiver, Peppermint and Sage are some essential oils that contain sesquiterpene alcohols.

- **Sesquiterpene Hydrocarbons:** Sesquiterpene hydrocarbons are anti-inflammatory and anti-allergenic. Noteworthy is German Chamomile, an anti-inflammatory par excellence. This oil contains chamazulene, which lends it its dark blue color as well as valuable calming and anti-inflammatory effects.

- **Aldehydes:** Oils that contain this group generally have sedative, antiviral effects. Lemongrass, Citronella, Melissa, Eucalyptus citriadora and Lemon verbena all contain aldehydes that give them a characteristic lemony scent. Highly diluted, aldehydes also exhibit anti-inflammatory effects. Dilution is a must due to the potential skin irritating qualities of this group. Citral and citronellol are aldehydes found in essential oils.

- **Oxides:** Oxides have an expectorant effect, as in the case of cineole found in Tea Tree and Eucalyptus essential oils. They are useful in small amounts in blends for congestion – valuable since animals can't very well blow their noses.

The Essential Oils

*(Recommended for use with dogs, horses and large animals – **not** for cats!)*

In this section, I have listed information for 52 essential oils that are used in the recipe sections of this book. Since there is no reason why you can't create a variety of blends using fewer oils, I have designated 20 of these oils as "Top 20 Must Have Essential Oils". High quality essential oils are expensive, and I have taken that into account when writing this book. You can incorporate aromatherapy into your animal's holistic protocols safely and effectively without needing to empty your wallet.

Top 20 Essential Oils for Dogs at a Glance

Carrot Seed	Mandarin,
Cedarwood,	Green
Atlas	Marjoram,
Chamomile,	Sweet
German	Myrrh
Chamomile,	Niaouli
Roman	Orange, Sweet
Clary Sage	Peppermint
Eucalyptus	Ravensare
radiata	aromatica
Geranium	Rose
Ginger	Thyme
Helichrysum	chemotypes
Lavender	Valerian

Sweet Basil essential oil is helpful for restoring mental balance, focus and clarity. For this reason, I add it, in very small amounts, to blends for animals that are suffering from nervousness or anxiety. Sweet Basil contains moderate amounts of the phenylpropane methyl chavicol (about 30%). Since essential oils bearing this chemical group can cause potential irritation, I use this oil sparingly with animals.

Sweet Basil is one of the key oils found in my blend for dogs with separation anxiety. The linalol chemotype is desirable for use because its methyl chavicol content is even lower.

The scent of Sweet Basil is an acquired taste, another reason why it is best to use it in very small amounts.

1. BASIL, SWEET,
Ocimum basilicum

METHOD OF DISTILLATION:	Steam distillation
PART OF PLANT:	Leaves, flower tops
PRODUCTION:	France, Italy, Egypt, U.S.A.
COLOR:	Pale yellow
SCENT:	Green, herbal, slightly spicy and heady
DOMINANT CHEMICAL GROUP:	Monoterpene alcohols, phenylpropanes

2. BAY LEAF,

Pimenta racemosa

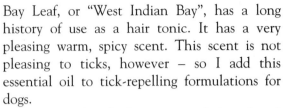

Bay Leaf, or "West Indian Bay", has a long history of use as a hair tonic. It has a very pleasing warm, spicy scent. This scent is not pleasing to ticks, however – so I add this essential oil to tick-repelling formulations for dogs.

Despite a rather high content of the phenol eugenol (which is also present in Clove Bud essential oil), Bay Leaf essential oil has only a moderate potential for irritation. When used in small amounts with other essential oils and properly diluted, this possible safety hazard appears to disappear altogether. The benefits of this oil as a hair (and fur) tonic and antimicrobial are apparent. For this reason, I enjoy using this oil in place of Clove, which is so dermocaustic that even the highest dilution still poses a sensitization risk.

I also like to use this oil in soy wax candles and diffusers and to add a few drops to a natural shampoo base. It is an excellent deodorizer.

METHOD OF DISTILLATION:	Steam distillation
PART OF PLANT:	Leaves
PRODUCTION:	West Indies
COLOUR:	Dark yellow
SCENT:	Warm, spicy, balsamic
DOMINANT CHEMICAL GROUP:	Phenylpropane, phenols

Bay Laurel, or "Laurel Leaf", essential oil has an unusual combination of chemical groups in its makeup which lend it a variety of unique characteristics. This is one of my favorite oils for human use. It has a distinctive and energizing aroma.

With dogs I prefer to use only a very small amount in blends for boosting the immune system. This is because it is a powerful oil with a potential for skin sensitization. When properly diluted and used in combination with other oils, this potential appears to be greatly minimized. Regardless, I still take great care in the use of this wonderful oil with dogs; as you will see in the recipe section – I often use only 1 or 2 drops in an entire recipe.

If you do end up purchasing this oil, don't ignore its many wonderful uses for yourself. Perfect to use during flu season, to ward off sickness when travelling, or in a diffuser to sanitize room air, it is a must-have in any aroma-medicine chest.

3. BAY LAUREL,
Laurus nobilis

METHOD OF DISTILLATION:	Steam distillation
PART OF PLANT:	Leaves, branches
PRODUCTION:	France, Spain, Italy, Morocco
COLOR:	Greenish yellow
SCENT:	Spicy, medicinal
DOMINANT CHEMICAL GROUP:	Oxides, phenols, Monoterpene hydrocarbons, esters

4. BERGAMOT,

Citrus bergamia

Bergamot is a citrus oil that combines the toning, strengthening and balancing effects of the monoterpene alcohols with the soothing, relaxing and uplifting qualities of the monoterpene hydrocarbons.

The oil is a strong antifungal agent, making it useful in blends for the treatment of fungal conditions, such as canine ear infections due to yeast overgrowth. Bergamot is a key ingredient along with Lavender, Roman Chamomile and Niaouli in a blend I formulate for dogs with dirty ears, or ears with bacterial or yeast overgrowth. I have found the blend to be effective in clearing ear infections in dogs that have repetitive infections that are resistant to conventional veterinary treatments consisting of antibiotics, antifungal agents and steroids.

Photosensitization is prevalent with Bergamot due to the presence of the furocoumarin Bergaptene. Bergaptene-free (BF or FCF) versions of the oil are available for those who wish to take advantage of the oil without the risk of sensitization. I do recommend the BF/FCF Bergamot for animal use, despite the fact that the oil is partially rectified in order to remove the coumarins.

METHOD OF DISTILLATION:	Expression
PART OF PLANT:	Fruit rind
PRODUCTION:	Italy
COLOR:	Pale green
SCENT:	Sweet, citrusy, slightly balsamic and tea-like
DOMINANT CHEMICAL GROUP:	Monoterpene alcohols, monoterpene hydrocarbons

The warming and circulatory stimulant qualities of Black Pepper, combined with a low incidence of toxicity and irritation make this oil an ideal addition to topical massage blends for animals with sore muscles, joint pain, arthritis and hip dysplasia. I enjoy blending the oil with Peppermint, Juniper Berry and Spearmint to create a safe and effective, non-toxic massage oil for animals. The synergy of using Black Pepper along with these other oils allows me to avoid using potentially hazardous oils such as Birch or Wintergreen (both have extremely high levels of Methyl salicyate and are often adulterated). Black Pepper is not compatible with homeopathic treatments and is believed to antidote them, so use wisely if you are following homeopathic protocols with your animals.

5. BLACK PEPPER,

Piper nigrum

METHOD OF DISTILLATION:	Steam distillation
PART OF PLANT:	Seeds of dried fruit
PRODUCTION:	India, Indonesia, Madagascar
COLOR:	Colorless
SCENT:	Warm, fresh, spicy, peppery
DOMINANT CHEMICAL GROUP:	Monoterpene hydrocarbons

6. CARAWAY,

Carum carvi

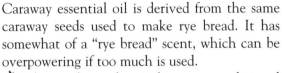

Caraway essential oil is derived from the same caraway seeds used to make rye bread. It has somewhat of a "rye bread" scent, which can be overpowering if too much is used.

The oil and seeds are traditional remedies for all sorts of digestive maladies – flatulence, poor appetite, indigestion and bad breath. I use Caraway essential oil in small amounts for blends for animals with these ailments.

The oil is extensively used by the pharmaceutical industry as a flavoring, and therefore has a history of safe and established internal use. Regardless, I recommend that the oil be sourced wisely from a trusted supplier since it is used internally.

METHOD OF DISTILLATION:	Steam distillation
PART OF PLANT:	Seeds of dried fruit
PRODUCTION:	Germany, Netherlands, Russia
COLOR:	Light brown
SCENT:	Harsh, warming, spicy
DOMINANT CHEMICAL GROUP:	Carvone, limonene

7. CARDAMOM,

Cardamom essential oil is similar in use to Caraway, and for this reason finds its way into many synergistic blends that I create for digestive problems. Its effectiveness for bad breath makes it a key ingredient in a formulation of oils I use for combating canine halitosis, along with Peppermint and Coriander Seed.

Cardamom is also used extensively by the pharmaceutical industry as a flavoring, for internal use. The internal use of such established spice oils is safe for animals in diluted amounts. Once again, source oils intended for internal use wisely.

METHOD OF DISTILLATION:	Steam distillation
PART OF PLANT:	Seeds of dried fruit
PRODUCTION:	India, Guatemala, Sri Lanka
COLOR:	Pale yellow
SCENT:	Warm, spicy, slightly woodsy
DOMINANT CHEMICAL GROUP:	Monoterpene alcohols and hydrocarbons, esters

8. CARROT SEED,

Daucus carota

Top 20 Must Have Essential Oils

Carrot seed is a valuable oil for use in skin care, particularly animals with dry, flaky skin that is sensitive to allergens and prone to infection. The oil is extracted from the seeds of the carrot plant and smells nothing like carrots themselves. Contrary to popular belief, it is not produced from the seeds of bright orange carrots that you buy in the grocery store. Rather, wild carrot, or Queen Anne's Lace, is the source of Carrot Seed oil. Queen Anne's Lace, although often referred to as a weed, is actually a valuable plant. The seed oil has a unique characteristic scent that is warm, nutty, herbal and intensely earthy all at the same time. Some find the scent comforting and pleasing, while others dislike it. Regardless, this is an excellent oil to add to any blend dealing with first aid, healing, scarring or skin conditions. The oil is extraordinarily gentle and has no notable potential for side effects. With 50% Caratol content, a sesquiterpene alcohol, Carrot Seed oil is well equipped to rejuvenate and stimulate tissue regeneration. Essential oils containing sesquiterpene alcohols are known for their anti-inflammatory, tonic and moderate antibacterial effects.

METHOD OF DISTILLATION:	Steam distillation
PART OF PLANT:	Seeds
PRODUCTION:	Mostly France, but also Egypt and India
COLOR:	Pale yellow
SCENT:	Warm, nutty, sweet, earthy, herbal
DOMINANT CHEMICAL GROUP:	Sesquiterpene alcohols

9. CEDARWOOD, ATLAS,
Cedrus atlantica

Top 20 Must Have Essential Oils

Atlas Cedarwood essential oil is a gently stimulating essential oil that increases circulation and stimulates the release of toxins. It is used in many human formulations to aid in the reduction of cellulite, but this is not a real concern with animals, of course! I use Atlas Cedarwood in conditioning blends for the skin and coat, because its circulation-stimulating effect is beneficial for dermatitis of all types The oil has an elegant, earthy and complex fragrance that makes it ideal for aromatic deodorizing blends. Fleas also appear to have a strong distaste for it.

The dominant chemical makeup of the oil is sesquiterpene hydrocarbons, which indicate tonifying properties, reduction of congestion in the circulatory and lymphatic system, and moderate antiseptic effects.

METHOD OF DISTILLATION:	Steam distillation
PART OF PLANT:	Wood
PRODUCTION:	Morocco
COLOR:	Deep amber
SCENT:	Deep, woodsy, smooth, warm, balsamic
DOMINANT CHEMICAL GROUP:	Sesquiterpene alcohols

10. CHAMOMILE, GERMAN, (BLUE CHAMOMILE)

Matricaria recutita

Top 20 Must Have Essential Oils

German Chamomile essential oil is a powerful, skin-soothing anti-inflammatory, thanks to the presence of chamazulene, a sesquiterpene hydrocarbon that lends an intense, deep blue color. Burns, allergic reactions and all types of skin irritations can be quickly calmed with German Chamomile. It is so gentle and non-toxic that it can be used undiluted on humans. However, when treating animals we take their sensitive noses into account and always dilute, even if the oil is extraordinarily gentle.

The costly oil is frequently adulterated with other blue oils, such as Blue Tansy or Moroccan Chamomile, which lack the healing properties that true German Chamomile possesses. For this reason, it is ultimately important to know your source when purchasing. Various chemotypes of German Chamomile also exist, the most therapeutic and desirable type being the alpha-bisabolol type.

METHOD OF DISTILLATION:	Steam distillation, CO^2 extraction
PART OF PLANT:	Flower petals
PRODUCTION:	Hungary, Eastern Europe
COLOR:	Deep blue
SCENT:	Deep, woodsy, smooth, warm, balsamic
DOMINANT CHEMICAL GROUP:	Sesquiterpene hydrocarbons

11. CHAMOMILE, ROMAN,

Anthemis nobilis

Top 20 Must Have Essential Oils

Roman Chamomile essential oil contains a rare profile of intensely calming and antispasmodic esters that make it valuable for soothing the central nervous system and relieving cramps, spasms and muscle pains. It also has analgesic effects, which make it an excellent addition to blends for wound care or teething pain. The fragrance of Roman Chamomile is very intense and needs to be used only in small amounts in blends. I personally can't stomach the scent of the oil, but others enjoy it immensely. (Sense of smell is entirely subjective.) It is gentle and non-toxic, but should always be used diluted with animals, as is the case with the majority of essential oils. The oil is high in price, but nevertheless is used in a vast amount of cosmetic, pharmaceutical and aromatherapy preparations.

METHOD OF DISTILLATION:	Steam distillation
PART OF PLANT:	Flower heads
PRODUCTION:	Britain, U.S.A., Italy, France
COLOR:	Pale blue turning yellow with storage
SCENT:	Fruity, fresh, apple-like
DOMINANT CHEMICAL GROUP:	Esters

12. CINNAMON LEAF,

Cinnamonum

zeylanicum

When using this oil, please make sure that you are using Cinnamon Leaf and not Cinnamon Bark. The bark oil is a powerful skin sensitizer that should never be used externally. The leaf oil is much gentler, but should still be used with the utmost care.

The warm and spicy fragrance of Cinnamon Leaf is very attractive, but it carries with it the risk of skin irritation. When I use this oil in a blend for external use, it is always highly diluted and in the presence of other essential oils. Used internally, the risk of irritation is no longer present, as this is the ideal use for this spice oil. It is an excellent digestive tonic with a long history of use. It has tonic effects and is a powerful antimicrobial. I add it to blends to decrease flatulence in dogs.

Used in a diffuser it is a powerful deodorizer and room air cleaner.

METHOD OF DISTILLATION:	Steam distillation
PART OF PLANT:	Leaves, twigs
PRODUCTION:	Madagascar, Sri Lanka
COLOR:	Yellowish brown
SCENT:	Warm, spicy
DOMINANT CHEMICAL GROUP:	Phenols

13. CITRONELLA,
Cymbopogon nardus

FLS

Citronella is well known as the insect-repelling substance in summertime candles and oil lamps, insect sprays, pet grooming supplies, and even as an ingredient in a no-bark training collar for dogs.

The numerous commercial uses of Citronella are linked to its comparative low cost. The oil should not be overused, however, for it is potentially irritating to the skin and also can cause toxicity. Several years ago I was in charge of an animal rescue raffle in which a gorgeous blanket was handcrafted out of golden retriever down and merino wool. Retriever owners from all over the world mailed packets of down to me, and I ended up with over 20 lbs of fur, which I had to carefully clean before sending off to be blended with the merino wool. Unsure about the presence of fleas in the fur, I decided to use Citronella in the wash water. An hour later in the unventilated basement washroom of my old home, and I was very sick – complete with numerous symptoms of toxicity: headache, dizziness, tremors, nausea and vomiting.

The moral of this story is that a tiny bit of Citronella is safe and effective to use with animals and humans. I like to use a small amount in flea-repelling blends, along with essential oils such as Clary Sage, Peppermint and Lemon.

Method of distillation:	Steam distillation
Part of plant:	Grass
Production:	Sri Lanka
Color:	Pale – medium yellow
Scent:	Intense, sweet, lemony
Dominant chemical group:	Aldehydes

14. CLARY SAGE,

Salvia sclarea

Top 20 Must Have Essential Oils

Not to be confused with common garden Sage, (*Salvia officinalis*), Clary Sage is a gentle and tolerable essential oil with an entirely different range of effects. While garden Sage essential oil is moderately high in ketones and thus mucolytic, Clary Sage is predominantly calming esters, which sedate the central nervous system. This makes Clary Sage a welcome addition to any calming blend. Garden Sage is by no means inappropriate to use with animals; it just must be used in very small amounts, properly diluted, and used for the appropriate reasons.

Clary Sage is appropriate to add to calming blends for animals in small amounts. Many human subjects note that Clary Sage creates a considerable euphoric effect when inhaled.

METHOD OF DISTILLATION:	Steam distillation
PART OF PLANT:	Flower tops, leaves
PRODUCTION:	Mediterranean, Russia, U.S.A., Morocco, France, Central Europe
COLOR:	Pale yellow – green
SCENT:	Warm, nutty, herbal
DOMINANT CHEMICAL GROUP:	Esters

Coriander Seed is a toning, balancing and strengthening essential oil that promotes and supports digestion. It is a circulatory stimulant and thus a good addition to blends for sore joints, muscles or arthritis.

The oil is frequently used in pharmaceuticals as a flavoring, and by the food industry to flavor liqueurs. The frequent internal use of this oil is regarded as safe in appropriate amounts. The mild, herbal scent of the oil makes it a welcome addition to a variety of blends, and it is mild and non-toxic.

15. CORIANDER SEED,

Coriandrum sativum

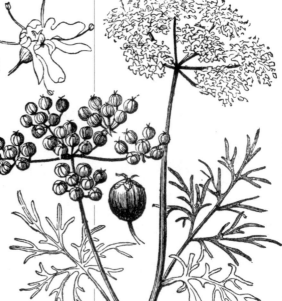

METHOD OF DISTILLATION:	Steam distillation
PART OF PLANT:	Seeds
PRODUCTION:	Russia, Yugoslavia
COLOR:	Colorless – pale yellow
SCENT:	Sweet, herbal, woodsy, slightly spicy
DOMINANT CHEMICAL GROUP:	Monoterpene alcohols

16. EUCALYPTUS RADIATA,

Eucalyptus radiata

Top 20 Must Have Essential Oils

Eucalyptus radiata essential oil is suitable for a variety of uses. It is the gentlest of all types of Eucalyptus oil and features a broad spectrum of tonifying terpene alcohols in its chemical makeup, which are well tolerated and metabolized. Eucalyptus is well known as a remedy for congestion, specifically *Eucalyptus globulus*, which is the type of Eucalyptus commonly available and found in remedies such as commercial chest rubs. The radiata type has a much more pleasing aroma that is softer, smoother and less harsh and medicinal.

The oil has antiviral, anti-inflammatory and expectorant effects. Due to its gentleness, it is very appropriate to use in blends for animals for congestion, and also makes an excellent diffuser room air cleaner, deodorizer and flea repellent. However, this oil can antidote homeopathic treatments, thus is not recommended for use in tandem with homeopathic protocols.

METHOD OF DISTILLATION:	Steam distillation
PART OF PLANT:	Leaves, branches
PRODUCTION:	Spain, Portugal, Brazil, China
COLOR:	Colorless
SCENT:	Camphorous, woodsy
DOMINANT CHEMICAL GROUP:	Terpene alcohols

This essential oil, of biblical fame, has a multitude of uses. It is indicated to strengthen a weakened immune system, and is a good choice for any blend for a sick or elderly animal that needs a systemic "boost".

It is both non-toxic and non-irritating, and can be used in a variety of manners for all sorts of skin ailments, due to its anti-inflammatory and antibacterial qualities.

The oil is believed to have rejuvenating and regenerating qualities on the skin and for this reason is a popular ingredient in products for wrinkles and scars.

17.

FRANKINCENSE,

Boswellia carterii

METHOD OF DISTILLATION:	Steam distillation
PART OF PLANT:	Resin
PRODUCTION:	Africa, China
COLOR:	Pale yellow – green
SCENT:	Fresh, green with warm and balsamic undertone
DOMINANT CHEMICAL GROUP:	Monoterpene hydrocarbons

18. GERANIUM,

Pelargonium graveolens

**Top 20 Must Have
Essential Oils**

Geranium essential oil has a very pleasing, soft floral aroma with a rose overtone. Because of this, it is frequently used to adulterate distillations of Rose to stretch yield. On its own, Geranium is a highly useful, gentle oil that belongs in every pet owner's aromatic apothecary. It is reasonably priced and has a multitude of uses. Geranium is predominantly composed of terpene alcohols, which explains its tonic and strong antifungal effects.

I add Geranium to blends for skin ailments, especially when a yeast overgrowth has been diagnosed. It is one of many antifungal essential oils that are suitable to use in the prevention and treatment of fungal ear infections in animals, especially in floppy-eared dogs. Geranium is also a necessary part of any effective tick repellent. Ticks are stubborn parasites, but the scent of certain essential oils sends them running. Geranium is one of several oils that can be used to create pesticide-free, safe and eco-friendly tick repellents for dogs.

METHOD OF DISTILLATION:	Steam distillation
PART OF PLANT:	Flowers, leaves, stalks
PRODUCTION:	Reunion, China, Russia
COLOR:	Yellowish green
SCENT:	Sweet, floral, rose-like
DOMINANT CHEMICAL GROUP:	Terpene alcohols

19. GINGER,
Zingiber officinale

**Top 20 Must Have
Essential Oils**

Ginger essential oil, distilled from the Ginger rhizome (root), is an acquired taste. Its distinctive smell is quite different from what many people expect. In other words, it does not smell like ginger snap cookies or ginger ale, although some of the expected nose-crinkling spiciness is present. I have found sourcing ginger to be a challenge, primarily due to the wide range of aromas present in different distillations. Don't settle for Ginger that smells stale, musty or somewhat rank. Fresh, warm and spicy are a must! Ginger is moderately low in price compared to other essential oils and adulteration is not common.

Ginger is wonderful to add to blends for use with dogs that have motion sickness. Many people give carsick dogs ginger snaps to thwart nausea, but a drop of Ginger on a dog biscuit works equally well without the sugar present in cookies. Ginger is also pleasant to add to blends with citrus oils in the creation of aromatic, deodorizing shampoos or sprays. It is also an effective digestive aid and can be used in massage blends for animals that have strains, sprains, dysplasia or arthritis. The warming effect of the oil combined with massage increases blood flow to the area of application. Ginger is non-toxic, non-irritating and safe to use in small amounts, properly diluted.

Method of distillation:	Steam distillation
Part of plant:	Root
Production:	China, India
Color:	Pale yellow, amber
Scent:	Warm, spicy, fresh
Dominant chemical group:	Sesquiterpene alcohols

20. GRAPEFRUIT,

Citrus paradisi

The heavenly scent of Grapefruit essential oil is uplifting, calming and just plain delightful. It can be added to blends for calming, deodorizing and also repelling insects, particularly fleas, due to their distaste for the monoterpene hydrocarbon limonene, of which Grapefruit contains 90%.

Like other citrus oils, it has a clarifying and tonic effect on the skin and tissues and is even believed to stimulate hair growth. It is useful in small amounts for animals that have an imbalanced sebum production resulting in skin problems.

The oil is non-toxic and, unlike other citrus oils, does not cause photosensitivity. It has a shorter shelf life than other citrus oils, so care should be taken to prevent oxidation, which can lead to skin irritation.

Organic quality is important, since most of the oil produced is from the U.S.A., where pesticides are used.

METHOD OF DISTILLATION:	Expression
PART OF PLANT:	Rind
PRODUCTION:	U.S.A., Brazil, Israel
COLOR:	Yellow – green
SCENT:	Fresh, crisp, bright, citrusy
DOMINANT CHEMICAL GROUP:	Monoterpene hydrocarbons

21.
HELICHRYSUM,
Helichrysum italicum

Top 20 Must Have Essential Oils

Helichrysum essential oil is by far one of the most amazing essential oils I have ever used. Unfortunately, it is also the most horrible smelling oil I have ever used, as well. I personally think that is smells like squashed bugs, yet have heard others "ooh" and "ahh" after smelling a sample and describe their experience to be that of smelling nectar, honey or ambrosia. Never forget that smell is, as I have said several times already, entirely subjective. Regardless of how the oil smells, there is no doubt as to its incredible therapeutic value. This has also recently driven the price of Helichrysum sky-high, so watch carefully for adulterations and always ask your supplier questions. The oil is also known as Immortelle or Everlasting. The oil is composed of calming esters and sesquiterpene hydrocarbons, yielding its analgesic, anti-inflammatory and regenerative effects. It is excellent for skin (undiluted). I of course recommend that Helichrysum is used diluted at all times with animals. Luckily, this is an oil which is most effective when it is highly diluted, so this makes it more affordable to use and also makes it more tolerable to smell, if you are one of those people who don't agree that it smells like honey.

METHOD OF DISTILLATION:	Steam distillation
PART OF PLANT:	Flower tops
PRODUCTION:	Italy, Spain, France
COLOR:	Pale yellow – orange
SCENT:	Heavy, honey-like, herbal
DOMINANT CHEMICAL GROUP:	Esters, sesquiterpene hydrocarbons, ketones

22. HYSSOP DECUMBENS,

Hyssop officinalis ch decumbens

Not to be confused with Hyssop officinalis, the decumbens chemotype is extremely gentle while being a powerful antiviral and antibacterial. The oil is non-toxic, non-irritating and is an antidepressant. A high price tag is attached to this oil, but it is well worth it. It is also known as creeping hyssop. Make sure that you purchase and use the decumbens chemotype, for Hyssop officinalis is high in ketones.

METHOD OF DISTILLATION: Steam distillation

PART OF PLANT: Leaves and flowering tops

PRODUCTION: France

COLOR: Pale yellow

SCENT: Slightly medicinal, green, herbal

DOMINANT CHEMICAL GROUP: Terpene alcohols, oxides

Juniper Berry oil is distilled from the berries of the juniper tree. The wood oil should be avoided due to its frequent adulteration with turpentine and its nephrotoxic (kidney) effects. Stimulating to the circulatory system, the oil is a welcome addition to blends for joint or muscle pain, arthritis or dysplasia. The berry oil is non-toxic and non-irritating in proper, diluted amounts.

Juniper Berry is also helpful for balancing oily skin, and for acne, eczema and hair loss.

Julia Lawless' *Illustrated Encyclopedia of Essential Oils* indicates that the oil is effective for repelling ticks,[20] but I personally have not used it in tick-repelling formulations. Other combinations of oils work especially well for repelling ticks, in particular, Geranium, Myrrh, Opoponax and Rosewood.

23. JUNIPER BERRY,

Juniperus communis

METHOD OF DISTILLATION:	Steam distillation
PART OF PLANT:	Fruit (berries)
PRODUCTION:	Italy, France, Austria, Spain, Germany, Canada
COLOR:	Colorless – pale yellow
SCENT:	Woodsy, balsamic
DOMINANT CHEMICAL GROUP:	Monoterpene hydrocarbons

24. LABDUNUM,

Cistus ladaniferus

Labdunum is also known as Cistus, or Rock Rose, and is distilled from the crude resin, twigs and leaves of the plant. The oil has a particularly unusual aroma, but its benefits outweigh any potential aversions.

I add Labdunum specifically to blends for wound care, and it was an ingredient in the first blend I ever created for use with animals, a blend of Labdunum, Lavender, Niaouli and Helichrysum which I call "Boo Boo Juice".

The oil is antibacterial, and astringent. Kurt Schnaubelt, in his book *Advanced Aromatherapy*, states that Cistus oil effectively stops bleeding and prevents hematomas.[21]

METHOD OF DISTILLATION:	Steam distillation
PART OF PLANT:	Resin, leaves, twigs
PRODUCTION:	Spain, Mediterranean
COLOR:	Dark yellow – orange
SCENT:	Rich, sweet, heavy, herbaceous
DOMINANT CHEMICAL GROUP:	Monoterpene hydrocarbons

25. LAVENDER,
Lavandula angustifolia

**Top 20 Must Have
Essential Oils**

Lavender is by far the most famous essential oil of all, and it's for good reason. Far and wide, people consider Lavender the one essential oil that they would not want to be without! This oil has numerous therapeutic properties as well as a pleasing scent and gentleness that is not found in the majority of essential oils. Lavender is one of few essential oils that can safely be used "neat", or undiluted.

Lavender can be used in blends for many common animal ailments, but I find it particularly well suited to any blend that is for skin conditions, first aid and healing purposes. The supreme gentleness of the oil in combination with antibacterial, antipruritic (anti-itch) and powerful regenerative properties make Lavender the perfect choice. The oil also acts as central nervous system sedative, thus it is known as a calming oil. This calming effect can be further synergized through blending with other calming oils. Lavender hybrids, known as Lavandin, share some similar therapeutic properties, but are considered to be harsher oils. For this reason, true Lavender, *Lavandula angustifolia* is most appropriate. Refrain from purchasing Lavenders labeled as "Lavender 40/42". This is Lavender to which synthetic Linalyl acetate has been added. There are many varieties of Lavender produced for aromatherapy purposes, all with varying

LAVENDER,

continued...

chemical compositions. Some of these types include the Mailette and Matherone varieties, which are produced by French artisan distillers.

Method of distillation:	Steam distillation
Part of plant:	Flower tops
Production:	France, Britain, Russia, Hungary, U.S.A.
Color:	Colorless
Scent:	Sweet, floral, herbal
Dominant chemical group:	Esters

Lemon essential oil is a strong antibacterial that also has the calming effects of other citrus oils. It is highly photosensitizing, so should not be applied directly to the skin and should be highly diluted in topical blends, with other oils composing the majority of the blend.

Lemon essential oil is an effective deodorizer and room air cleaner (great to use in a nebulizing diffuser). I like to add it to insect-repelling blends along with Clary Sage, Peppermint and Citronella to deter fleas, flies, mosquitoes and no-see-ums (midges). Add Lemon essential oil to a base of soy wax to make an anti-pet-odor candle, along with Citrus, Mint or Pine oils. The use of Lemon essential oil in candles, diffusers or room sprays not only disinfects room air, but also can cut right through the smell of musty, wet dog.

As with all citrus oils, organic oils are a must due to pesticides used in conventional citrus farming.

26. LEMON,
Citrus limon

METHOD OF DISTILLATION:	Expression
PART OF PLANT:	Rind
PRODUCTION:	Worldwide
COLOR:	Yellow
SCENT:	Crisp, sharp, bright, citrusy
DOMINANT CHEMICAL GROUP:	Monoterpene hydrocarbons

27. LEMONGRASS,

Cymbopogon citratus

Lemongrass bears many similarities to Citronella, but has a much smoother, more refined scent. It also can be a potential skin sensitizer, so use with great care and in dilute amounts. The very strong, sweet scent of this oil demands that it be used in small amounts anyway; use of larger amounts almost always results in a headache.

The oil has an intensely calming effect, and is also antiviral due to the presence of the aldehyde citral. While Lemongrass and Citronella can often be used interchangeably, Citronella appears to be more apt to repel insects.

METHOD OF DISTILLATION: Steam distillation

PART OF PLANT: Grass

PRODUCTION: West Indies, Sri Lanka, Asia

COLOR: Yellow – amber

SCENT: Intensely sweet, grassy, citrusy

DOMINANT CHEMICAL GROUP: Aldehyde

Green Mandarin essential oil is the sweetest of all citrus oils. The fragrance can only be described as candy-like and intensely calming, due to the presence of trace amounts of anthranilic acids. Green Mandarin is the only citrus oil in which this specific compound exists, making it an excellent addition to any blend for calming fear, anxiety or stress.

Like most citrus oils, this Mandarin has some photosensitizing properties and sun exposure after direct topical application should be avoided. This is not a situation that is run into often, since most animals have a dense coat of fur which prevents direct skin contact, but there are some breeds of hairless dogs. This safety warning is for them. Green Mandarin can be difficult to find, and only a few suppliers carry it.

Be careful that unscrupulous suppliers are not passing off Red Mandarin essential oil as the green variety and charging a higher price tag for it! An organic distillation is preferable, as with all citrus oils.

28. MANDARIN, GREEN,

Citrus reticulata

Top 20 Must Have Essential Oils

METHOD OF DISTILLATION:	Expression
PART OF PLANT:	Fruit rind
PRODUCTION:	Italy, Spain, Brazil
COLOR:	Pale orange – red
SCENT:	Sweet, citrusy, candy-like
DOMINANT CHEMICAL GROUP:	Terpene hydrocarbons

29. MARJORAM, SWEET,

Origanum marjorana

Top 20 Must Have Essential Oils

Sweet Marjoram essential oil is multi-purpose, with a pleasing, smooth herbal fragrance. Its chemical composition of terpene alcohols and terpene esters give it a calming, spasmolytic effect as well as strong antibacterial effects similar to Tea Tree and Niaouli. Kurt Schnaubelt recommends Sweet Marjoram as a replacement oil for Tea Tree, when one tires of its harsh and medicinal scent.

I use Marjoram as a key ingredient in certain calming blends for dogs, in combination with other soothing and grounding essential oils. It can also be used in blends for bacterial skin infections, wound care and insect repelling. I have also found that Marjoram has a profound effect on the undesirable behaviors of un-neutered male dogs. Whether the cessation of canine sexual urges is due to the calming effects of the oil or the folk use history of Marjoram as an anaphrodisiac, I'll never know. All I know is that several guide-dog-training groups swear that aromatherapy is responsible for calming down over-amorous males so that training sessions can continue.

METHOD OF DISTILLATION:	Steam distillation
PART OF PLANT:	Flower heads, leaves
	Mediterranean, Egypt, North Africa
COLOR:	Pale yellow
SCENT:	Intensely herbal, slightly spicy
DOMINANT CHEMICAL GROUP:	Terpene alcohols, terpene esters

Myrrh essential oil has a deep, warm, earthy fragrance and is valued for its anti-inflammatory properties. It also has noted antiviral properties. The oil extracted from the resin found on the *Commiphora myrrha* shrub has a long history of use, from numerous biblical references to its use by the Egyptians to mummify bodies.

I use Myrrh in blends for puppy teething pain, treating irritated or inflamed skin conditions, or in immune system-boosting blends. Several of my clients follow holistic vaccine protocols for their puppies, and rely on antiviral and antibacterial blends of essential oils to protect their young pups from infections such as parvovirus and kennel cough, or bordatella. Myrrh is also an important ingredient for repelling ticks.

30. MYRRH,

Commiphora myrrha

Top 20 Must Have Essential Oils

METHOD OF DISTILLATION:	Steam distillation
PART OF PLANT:	Resin
PRODUCTION:	Africa, Asia
COLOR:	Amber
	Warm, balsamic, earthy
DOMINANT CHEMICAL GROUP:	Terpene hydrocarbons, sesquiterpenes

31. NEROLI,

Citrus aurantium

Neroli essential oil is distilled from the blossoms of the orange tree. Three different essential oils are obtained from different parts of the tree, and Neroli is the most exquisite and precious of all. The oil is an expensive, albeit effective addition to any type of blend for calming, stress reduction or anxiety. It can also be used in blends for topical massage for female dogs that are in labor, to ease pain and stress.

The high cost of this oil makes its use prohibitive. "Neroli sur petitgrain", or orange blossoms co-distilled with the immature fruits, leaves and twigs (Petitgrain) yields a greener, more herbaceous scented oil, which lacks the precious nature of pure Neroli, but still has therapeutic calming effects.

The oil is non-toxic, non-irritating and safe to use in topical blends for animals.

METHOD OF DISTILLATION:	Steam distillation
PART OF PLANT:	Flower petals
PRODUCTION:	Italy, Tunisia, Morroco, Egypt, France
COLOR:	Yellow – orange
SCENT:	Sweet, floral, honey-like
DOMINANT CHEMICAL GROUP:	Monoterpene alcohols

Niaouli is a gentle relative of the immensely popular Tea Tree, *Melaleuca alternifolia*. Niaouli is preferable to Tea Tree for a variety of reasons, most notably its more pleasing scent, antihistaminic properties and powerful antibacterial effects with less potential for skin irritation.

Niaouli is the perfect oil to add to blends for any type of allergies manifesting themselves in the ears and skin, as well as for first aid purposes. It is a key ingredient in a blend of oils I use for cleaning and preventing ear infections in dogs. It is gentle, tolerable and whereas the quality of many Tea Tree distillations is questionable (Tea Tree is a trendy oil, remember that essential oil adulteration is especially victim to the principles of supply and demand!) I use and recommend this oil in place of Tea Tree. Niaouli is also known as "MQV".

32. NIAOULI,

Melaleuca quinquenervia viridiflora

Top 20 Must Have Essential Oils

METHOD OF DISTILLATION:	Steam distillation
PART OF PLANT:	Leaves, branches
PRODUCTION:	Australia
COLOR:	Pale yellow
SCENT:	Fresh, medicinal
DOMINANT CHEMICAL GROUP:	Terpene hydrocarbons, terpene alcohols, sesquiterpene alcohols

33. NUTMEG,

Myristica fragrans

Nutmeg essential oil has a history of controversial use. Too much of it is believed to cause hallucinations due to the myristicin content, but the bulk of the oil (approximately 85%) is composed of benign monoterpene hydrocarbons.

Nutmeg can safely be used in small amounts, properly diluted. It has a history of safe internal use due to its prevalence in pharmaceutical preparations as a flavoring.

I use Nutmeg in small amounts in blends for canine flatulence. The oil has a history of use in reducing gas production and flatulence, and also aiding indigestion and nausea.

It is also stimulating to the circulatory system, and its warming effects can be beneficial in topical massage oils for animals.

METHOD OF DISTILLATION:	Steam distillation
PART OF PLANT:	Seed
PRODUCTION:	Indonesia, Sri Lanka, West Indies
COLOR:	Colorless – pale yellow
SCENT:	Spicy, nutty, warm
DOMINANT CHEMICAL GROUP:	Monoterpene hydrocarbons

Opoponax essential oil is hard to find, but is a key ingredient in blends for repelling ticks. It is also known as Sweet Myrrh. I use Opoponax essential oil in my tick-repellent blend, along with Myrrh, Geranium, Lavender and Rosewood. This blend has been extremely successful in repelling ticks from dogs, even in areas with high tick populations. Dog owners using the tick repellent blend report that the number of ticks they find on their dogs after walks or hikes in infested areas is few to none. The use of essential oils as pest repellents becomes more and more important on a daily basis as an increasing number of pet owners seek to discontinue the use of monthly topical repellents which contain synthetic pesticides or have potential toxicity.

Essential oils repel insects due to their scent, so unfortunately, they need to be applied frequently. Fortunately, certain blends have pleasing aromas and animals enjoy the human touch.

34. OPOPONAX,

Commiphora erythraea

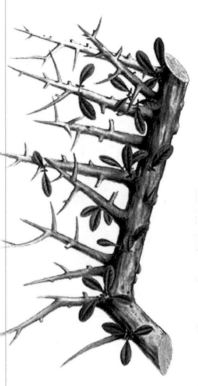

Method of distillation:	Steam distillation
Part of plant:	Resin
Production:	Somalia, Ethiopia
Color:	Yellow – orange
Scent:	Sweet, spicy, warm
Dominant chemical group:	Sesquiterpene alcohols

35. SWEET ORANGE,

Citrus sinensis

Top 20 Must Have Essential Oils

The crowd-pleasing fragrance of Sweet Orange essential oil makes it a joy to use, but common sense precautions must be taken. The oil is an excellent addition to any calming, deodorizing or flea-repelling blend. It also has a clarifying effect on skin that produces an excess of sebum, and is tonifying.

An organic oil should be used due to the potential for toxic pesticide residue in conventionally farmed distillations. Direct skin contact should be avoided due to photosensitization, and like all citrus oils, storage should involve minimal bottle headspace and, possibly, refrigeration to prevent oxidation.

Sweet Orange is one of my favorite essential oils because it is bright, clean and sunny, always sure to raise the spirits. While its therapeutic values are limited it is nevertheless a welcome oil to add to any blend that you are trying to "improve" the scent of for aesthetic purposes.

METHOD OF DISTILLATION:	Expression
PART OF PLANT:	Fruit rind
PRODUCTION:	U.S.A., Mediterranean, Brazil, Italy
	Medium orange
SCENT:	Sweet, citrusy
DOMINANT CHEMICAL GROUP:	Terpene hydrocarbons

36. PALMAROSA,
Cymbopogon martinii

Palmarosa is an attractively scented, inexpensive essential oil which can be used in a variety of ways. It is both antibacterial and antiviral and non-toxic to the skin.

Its fragrance is very similar to Rosewood and Geranium, and it can be used interchangeably with Rosewood (which incidentally, is frequently adulterated with Palmarosa or in other cases, Palmarosa is sold as Rosewood). Many aromatherapists prefer Palmarosa to Rosewood because there is a stigma attached to the use of Rosewood – the belief that the wood of this endangered tree is harvested specifically for essential oil distillation. In truth, Rosewood essential oil is distilled from the sawdust and branches left after rosewood trees are processed for the production of lumber.

METHOD OF DISTILLATION:	Steam distillation
PART OF PLANT:	Grass
PRODUCTION:	West Indies
COLOR:	Pale yellow
SCENT:	Floral, sweet, geranium-like
DOMINANT CHEMICAL GROUP:	Monoterpene alcohols

37. PATCHOULI,

Pogostemon cablin

Patchouli essential oil is an earthy scent that evokes memories of the sixties for many. I enjoy blending it with other deep and earthy-scented oils and with citrus oils to create deodorizing shampoos for dogs. The oil itself has gentle circulation-stimulating effects that are beneficial for skin and coat and also acts as an insect repellent. If you don't care for the scent of patchouli, then this is one to best leave on the shelf.

METHOD OF DISTILLATION:	Steam distillation
PART OF PLANT:	Leaves (dried)
PRODUCTION:	India, China, Malaysia, South America
COLOR:	Amber
SCENT:	Earthy, woodsy, herbaceous
DOMINANT CHEMICAL GROUP:	Sesquiterpene hydrocarbons and alcohols

Peppermint essential oil is produced worldwide, primarily for industrial and pharmaceutical purposes. The majority of the oil produced is used in menthol cigarettes. Distillations of Peppermint contain varying levels of ketones, thus a low-ketone distillation is preferred. The aroma of low-ketone Peppermint oil will be softer, sweeter and smoother than the typical harsh, almost medicinal-like scent which indicates the presence of high levels of ketones found in hastily distilled Peppermint.

Next to Lavender, Peppermint surely has the most uses. I find it indispensable. It is stimulating, but some people swear that it calms them. The oil stimulates circulation and is therefore an excellent addition to a massage oil for animals with injuries, sprains, strains, arthritis or dysplasia.

Peppermint oil is an excellent replacement for high-ketone Pennyroyal in insect-repelling blends. It successfully repels fleas, flies, mosquitoes and the ubiquitous no-see-ums.

Other uses for Peppermint include relief of pain and itching, reducing mouth odor, and with Ginger, as an effective remedy for carsickness.

38. PEPPERMINT,
Mentha piperita

Top 20 Must Have Essential Oils

METHOD OF DISTILLATION:	Steam distillation
PART OF PLANT:	Leaves
PRODUCTION:	Worldwide
COLOR:	Pale yellow – green
SCENT:	Sweet, minty, herbal
DOMINANT CHEMICAL GROUP:	Terpene alcohols, ketones

39. PETITGRAIN,

Citrus aurantium

Petitgrain is yet another essential oil distilled from the orange tree. This time, the leaves, branches and immature fruits are used. The oil is most prized for its calming effects, and it is non-toxic to use, making it ideal to use with animals and children.

Different types of Petitgrain are also available, with varying ester content. Mandarin Petitgrain is the most intensely calming. Lime and Bergamot Petitgrain are also distilled in small quantities for aromatherapy use. Sweet Orange Petitgrain is often referred to as "Petitgrain Bigarade".

I use Petitgrain in calming blends and also for its delicate fragrance.

METHOD OF DISTILLATION:	Steam distillation
PART OF PLANT:	Leaves, branches, immature fruits
PRODUCTION:	France, Paraguay, North Africa
COLOR:	Pale yellow
SCENT:	Fresh floral, citrus, green
DOMINANT CHEMICAL GROUP:	Esters

Ravensare aromatica is a chemotype of *Cinnamonum camphora*. It is a gentle and tolerable antiviral and antibacterial essential oil that is similar in scent and activity to Eucalyptus radiata. It is distilled in Madagascar, where natives call it "ravintsara", which means "the good leaf".

The oil is supportive to the immune system and has tonifying effects.

I use Ravensare in blends for animals with compromised immune systems or for young dogs that are prone to infections until their full range of immunity and vaccinations are established.

I also like to use a combination of Ravensare, Eucalyptus radiata and Niaouli in place of any blend calling for Tea Tree.

40. RAVENSARE AROMATICA,
Cinnamonum camphora

Top 20 Must Have Essential Oils

METHOD OF DISTILLATION:	Steam distillation
PART OF PLANT:	Leaves
PRODUCTION:	Madagascar
COLOR:	Pale yellow
SCENT:	Herbal, medicinal, camphor-like
DOMINANT CHEMICAL GROUP:	Terpene alcohols

41. ROSE,

Rosa damascena

Top 20 Must Have Essential Oils

Rose is the queen of flowers, and the price of the essential oil or the absolute definitely reveals this. The attractive scent of Rose is undeniable, thus it makes a luxurious grooming product, spray or shampoo for any dog.

Rose is also stabilizing to the central nervous system, making it a suitable addition to blends for fearful animals.

The oil has a gentle tonifying effect on the skin, and I like to add a small amount of it to blends for itchy, irritated or dry skin.

METHOD OF DISTILLATION:	Steam distillation
PART OF PLANT:	Flower heads
PRODUCTION:	Bulgaria, Turkey, France
COLOR:	Pale yellow – green
SCENT:	Rich, deep, floral
DOMINANT CHEMICAL GROUP:	Terpene alcohols

42. ROSEMARY,
Rosmarinus officinalis

Rosemary essential oil is unfortunately widely adulterated and it has a "bad rap" for raising the blood pressure and inducing seizures, neither of which has been proven in any sort of informal or formal research studies. Regardless, I adhere to the "warnings" and suggest that those who are prone to seizures or have high blood pressure use Rosemary with caution.

There are several distinct chemotypes of Rosemary available, but the verbenone chemotype is the gentlest and most desirable for use with dogs. It contains verbenone, a ketone – but in low amounts which are very gentle and tolerable in use. The oil is mucolytic, acting as an expectorant, and also aids in cell regeneration.

It is believed that Rosemary (like Bay Leaf) is responsible for promoting and maintaining hair growth. For this reason, I include this oil in blends for healthy skin and coat for dogs. I also enjoy using it in small amounts because of its refreshing, spicy herbal fragrance.

METHOD OF DISTILLATION:	Steam distillation
PART OF PLANT:	Leaves, flower tops
PRODUCTION:	France, Spain, Tunisia
COLOR:	Colorless – pale yellow
SCENT:	Herbaceous, camphorous, minty
DOMINANT CHEMICAL GROUP:	Monoterpene alcohols and hydrocarbons

43. ROSEWOOD,

Aniba roseadora

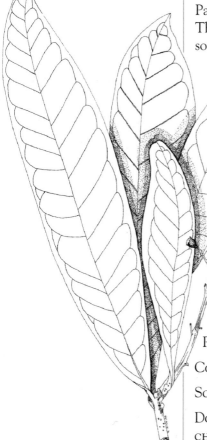

Rosewood essential oil is an extremely gentle, tonic oil which is excellent for skin conditions. It is most commonly used in perfumery, but has aromatherapy uses as a cellular stimulant and aids in tissue regeneration. Its scent is very similar to Geranium and Palmarosa.

Rosewood is frequently adulterated with Palmarosa, or Palmarosa is sold as Rosewood. These oils are very similar in scent and action, so this is not a problem for therapeutic value. The issue is that many will charge more for the Rosewood but be selling you Palmarosa instead. The oil has antibacterial and antiviral properties, and ticks are repelled by the scent of it, in combination with other oils such as Myrrh, Bay Leaf and Opoponax.

METHOD OF DISTILLATION: Steam distillation

PART OF PLANT: Wood (sawdust and twigs)

PRODUCTION: Brazil

COLOR: Colorless

SCENT: Sweet, herbal, rose-like

DOMINANT CHEMICAL GROUP: Monoterpene alcohols

Sage is an unfortunately misunderstood essential oil. Open just about any aromatherapy book and you will see warnings galore for this useful oil. Sage is part of the ketone group, and ketones are an essential oil component that can be both neuro- and nephrotoxic. However, Sage has only a moderate ketone content – low in comparison to oils such as Pennyroyal or Thuja. Kurt Schnaubelt agrees that Sage can be used safely. In his book *Advanced Aromatherapy*, he states that "Of all of the oils having a high thujone (ketone) content, sage is the most common. Its frequent use points to a relatively low toxicity and therefore is evidence that safe oil is less toxic than the thujone it contains, were the thujone taken as an isolated substance."[22]

Ketones are stimulating and aid in tissue regeneration, as well as having both antibacterial and antiviral effects.

It is for these reasons, that Sage can be beneficial when used in blends for quickly spreading conditions such as hot spots, technically known as moist acute pyoderma. I use Sage essential oil in my blend for hot spots in small amounts combined with other essential oils. With animals, Sage should always be used in the smallest amount necessary to produce a desired effect, due to its ketone content.

44. SAGE,

Salvia officinalis

METHOD OF DISTILLATION:	Steam distillation
PART OF PLANT:	Leaves
PRODUCTION:	Worldwide
COLOR:	Pale yellow
SCENT:	Fresh, herbal, medicinal
DOMINANT CHEMICAL GROUP:	Ketones, oxides

45. SPEARMINT,

Mentha spicata

Spearmint essential oil has a smoother, more refined scent than Peppermint, but a similar range of action. Surprisingly, it is Peppermint which is more commonly used, perhaps because few distillations for therapeutic grade spearmint exist (most is produced for the food and flavorings industries, used in candies, cigarettes and for baking).

I enjoy using Spearmint in combination with Peppermint in blends to synergize the effects of the two mints. Mint essential oils repel fleas and other pesky insects, and a massage containing mint stimulates circulation and blood flow to the area, speeding the healing process.

METHOD OF DISTILLATION:	Steam distillation
PART OF PLANT:	Leaves
PRODUCTION:	U.S.A., Hungary, Spain
COLOR:	Pale yellow
SCENT:	Fresh, minty, warm
DOMINANT CHEMICAL GROUP:	Monoterpene alcohols, ketones

46. SPIKENARDE,
Nardostachys jatamansi

Spikenarde essential oil is similar in fragrance to Valerian, and has a similar range of action. It is intensely calming and grounding, and is considered to be a "spiritual oil" due to its presence in the Bible where Mary anointed the feet of Jesus with Spikenarde before the Last Supper.

The oil is also rejuvenating and regenerating to the skin, making it suitable for blends for dogs with problem skin.

The oil is commonly interchanged with Valerian, and much Valerian sold is often actually Spikenarde. It is non-toxic and non-irritating. While many describe the scent as being repugnant, like "dirty socks," others find the scent soothing, calming and centering. When blended with other essential oils it rounds out a blend, providing depth, warmth and earthiness.

METHOD OF DISTILLATION:	Steam distillation
PART OF PLANT:	Root
PRODUCTION:	India, China
COLOR:	Amber
SCENT:	Sweet, woody, earthy
DOMINANT CHEMICAL GROUP:	Sesquiterpene hydrocarbons

47. TANGERINE,

Citrus reticulata

Tangerine and Mandarin, or "Satsuma," are often used interchangeably, but differences do exist. The two oils actually represent different chemotypes in that Tangerine does not contain any of the calming methyl anthranilate that is present in Mandarin (especially Green Mandarin).

Tangerine, lacking this intense calming component is closer to Sweet Orange – uplifting and clearing depression, revitalizing. Tangerine has a softer, more delicate scent than Sweet Orange.

I use Tangerine in citrus blends for aesthetic fragrance purposes, in topical blends for dogs with malaise and fatigue (Tangerine is not phototoxic as Sweet Orange is), and also in blends for canine flatulence, as the oil aids in digestion.

As with all citrus oils, quality is imperative because of pesticides, therefore an organic oil should always be used.

METHOD OF DISTILLATION:	Steam distillation
PART OF PLANT:	Rind
PRODUCTION:	U.S.A., Spain, Italy
COLOR:	Yellow – orange
SCENT:	Fresh, bright, citrusy
DOMINANT CHEMICAL GROUP:	Monoterpene hydrocarbons

Thyme linalol is one of six known Thyme chemotypes. Our previous discussion of chemotypes on page 20 reveals the circumstances under which a plant may exhibit polymorphism and produce chemotypes of varying chemical composition. Thyme linalol is the gentlest and most useful of the Thyme chemotypes.

With its high linalol content, it is relaxing, antibacterial and antifungal, with none of the harshness and skin irritation associated with common Thyme, often referred to as "Red" or "White" Thyme, which has a very high phenol content.

Thyme linalol is excellent for skin problems, as it can help to clear and prevent a variety of imbalances as well as act as a balancing tonic.

48. THYME LINALOL

Thyme vulgaris ch linalol

Top 20 Must Have Essential Oils

METHOD OF DISTILLATION:	Steam distillation
PART OF PLANT:	Leaves, flower tops
PRODUCTION:	France
COLOR:	Colorless – pale yellow
SCENT:	Herbaceous, green, slightly medicinal
DOMINANT CHEMICAL GROUP:	Monoterpene alcohols

49. THYME THUJANOL

Thyme vulgaris ch thujanol

Top 20 Must Have Essential Oils

Thyme thujanol is another Thyme chemotype which has all of the effects and benefits of Thyme linalol in addition to being an immune system stimulant, liver detoxifier and antiviral. Kurt Schnaubelt recommends Thyme thujanol to be used in the prevention of Lyme's disease, applied immediately after a tick bite is discovered or a tick is found. It is for this purpose that I use Thyme thujanol with dogs. It is also useful in immune-boosting blends, or when a powerful antibacterial is needed without the caustic, skin irritating effects.

METHOD OF DISTILLATION:	Steam distillation
PART OF PLANT:	Leaves, flower tops
PRODUCTION:	France
COLOR:	Colorless – pale yellow
SCENT:	Herbaceous, green, slightly medicinal
DOMINANT CHEMICAL GROUP:	Monoterpene alcohols

50. VALERIAN,
Valeriana officinalis

Top 20 Must Have Essential Oils

Valerian essential oil is intensely calming and grounding. It is distilled from the root of the valerian herb, the same plant which calming valerian herbal supplements come from.

I add Valerian essential oil to blends for calming dogs that have separation anxiety or are fearful of loud noises, storms, fireworks or new situations.

Although many people describe the odor of this oil as "dirty socks", I find it to be intensely comforting, and it blends well with Sweet Orange, Petitgrain, Mandarin, Rose, Neroli, Marjoram and Vetiver.

Spikenarde essential oil is often sold as Valerian and marked up in price, so be cautious of your supplier for this hard-to-find oil. If you cannot find Valerian, Spikenarde is an appropriate replacement, as it has a similar fragrance and very similar qualities of calming and grounding.

METHOD OF DISTILLATION:	Steam distillation
PART OF PLANT:	Root
PRODUCTION:	Belgium, France, Netherlands
COLOR:	Brown
SCENT:	Warm, musty, woodsy
DOMINANT CHEMICAL GROUP:	Sesquiterpene alcohols

51. VETIVER,

Vetivera zizanoides

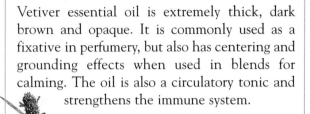

Vetiver essential oil is extremely thick, dark brown and opaque. It is commonly used as a fixative in perfumery, but also has centering and grounding effects when used in blends for calming. The oil is also a circulatory tonic and strengthens the immune system.

METHOD OF DISTILLATION: Steam distillation

PART OF PLANT: Roots

PRODUCTION: India, Indonesia, Sri Lanka

COLOR: Dark brown

SCENT: Earthy, grassy, balsamic

DOMINANT CHEMICAL GROUP: Sesquiterpene hydrocarbons

Ylang Ylang is an intensely heady and sweet floral essential oil that has a deeply calming, almost narcotic effect. I use it mostly for fragrance and calming purposes, but also to balance out the effects of other oils. For instance, in a blend for canine fatigue, I use a small amount of Ylang Ylang to temper any chance that the Rosemary essential oil used in the blend might be overstimulating.

Ylang Ylang is produced from a series of distillations of the flower petals, the first, or "Extra", yielding the most complete and highest quality oil. First, second and third distillations also exist. I avoid these, as the relative low cost of this oil (in comparison to other florals such as Rose, Jasmine or Neroli) makes its price entirely affordable. Also, its intense fragrance is such that only a tiny amount is ever needed in any given blend.

52. YLANG YLANG,
Cananga odorata

Method of distillation:	Steam distillation
Part of plant:	Flower petals
Production:	Madagascar
Color:	Pale yellow
Scent:	Intense, sweet, floral
Dominant chemical group:	Sesquiterpene hydrocarbons

The Hydrosols

(Recommended for all animals, but particularly for cats, rabbits and other small animals.)

Hydrosol monographs were written using *Hydrosols: The Next Aromatherapy* by Suzanne Catty as a reference.[23] I focus on ten common hydrosols in this section, but numerous others exist and are explored in detail in the hydrosol monograph section of Catty's book.

1. CHAMOMILE (ROMAN),

Anthemis nobilis

This delicately sweet-smelling hydrosol is excellent for all-purpose use. It is supremely gentle and excellent for all sorts of skin irritations and ailments, as well as for calming nervous tension and anxiety.

PART OF PLANT:	Flowers
SCENT:	Sweet, honey-like
PH:	3.0 – 3.3
SHELF LIFE:	Up to 2 years

2. CORNFLOWER,

Centaurea cyanus

Cornflower hydrosol has a subtle, almost undetectable fragrance. It is excellent for use topically on the skin, for any sort of skin condition – but especially for dry, devitalized skin. It is extremely gentle and has a cooling feeling on the skin.

PART OF PLANT:	Flowers
SCENT:	Subtle, delicate, floral
PH:	4.7 – 5.0
SHELF LIFE:	Up to 12 months

A lush flowery-scented hydrosol, reminiscent of roses. It is anti-inflammatory and thus perfect for inflamed skin conditions and wound care. Its beautiful scent makes it a sweet kitty perfume, which is emotionally uplifting.

3. GERANIUM,
Pelargonium graveolens

PART OF PLANT:	Leaves, flowers
SCENT:	Rich, intense, sweet, rose-like
PH:	4.9 – 5.2
SHELF LIFE:	12 – 16 months

A somewhat green and tea-like scent, which is very different from Roman Chamomile. A must-have for skin problems and wound care, due to its powerful anti-inflammatory nature. Suzanne Catty states that this hydrosol is "Extremely energetic, powerfully calming and emotionally comforting".

4. GERMAN CHAMOMILE (BLUE CHAMOMILE)
Matricaria recutita

PART OF PLANT:	Flowers
SCENT:	Green, tea-like
PH:	4.0 – 4.1
SHELF LIFE:	Up to 14 months

5. LAVENDER,

Lavandula angustifolia

Another all-purpose, must-have hydrosol, with the recognizable scent of lavender, but deeper and sweeter like honey and nectar. It has cooling and healing properties and relieves itching and irritation quickly. Lavender is excellent for wound care and cleaning and is soothing to the emotions.

PART OF PLANT:	Flowers
SCENT:	Floral, herbal
PH:	5.6 – 5.9
SHELF LIFE:	Up to 2 years

6. LEMON VERBENA,

Lippia citriadora

Lemon Verbena is stress-relieving and highly relaxing hydrosol with a light and delicate lemony scent. Strong anti-inflammatory properties make it useful for skin and wound care, ear cleaning and also, gum and teeth inflammation.

PART OF PLANT:	Leaves
SCENT:	Light, citrusy
PH:	5.2 – 5.5
SHELF LIFE:	18+ months

The scent of heaven – a deliciously fragrant hydrosol with a complex floral and fruity scent, Neroli should be an ingredient in any calming blend due to its light sedative action. It is physically and emotionally supportive and nurturing – perfect partner to flower and gemstone essences.

Part of Plant:	Flowers
Scent:	Floral, citrus
Ph:	3.8-4.5
Shelf Life:	2 years +

7. NEROLI (ORANGE BLOSSOM)
Citrus aurantium

If you know the divine scent of a fresh rose, this is it. The hydrosol smells exactly like the treasured flower. Rose is useful for all types of skin problems, wounds, bites, scratches or cuts. It is emotionally calming and supportive especially when blended with Roman Chamomile and Lavender

Part of Plant:	Flowers
Scent:	Floral, sweet, just like a fresh rose
Ph:	4.1 – 4.4
Shelf Life:	Up to 2 years

8. ROSE,
Rosa damascena

9. ROSEMARY,

Rosmarinus officinalis

Rosemary hydrosol is an excellent flea repellent due to its intense green, herbal scent. It is stimulating and revitalizing and good for deodorizing. It has been shown to be a powerful antioxidant, similar in action to Witch Hazel.

Part of Plant:	Leaves
Scent:	Herbal, green
Ph:	4.6 – 4.7
Shelf Life:	18 – 20 months

10. WITCH HAZEL,

Hamamelis virginiana

This is a most subtly scented hydrosol – plantlike but not identifiable. The real thing does not contain the rubbing alcohol found in drugstore versions (avoid those!). A powerful anti-inflammatory and antioxidant, making it a must for healing, its uses are limitless, making it a must-have.

Part of Plant:	Bark
Scent:	Herbal, woodsy
Ph:	4.0 – 4.2
Shelf Life:	8 – 12 months

Section 4

Man's (and Woman's!) Best Friend: Aromatherapy for Dogs

Canine aromatherapy has been my specialty for the last ten years, and for good reason. With a selection of pure essential oils and knowledge of basic essential oil chemistry and appropriate dilutions and dosages for dogs, aromatherapy provides an entire pharmacopeia of home remedies for a plethora of common canine ailments.

I feel that aromatherapy and dogs are a perfect combination. Dogs, with their keen sense of smell and innate curiosity are ideal subjects for the use of essential oils and hydrosols. I have yet to meet a dog that did not perk up his ears and eagerly try to sniff whatever it was that I had to offer. I have had pet owners tell me how their dogs, who would previously run and hide from an ear cleaning or bath, now eagerly await their grooming session with all natural, essential-oil-containing formulations.

When giving aromatherapy remedies to dogs, I always use the highest quality oils, highly diluted in base oils at a fraction of the human dose, while avoiding certain oils altogether, and have never had a dog experience any type of negative reaction, toxicity, irritation or other undesirable effects. Dr. Susan Wynn, DVM, sums up a similar rationale for treating animals with herbs and essential oils in "Pet Metabolism Dictates Dosage: Natural Treatments for Animals Should Reflect Bioindividuality," an article written for the *Nutrition Science News*. Dr. Wynn tells us that "The pharmacologic actions of numerous herb and multivitamin therapies work similarly in both animals and people, and treatment recommendations usually involve proportionate dosages. In many cases, however, the physiology of other species is sufficiently different from that of humans to require more cautious dosing or even avoidance of certain substances."[24]

While only one book has been written covering canine aromatherapy, and while very few vets (or aromatherapists) practice it, a fair amount of information exists on the internet and in general holistic pet care books. However, much of this information is dubious and contradictory. I have come across numerous instances of information that is downright dangerous, as well as nonsensical. One website recommends a blend of three of the most toxic oils in existence to repel fleas – Rue, Wormwood and Thuja. Another website recommends the use of undiluted essential oils high in phenols (dermocaustic and nephrotoxic) in large amounts applied to the spine of animals to release toxins. Another website suggests that absolutely no essential oil should be given to an animal internally without being prescribed by a holistic vet – a tough thing to manage when you'd be hard-pressed to find a vet who even acknowledges aromatherapy, much less has studied it in enough depth to know what is and is not safe to administer internally.

The situation is no better when one turns to books for advice. The fact of the matter is that just because something is in print does not mean that it is gospel. Always take into account the full message and context of a work, as well as the training of the author. Look into an author's credentials and education if you feel the need to. It is the welfare of your pet that should be of the greatest concern.

Also, while a vet may know much about animal physiology and medicine, many vets may be very much in the dark about aromatherapy and essential oils. Ironically, much of the questionable information I have seen is presented in none other than books written by veterinarians! Some vets may base their information on the action of herbs, which are different than that of essential oils, others on sourcebooks detailing human aromatherapy treatment, just because they are writing a book on holistic pet health and want to present all possible angles.

I experienced this just yesterday when a new client contacted me for a brief consultation in regards to her cat. She had just learned that essential oils could be harmful to cats and was concerned because following the advice of a book written by a veterinarian, she had been giving her cat 1 drop of Spruce essential oil on a daily basis for liver detoxification. Spruce essential oil is dominantly monoterpene hydrocarbons, which cats cannot metabolize. (more about this in the feline section, Section 5). Thankfully, some veterinarians, such as Dr. Susan Wynn, have done adequate research into the metabolic differences between different animal species. The awareness of this type of information can be lifesaving when it comes to our pets. Obtaining accurate and safe information about the use of essential oils with animals is of paramount importance, due to the fact that the oils are such concentrated substances, with varied chemical make-ups.

In this section we will cover a variety of topics, including the canine–human bond, how canine aromatherapy is being used today, essential oils used in tandem with other modalities, specific safety considerations for dogs, and common canine ailments that can be helped with essential oils along with helpful recipes. Please refer to Section 1 of this book for basic aromatherapy information as well as specific information concerning the pathways through which aromatherapy works with animals.

Unfettered Loyalty – the Dog

The canine–human bond is strong, there is no doubt about that. Dogs have been domesticated over the course of thousands of years, evolving from wild pack animals to tame and obedient companions that seemingly never leave our sides. Many of us see our dogs as family members, and in our modern, convenience-driven society, dogs have even become a veritable replacement for children, or possibly a stand-in "partner" for those who choose to lead a solitary life.

Is it any wonder that the pet-care industry has blossomed? Ten years ago, cashmere dog sweaters, $200 bottles of French dog perfume, ostrich leather collars and leads, and plush faux-fur dog beds were nowhere to be seen. Yet here we are today with dog spas, doggie daycare centers, personal dog trainers, dog masseuses, dog chiropractors and canine acupuncturists, and Reiki practitioners. To many, the dog is a cherished and privileged member of the pack. These frills and luxuries are merely ways of attempting to strengthen the canine–human bond. This bond is reciprocal: we dote upon our dogs and in turn they give us love, affection, obedience and loyalty, although the large number of dogs presently sitting in shelters tells us that this is not always the case, but this book is about aromatherapy, not the ethics of animal rescue, pet ownership and euthanasia. Aromatherapy is a way to support and nourish the human–canine bond while also improving the health of the dog you are caring for. It also comes with a much lower price tag, and the very nature of aromatherapy makes it beneficial for both dog and owner.

Aromatherapy is one of the most precious "gifts" that can be bestowed upon a dog. Domesticated canines are a far cry from their wolf relatives, but only because they've been stripped of their wild freedoms. In most cases, they are fed by humans, cleaned and brushed by humans, and medically cared for by us as well. Wolves and wild dogs, however, remain close to nature – because it is all that they know. This does give them a competitive edge over their domesticated counterparts. Although they typically have a more arduous existence and a shorter lifespan, they do eat an available diet which is best for them – scavenging for prey and small animals, eating plants, grasses and herbs, fruits, nuts and berries. I have experienced my own dogs foraging in the herb garden on numerous occasions, or eating grasses and treasures found in the neighbors' vegetable garden. The domesticated dog doesn't exactly get this in his kibble unless he has room to roam, or a master who is extremely well educated and feeds a "BARF" diet – Bones And Raw Food.

When wild dogs or wolves are sick, they seek out certain foods, plants and herbs to aid in boosting them back to health. Horses also do this. In *Veterinary Aromatherapy*, naturopath Nelly Grosjean states that "Dogs naturally purge their systems if they live outside and in the country: when they are out, they will carefully choose those specific plants they need. When a dog becomes 'civilised', it loses this instinct."[25] This is an important aspect of using aromatherapy, and also herbs, with dogs. It is also the basis of a form of aromatherapy that relies on the use of kinesiology, in which the animal chooses the essential oil it wants to receive in a treatment. Kinesiology is preferred by aromatherapists in the United Kingdom, where it is primarily used with horses. It is based on the premise that since in the wild animals self-medicate themselves with certain plants and herbs, they should be allowed to choose which essential oil they want in a treatment. While this sounds wonderful, I have yet to find a dog who was not interested in any aromatic formulation – be it essential oil or hydrosol based – which was presented to him, and for this reason have based my practice of aromatherapy on synergistic topical blends. Nevertheless, the use of herbs and plant extracts allows us to give a little bit of the wild back to our dogs, bringing them closer to that which was once part of their very existence. Plant-based therapy is a link to the evolutionary process of canines. It is a biochemically compatible therapy. It is the least we can do in return for their unwavering love, devotion and loyalty.

Wild and Wacky Canine Aromatherapy

Canine aromatherapy is still in its infancy in terms of general acceptance. While aromatherapy is well known to the masses due to repeated exposure to "smelly stuff" by the perfume and toiletries industries, few are aware of the true holistic capabilities of aromatherapy, much less canine aromatherapy. Very few veterinarians see aromatherapy as a viable form of holistic care. Those who do, and who practice it from a safe and educated point of view, I consider blessed! Mass-produced canine aromatherapy products are now available in the aisles of pet superstores, further skewing the public's viewpoint of what the modality truly is. These are not really aromatherapy products. They are synthetic chemical soups and fake scents designed to entice you into pampering your pet and making your home supposedly smell better (at the expense of your health and your poor dog's sense of smell).

Last year (2001), I sent a series of press releases over the national public relations newswires in hopes of garnering interviews and radio talk show appearances about aromatherapy for pets. While I did receive several valuable appearances on various reputable programs, I also received a large number of requests for interviews based solely on the premise that aromatherapy for dogs was a wild and crazy idea! One such request involved my being contacted and interviewed over the phone by the television program *Ripley's Believe It or Not*. In the end, they opted not to do the segment because in the interview I told them just how believable and demonstrably effective aromatherapy truly was – not exactly what they wanted to hear for their program! Several other radio appearances involved the program hosts introducing me as a wacky sort of pagan witch-woman doing aromatherapy for dogs… only to have their premise soon dispelled when I described what aromatherapy was actually capable of and explained how it was hardly what their original impression had led them to believe. It is my hope that the many press appearances I made in 2001 exposed more people to the purity of aromatherapy as an alternative healing method, while clearing some of the new-age stigma from the air.

Canine Aromatherapy: Case Studies and Observations

With each passing year, I learn of more and more people utilizing aromatherapy with dogs. Some of these instances are downright frightening, but others are highly commendable uses of aromatherapy formulations for common canine ailments. I have had the pleasure of meeting and working with many wonderful people in the last ten years. Some were already using aromatherapy with their dogs when I met them. Others began using my recipes and have naturally progressed to their own formulations. Here is a view of how some professionals and some "regular" dog owners are using aromatherapy today. Seeing how aromatherapy is being used by various persons is essential to understanding how it can translate into use with your own dog. It also lends credibility and substance to a truly wonderful holistic healing modality that is so often misinterpreted.

DR. KAREN BECKER, DVM – NATURAL PET ANIMAL HOSPITAL, TINLEY PARK, ILLINOIS

Dr. Becker is the first vet I learned of who used aromatherapy with pets. Today, Dr. Becker relies on a variety of essential oils and hydrosols for use in the routine course of exams.

We diffuse relaxing Lavender in the waiting room and some exam rooms; we nebulize oils for certain respiratory conditions and also mix oils with jojoba and use them topically.

Most recently, I have used several therapeutic oils for Gemini, my 11-year-old Rottweiler. She ruptured several intervertebral discs and had a lot of muscular pain associated with the injury. I used a blend of Marjoram (for its musculoskeletal analgesic effects) and Rosemary (as a neurological stimulant). I really encourage pet owners to use aromatic massage for musculoskeletal conditions for several reasons. First, the oils themselves have therapeutic properties. Second, the massage benefits pets by improving circulation, reducing muscular tension and removing cellular toxins from the tissues. Third, I have found that pets and owners begin to look forward to their daily aromatic massages, which also become a wonderful bonding time for both of them.

The rich vasculature in pets' nasal membranes makes intranasal absorption of nebulized substances very therapeutic. Veterinarians often administer drugs for respiratory conditions via nebulization. This form of therapy is often times less stressful for pets (especially birds and exotic animals) and delivers medication directly to the affected area, including the nasal passages, sinuses, trachea and lungs or airsacs.

Recently, a two-year-old Doberman, "Hotshot," presented to me for complementary therapy to address his intranasal aspergillosis, a resistant fungus that was growing in his sinuses. Systemic and topical drug therapy was not improving his condition and the owner was concerned he was getting worse. We elected nebulization therapy, in conjunction with his weekly drug treatments at the state veterinary hospital. Hotshot's owner learned how to nebulize him at our hospital, then continued the treatments at home with a portable machine. We used a dilute combination of Tea Tree (Melaleuca alternifolia) and Eucalyptus oils in sterile bronchosaline. The owner noticed an immediate improvement in the dog's energy level and in his ability to breathe through his nose. The university was impressed with Hotshot's unusually quick recovery from this sometimes difficult-to-treat fungus.

We use aromatherapy on a daily basis at Natural Pet Animal Hospital. We keep spritz bottles of Chamomile hydrosol in each room, to help calm nervous pets and owners. We also keep spritzers with Citronella and Orange essences handy, in case pets come in with fleas or other external parasites. Specific oils can also be applied to cotton balls and taped outside pets' cages, so each pet receives the benefits of oils that address its unique issues. We have electrical diffusers that plug into hallway outlets, and even add bacteriocidal oils (including Thyme, Tea Tree, Lemongrass) to the ozone-ionizer machine we keep in the isolation ward. Because our hospital is licensed to care for injured and orphaned wildlife, we often reduce the stressfulness of captivity for these animals by spraying the cage with aromatic blends before putting the animal in the cage.

Keep in mind, however, that animals have a more acute sense of smell than we do, and that a pleasant level of smell for us may be too concentrated for pets. Mixing oils with similar properties can also create a synergistic effect, and the oils may need to be extensively diluted, depending on the animal and the condition. Certain essential oils can be contraindicated for some conditions and can be toxic, if not used or diluted correctly. Some oils may be irritating to the skin or mucus membranes. And remember, some oils should not be ingested. It's best to contact an experienced animal aromatherapist or holistic veterinarian before treating your pet yourself.

DR. CROSBY ROPER, DVM, CVA – BAY PARK PET CLINIC, SAN DIEGO, CALIFORNIA

As sensitive as our olfactory system is, it pales in comparison to that of dogs and cats. It makes sense then to take advantage of the use of essential oils when treating animals. *Essential oils are used for odor control, patient conditioning, and client and staff conditioning at the Bay Park Clinic. Calming and stress-relieving essential oils such as Lavender, Chamomile and Valerian are diffused in the client areas, while energizing citrus essential oils are used in treatment and surgery areas to enhance the mental and physical stamina of the staff. With the simple use of a diffuser, we feel that we improve our client's perception of the practice, make their visit less stressful and enhance the effectiveness of our treatments.*

DR. STEPHEN R. BLAKE, DVM – SAN DIEGO, CALIFORNIA

I have been using aromatherapy for the past six years in my practice as an adjunct therapy to my classical homeopathic, glandular, acupuncture, nutritional, Bach Flower and colostrum healing modalities.

I do not use aromatherapy exclusively in any of my cases except in acute cases, although I still would use homeopathy in aiding in the healing process.

The following is an excerpt from an article on aromatherapy that Dr. Blake wrote for the American Holistic Veterinary Medical Association:

In my general practice, I diffuse Frankincense in my exam room and give the patient a light massage with the oil on my hands. Both dogs and horses are very conformable with this application. You only place a few drops in your hands, rub them together and then lightly massage the animal for a few seconds. This procedure calms both the caregiver and the patient. It is also antiviral, antibacterial and antifungal. This reduces the chance of my next patient being exposed to any contagious etiologies. I use this same oil directly on the gums of dogs that have severe gum disease. The effect is dramatic and most dogs are very conformable with doing this.

When I have a possible cruciate or joint injury, I have the owner massage a dilution of 1 drop Lemongrass to one teaspoon of Sweet Almond oil twice per day into the area. You use a very small amount of the oil. Lavender is an excellent oil to use on burns, eczema, insect bites, wounds or areas where there is excess itching.

I have used a blend of Spruce, Frankincense, Rosewood and Blue Tansy as the chiropractor in a bottle for my musculoskeletal cases. I have the caregiver apply 1 drop of the blend to each of the pads of all four feet and massage it into the feet. I have them do this on a couch or table and then immediately after the massage is done, put them on the floor. They will shake off and in doing so, self adjust themselves. If they do not shake from head to tail, I have them repeat the procedure until they do. The oils help to align the body and mind. I also feel that since the massage and the oils are stimulating all of the acupuncture meridians, which are being absorbed into the ting points. This combination of massage, essential oils, self adjusting and ting point stimulation, results in fewer acupuncture or chiropractic treatments because of the proactive part the caregiver plays in maintaining the healing process. I have them do this one to four times per day depending on the response of the patient to each treatment. Once they are stable, I reduce the frequency of treatments to match the progress of the case."

Dr. Sandra Priest, DVM – Four Winds Holistic Animal Services, Knoxville, Tennessee

Sandra Priest is a holistic veterinarian, Reiki master, animal chiropractor, homeopath and B.E.S.T. practitioner. She uses essential oils and hydrosols in a variety of ways to complement her practice.

I have used essential oil blends to treat bacterial and yeast ear problems with good results. In some instances, the essential oil blends were able to resolve recurrent infections that had not responded to drugs and other therapy. These products are well tolerated by the animals. I have seen very few side effects. I have also used these same blends topically to treat nail bed fungal infections. Conventional therapy involves the use of potent systemic antifungal drugs. Essential oils offer a gentle, effective alternative that is easy for the caregiver to administer and is well received by the animals.

I have also used anti-anxiety blends successfully with animals that are being boarded. In some cases, simply putting a towel with a few drops of the blend in their cage is sufficient to bring about a more relaxed state. Other blends have been useful in helping to maintain a more calm atmosphere in households where there are several intact males. These blends were effective when a few drops were placed on towels, which were then located on or near the animals' crates.

The best results are achieved with aromatherapy when energetic as well as physical properties match patient requirements. Like all substances, essential oils and hydrosols have energetic characteristics (electrochemical and electromagnetic properties). These characteristics combine to form a "signature" which varies from oil to oil and from blend to blend. Some signatures are very light and airy while others are more densely physical in their resonance. When the energetic signature of the product used is similar to the resonance of the patient, healing properties are enhanced and the patient has more opportunities for improvement. When there is dissonance between the product signature and patient resonance improvement may still occur but it will be slower and without benefit of synergy between energetic and physical properties of the product and patient. If there is sufficient dissonance between product and patient resonance, no physical benefit from the product will be obtained. In extreme cases some disordering of patient energetics may occur.

DR. PAUL WEISETH, DVM – ALL ANIMAL VETERINARY HOSPITAL, PORT ANGELES, WASHINGTON

Paul Weiseth is a holistic veterinarian who devotes a significant amount of his practice to the use of pure, therapeutic grade essential oils with animals. Essential oils are used on a daily basis for ear cleansing, wound care, calming, digestive problems, hot spots, insect repelling and easing the transition from life to death.

The latter is one of the most interesting uses of essential oils with dogs which Dr. Paul relies on. The treatment consists of a series of seven diluted essential oil blends which are used daily with terminally ill or euthanasia patients. Dr. Paul shared the following information about the process with me during the course of our correspondence:

I have a protocol, the Terminally Ill Energy Transition Set, which I use for terminally ill animals (and euthanasia patients) that helps tremendously with the transition. Some terminally ill cancer patients will go ahead and release their attachments to owners and die peacefully at home. I apply the oils in the following sequence:

1. Oil of Acceptance – aids in acceptance of transition into next life.

2. Gathering – pulls energy together for moving into next life.

3. Harmony – calms energy in preparation for moving on.

4. Forgiveness – to let go of attachments to the past.

5. Release – for letting go of fear and anger in the transition.

6. Surrender – in order for the spirit to let go in moving on to next life.

7. White Angelica – And now you may walk with the angels…

Each kit is provided with seven ⅛ oz (approx 3.5 ml) numbered vials. Apply small amounts of the essential oils to the head, ear tips and along the spine of your pets. Each vial has the words supplied to help you convey your message of releasing them from this life and assisting them in their transition to the next world. As you allow your spirit to be touched by the oils you will intuitively sense the timing for moving from one oil to the next. Use our suggested wording as a guide to help you convey your individual spiritual message through your pet's transition. This process helps all of us to have a sense of providing for our pets the most meaningful good-bye possible.

SUZANNE WARFIELD – WILLOWOOD TOY DOG KENNEL, AUBURN, PENNSYLVANIA

Willowood Toy Dog Kennel is a stress-free boarding experience for all small dogs. I breed Pomeranians and Japanese Chin, as well as show these dogs and handle toy breeds for other people. I carry holistic products and feed my dogs all natural diets. I also rely heavily on Lavender essential oil in my work. It is part of the relaxing atmosphere I work hard to provide to my clients. It keeps any fleas at bay, and a touch of the diluted oil at shows takes the edge off show stress. I have very happy, mellow, smiling dogs! I have also found Lavender to be a great calming oil to use for whelping. I use Lemon essential oil in my cleaning supplies at the kennel. It deodorizes and raises spirits, making the kennel a cleaner, brighter place.

CHRISTIE KEITH, BREEDER – CABER FEIDH SCOTTISH DEERHOUNDS, CAZADERO, CALIFORNIA

At Caber Feidh Scottish Deerhounds, we have been raising our dogs and cats holistically since 1986. Over the years we have used essential oils on our own dogs, and on rescues we've worked with, and hydrosols on our cats. I particularly like using essential oils on rescue dogs; you get the healing and hygienic benefits of the oils, as well as a calming effect, and it often helps with the bad smell many previously neglected animals will have. I've often used a mixture containing German Chamomile on hot spots; it's very soothing and helps speed healing. Another favorite "trick" of mine is to diffuse essential oils in the room when I have puppies; a bit of Lavender can be very calming, and I also like using Neroli for its lovely, fresh smell. A few drops of Lavender rubbed in my hands and gently cupped over the muzzle of a stressed out dog can also be a great help!

I find hydrosols useful when a dog is on a homeopathic remedy, as many of the stronger essential oils can conflict with homeopathic treatments.

TIFFANI BECKMAN, VETERINARY TECHNICIAN/CO-OWNER – FEED THIS! INC., NUTRITIONAL CONSULTING AND RAW DIETS FOR DOGS, FORESTVILLE, CALIFORNIA

I co-own Feed This! Inc., a raw pet food business for dogs and cats. We see many people with unhealthy animals looking for an alternative to drugs, chemotherapy, radiation, steroids and other Western medications. After starting the foundation of a proper diet for ill and healthy animals alike, we like to remind owners that there are many forms of holistic healing out there, including the safe usage of essential oils. Holistic means looking at the entire animal – physically, emotionally, mentally and spiritually. Together, diet and aromatherapy can work holistically to address the roots of problems and work towards a cure.

Several clients who have dogs with ear problems have used a diluted Tea Tree wash and found that it helped and didn't smell nearly as bad as chemical cleaners. The dogs themselves didn't seem to mind it as much as the chemicals, either. My business partner *Cathy* uses a combination of *Valerian, Vetiver, Mandarin Petitgrain* and *Sweet Orange* on her boarding dogs that get anxious when their owners leave.

Cutie-Que, my Aussie-Border collie, was started on the raw diet at eight weeks of age when I rescued her from the pound. Her detoxification period, while short-lived, showed itself in very itchy skin. I rinsed her daily with a combination of ¹/₂ water, ¹/₂ white vinegar with a few drops of *Lavender* and massaged it in well. This helped the itching immensely. I now tell all our clients to do this with their detoxing dogs who have itchy skin.

We believe that a proper raw diet can work wonders on most animals. But pairing it with other holistic modalities such as essential oils can make an even bigger impact in the lives of our beloved pets.

■ Judith Botsford – Greyhound Adoption Service, Salisbury, MA

I use essential oils holistically with my Greyhounds. Due to their low body fat, they tend to not tolerate chemicals well. Aromatherapy offers an effective alternative to conventional chemical treatments, especially traditional flea and tick repellents. Ticks, wherever you are, are unpleasant. Where I live, Lyme's disease is very common and Erlichea is becoming more so. This makes tick control even more important. Essential oils are effective for repelling both fleas and ticks and as a bonus, they make good mosquito repellents as well!

The first winter I had Juno, a rescued greyhound, she developed a rash on her lower abdomen. The vet gave me a cortisone cream to rub on it that did clear it up. But the rash quickly reappeared. This cycle continued over several weeks until I started using a skin-soothing blend of essential oils and hydrosols in a spritz form instead of the cream from the vet. Since using the spritz, Juno's rash has never re-occurred.

■ Judy Bechtel, Aromatherapist and Owner – Soothe My Soul Aromatherapy and Skin Care, Pennsylvania

My dog Bud, a brindle male boxer, has recently had some problems with his rear left leg. Our vet has ruled out Lyme's disease, rheumatoid arthritis and a ruptured cruciate ligament. I think the condition came from a fall on his rump when he jumped up to chase a squirrel running down the phone line in our backyard. I have been using an anti-inflammatory blend that I make, called arthritis blend. It has *Peppermint, Cypress, Juniper Berry* and *Lavender* in it. It has been working quite well and he hasn't been holding the leg up (only when he runs for too long) since

I've been applying it a couple of times a day. I didn't want him to take Rimadyl, which was the vet's usual first course of treatment.

EDIE BENNETT, AROMATHERAPIST AND OWNER – CRESCENT MOON AROMATHERAPY, ORANGE, CALIFORNIA

My Sheltie, Devon, has recurrent skin infections. This has become very expensive to treat through conventional veterinary means. The infections were diagnosed as being fungal, so I opted to formulate a blend of antifungal essential oils in lieu of the vet's recommended medications, which had temporarily cleared up the condition, only to have it return several weeks later.

Using a highly dilute blend of Thyme linalol, Lavender and Tea Tree essential oils in a base of aloe vera, I applied the solution to Devon's tummy every day. By the fourth day, all the redness was gone, and the oozing and crusty sores drying and healing well. In addition, he seems to enjoy the treatments, and smells very nice in the process. Essential oils accomplished the healing process much faster than the antifungal ointment prescribed by our vet, and the condition has not recurred.

CELESTE O'MALLEY, OWNER – THE HANDSOME HOUND DOG AND CAT GROOMING, BENNINGTON, VERMONT

Beleigh, a Soft Coated Wheaten Terrier is an exceedingly difficult dog to groom, due to her intense attachment to her owner. I began to groom her about four years ago, and she had been to two other groomers before me, who found her practically impossible to work with.

She hates to be brushed and bathed, and after about five months of grooming her, I told the owner I just didn't think I could do her any more because she was constantly biting and snapping. Her owner couldn't believe she could possibly be that bad, so I invited her to stay and watch – and she couldn't believe what she was seeing. We finally decided to have her stay and help me, especially with the bath. For two and a half years the owner stayed to muzzle and hold the dog while I performed the grooming.

I finally decided to try aromatherapy, and began bathing Beleigh with a natural shampoo containing calming essential oils such as Sweet Marjoram, Sweet Orange, Petitgrain, Valerian Root and Vetiver. I also used a spritz using the same oils to mist the air in the grooming area and in the cage. Thanks to essential oils, I can actually now groom Beleigh without the muzzle and without her owner holding her, although her owner does still stay where Beleigh can see her. An added benefit of incorporating aromatherapy into my grooming business is that it has a calming effect not only on me, but on everyone in the shop.

Canine Aromatherapy Safety Considerations

Safety considerations are crucial in using essential oils with dogs. There is no doubt that dogs, like all animals, are more sensitive to essential oils than humans are. While we share physiological similarities with our canine counterparts, they possess a much more powerful and acute sense of smell, which makes dilution absolutely necessary.

Also, most dogs are much smaller in size than humans. This needs to be taken into consideration when blending for a dog. A 4 lb. Chihuahua, a 150 lb. Newfoundland and a 150 lb. human should all receive different dilutions and dosages of essential oils. Dilution and dosage are two different things. *Dilution* refers to the amount of essential oil present in a formulation. *Dosage* refers to the amount of the final formulation that is used with the animal, usually expressed in terms of "drops" or "spritzes". With shampoos or grooming formulations, this is a basic function of the fact that it takes less shampoo to groom a small dog than a large one.

HERE ARE SOME BASIC GUIDELINES TO FOLLOW WHEN BLENDING FOR DOGS:

- Always use the highest quality essential oils, sourced from a trusted and reliable supplier.

- Always use essential oils within the context of other 100% natural ingredients. Don't add your carefully chosen oils to synthetic bases, such as liquid dishwashing soaps, laundry detergents or human shampoos that are synthetic.

- Don't rely on a single essential oil or hydrosol to provide the best results. I always formulate essential oils and hydrosols in blends with one another; the reason is the process of "synergy", which dictates that a blend of essential oils or hydrosols is more powerful than the use of a single oil alone. This is due to the complex makeup of essential oils and hydrosols. Blending three to five of these substances together increases the therapeutic benefits. Where one essential oil leaves off, another picks up and continues the healing process. Synergy helps to guarantee that a blend of essential oils will work together, doing their best to produce the desired effects. If all you have is a single essential oil, then one oil is, of course, better than none, but remember for optimum effects, opt for three to five oils.

- *Always D-I-L-U-T-E essential oils for use with dogs!* I suggest starting with 25% of the human dose, or a dose that is acceptable for a human toddler. This translates into 30 drops of essential oils in 8 oz (240 ml) of shampoo or other base, or 10 drops of essential oils in $^{1}/_{2}$ oz (15 ml) of base oil. Or, if you are good at math, a dilution of 1–2% (The essential oils making up a total of 1–2% of the final total volume of the formulation).

- Avoid essential oils that are high in phenols and ketones, as well as all essential oils considered toxic. (See Chart on page 22) Choose your essential oils from the 52 essential oils listed in this book for the safest, most effective results.

- Only give essentials oils internally when indicated in the recipes in this book, and only use essential oils regarded as safe for ingestion, such as Peppermint, Cardamom and other generally regarded as safe spice oils. All essential oils given internally must also be diluted to minimize the possibility of giving too much.

- Don't use essential oils on medium–large breed puppies younger than eight weeks. With small and toy breeds, avoid essential oils until after ten weeks. Use the smallest amount possible with all puppies. The safest use of aromatherapy with puppies, when in doubt, is hydrosols.

- Always introduce essential oils gradually and in small amounts to all dogs. Watch carefully for any indications that the dog is upset by the oil application. Using very small amounts of oil or letting the dog smell the oil blend before application usually alleviates any adverse effects. By adverse effects, I am referring to dogs whining, panting, drooling or rubbing their faces on the floor, usually on carpeting. These type of effects are not common in the use of aromatherapy with dogs, but certain highly sensitive dogs have on occasion been "upset" by the application of diluted essential oils.

- Use less diluted essential oil with small dogs than with large dogs! This is a way to automatically control dosage. In the recipes in this book, I will often recommend dosage as a range of drops or spritzes for application. Use the smallest recommended amount for small dogs, and the higher end of the range for large dogs. Medium-sized dogs obviously fall in the middle of the range.

- Use essential oils in moderation with all dogs, but especially with those who are of advanced age, pregnant or ill. I often will reduce the number of drops or spritzes used when a dog's health is compromised. I specifically avoid stimulating essential oils with pregnant animals, opting for calming and tonic oils instead. Some stimulating oils are Peppermint, Rosemary, Niaouli, Tea Tree, Spearmint, Ravensare and Eucalyptus.

■ Epileptic and seizure-prone dogs are of special concern. It is believed that certain essential oils, particularly Rosemary, can influence the onset of seizure activity in humans. While it has not been clinically researched, it has been observed in a variety of instances and for this reason should be taken into account. On the other hand, it is believed that the regular use of calming essential oils is gently sedative to the central nervous system and can thus prevent or reduce the frequency of seizures.

■ Always remember, that a dog can't tell you how it feels, what it likes or whether or not something is working. This is one of the reasons why the use of highly diluted essential oils, as well as the gradual introduction of the oils, is so important. When in doubt, always use less. With aromatherapy, less is more.

■ Do not use essential oils in the eyes, close to the eyes, directly on the nose or close to the nose, or in the anal or genital areas.

■ Discourage ingestion, but do not be concerned if your dog licks some formulation from its paws or fur. Not all recipes are intended to be taken internally. Those that are meant to be are clearly indicated in the instructions. The recipes in this book are all created with the consideration that all dogs will try to lick anything off of their coats. The ingestion of small amounts of essential oils will not be harmful. This book uses highly diluted blends and the safest essential oils.

Canine Aromatherapy and Other Holistic Modalities

Aromatherapy complements a variety of other holistic modalities, often creating a powerful synergistic effect. Due to the alternate methods in which aromatherapy achieves its effects, it often picks up where another modality leaves off, or vice versa. Aromatherapy offers a wide range of effects and is one of the most powerful forms of complementary care, but it doesn't work for everything. No form of holistic care is a magic pill. Many people find that supplementing an aromatherapy regimen with other holistic remedies provides the most powerful effect. There are numerous holistic modalities out there, and new ones appearing every day. I have included some of the most widely accepted, so that you may consider using them.

HERBALISM

The use of herbs and herbal tinctures is one of the most common and familiar forms of complementary care today. Dried and fresh herbs contain minute percentages of essential oils (remember that it takes huge amounts of plant material to produce a small amount of essential oil). Herbs, containing mostly water-soluble components, have a very different range of action than oil – or fat-soluble, essential oils. Herbs and essential oils have no known contraindications for tandem usage. In fact, simultaneous use can provide a supportive and synergistic effect.

For example, there is the use of herbs and essential oils to provide a calming effect with dogs. Herbal calming tablets given to a dog will take time to be digested and enter the bloodstream before having any effect. Essential oils work much faster than this, due to the fact that they are inhaled. I often suggest a protocol of calming herbs and aromatherapy for dogs suffering from separation anxiety. The owner can apply diluted essential oils via massage shortly after giving an herbal remedy. The essential oils will begin to work within minutes, and the effects can last up to 30–45 minutes, sometimes more. By the time the effects of the essential oils wear off, the herbs have begun working. In this manner, the combination of essential oils and herbs can be crucial in helping dogs with separation anxiety get through the first few hours of their owners' absence in a much calmer, at ease state. Often, getting past the initial trauma of the owner leaving is enough to greatly lessen and even eventually eliminate symptoms of separation anxiety when combined with training techniques.

SUPPLEMENTS

Various supplements are often involved in holistic care regimens. These supplements vary from vitamins and minerals to substances of plant or animal origin. The use of essential oils and hydrosols has no known interactions with any supplements.

HOMEOPATHY

Homeopathy is one of the few holistic modalities with which aromatherapy is believed to interfere. Many homeopaths believe that the use of any essential oils containing menthol or camphor may antidote homeopathic remedies. As a rule, the use of essential oils that do not contain these components is fine. Some holistic veterinarians are so exclusive to homeopathy that they discourage the use of anything aromatic, regardless of whether or not it contains camphor or menthol. If you are concerned about the use of essential oils with homeopathy, don't use essential oils within an hour before or after giving a homeopathic treatment.

Flower Essences

Flower essences and essential oils or hydrosols are remedies that I frequently combine, especially when I am using aromatherapy as a remedy to an emotional problem. One of the most important flower remedy formulations to have on hand is Bach Rescue Remedy™, a combination of the five flower essences Impatiens, Star of Bethlehem, Cherry Plum, Rock Rose and Clematis – which is indicated for all sorts of emotional crises. The remedy is beneficial for restoring balance. Other flower essence companies sell their version of Bach's famous formula, often referred to as five-flower formula. The addition of flower essences to aromatherapy blends can support and enhance the desired effect. With over 100 flower essences on the market, treatment enhancements can get very specific to an animal's needs.

Gemstone Essences

Gemstone essences are similar in principle to flower essences, and once again, do not conflict with aromatherapy treatments with essential oils or hydrosols. In fact, aromatherapy flower essences and gemstone essences can all be used safely side by side to increase the therapeutic value of a treatment. All three remedies work together to balance and calm an animal. Gemstone essences are a relatively recent newcomer to the holistic care arsenal. Hence, they are not being as routinely used by holistic vets as flower essences are.

Natural Diet

A natural diet is one of the most beneficial things that you can do for your dog's health. According to animal nutritionist Kymythy Schultze, author of *Natural Nutrition for Dogs and Cats: The Ultimate Diet,* "The closer we can simulate the diet that evolution designed our cats and dogs to thrive on, the closer we will be to providing nutrients in the form that our animal companions need to enjoy good health. Since few of us are willing or able to provide whole prey animals for our pets to eat, making a well-designed homemade diet of raw foods is the next best thing."[26]

I have experimented with numerous diets for dogs in the last ten years. There is no doubt that the BARF, Bones and Raw Food, diet is optimum for a dog's nutritional needs, but for many, it is difficult, time-consuming or costly to feed "raw". There are other options, such as pre-made raw food diets, high quality, human-grade kibble, or a combination raw–cooked diet.

My own personal experience with diet is that it is a crucial element in clearing up dog allergies, very common these days with dogs who are fed low-grade kibbles, exposed to all sorts of chemicals and cleaning supplies and prone to environmental allergies. My own Golden Retriever, Dublin, was afflicted with allergies for the first six years of his life. Being fed an inferior, mass-produced kibble for many years suppressed his immune system, and allergies manifested themselves in chronic skin and ear infections, treated with prednisone and round after round of antibiotics which further depleted his health. The combination of aromatherapy treatments for ears and skin along with a change in diet resulted in a "new dog" over the course of a year. I found a B.A.R.F. diet difficult to feed, due to expense and the amount of time required to prepare and maintain the necessary foods and supplements. I eventually weaned Dublin off of the B.A.R.F. diet and onto a high quality kibble with various supplements and small amounts of raw foods. His allergies have never returned.

The term "holistic" refers to treating the entire animal. A switch in diet combined with aromatherapy treatments designed to soothe and relieve symptoms and prevent recurrences is one of the most powerful holistic care synergies.

Reiki and Other Energy Healing

Reiki and other forms of energy healing are used with animals to balance the energy fields of the body, restoring natural flow and in turn physical health and vitality. Most energy healers have a ritual that they use before every treatment to clear any negative energy from the treatment area, and to clear themselves in preparation for their client. Essential oils can be diffused or misted into the air, or several drops can be massaged into the healer's hands and used to massage the air around the client, "cleansing" the aura in preparation to receive Reiki or other types of energetic treatments.

Massage

Essential oils are a natural complement to massage. Why just use your hands or an unscented massage oil, when you can add a few drops of pure essential oils to enhance and strengthen the effects of the massage? I believe that many canine massage therapists don't use essential oils because they are unsure about using them. Many are also reticent to use "oil" on a dog's fur because they automatically equate "oil" with the attraction of dust and dirt. This is the case with mineral oil, but not with lightweight vegetable and nut based oils that are conditioning and quickly absorbed by the skin and coat. Whether you are a dog owner or a professional animal massage therapist, massage is an excellent way to forge a therapeutic bond with any dog. The power of touch is unmistakable. Tellington Touch™ massage, a technique created by Linda Tellington-Jones, is a simple, easy to learn and exceedingly popular massage technique for dogs that has produced profound results in dogs with various behavioral problems.

But you needn't have a massage technique in mind to get the benefits of massage. The simple process of lightly touching and massaging your dog is enough to strengthen the bond of companionship, lightly stimulate circulation and relieve mild aches and pains.

Acupuncture and Acupressure

Calming aromatherapy essential oils and hydrosols are ideal to pair with acupuncture and acupressure treatments. Since an animal needs to lie still for these treatments, and many animals want to move around a lot or may experience anxiety at the onset of the treatment, the use of aromatherapy via nebulization, misting or a short massage is a superb way to soothe and calm a dog during the course of treatment.

Chiropractics

Again, as with acupuncture and acupressure, chiropractic treatments also involve an animal being required to stay still or in certain positions in order to be worked on. Calming essential oils can have a profound soothing effect on a dog, making treatments easier and as a result, more effective.

Canine Aromatherapy and Allopathic Medicine

Aromatherapy and essential oils can be safely used with Western conventional allopathic medicines without interfering with their effectiveness or range of action. There are currently no known interactions or reactions with any allopathic drugs, and there isn't any reason for there to be, mainly because essential oils work via entirely different mechanisms than modern synthetic medicines. Antibiotics are a perfect example. Essential oils possess strong antibacterial properties, yet they work in an entirely different manner than antibiotics do – and without any of the side effects or potential for antibiotic immunity.

Allopathic medicine typically makes use of synthesized medications for treatment, such as antibiotics, steroidal anti-inflammatories and even pain relief medications such as ibuprofen. All allopathic medications have one thing in common: they simply cover up symptoms, or "trick" the body into perceiving something other than what is actually there – usually at the cost of a depressed immune system. Essential oils, on the other hand, seek to change the landscape of the body, balancing and tonifying it for optimal health, while at the same time, alleviating symptoms and helping a dog owner to seek out possible causes for the imbalance. When essential oils and alternative care are employed and allopathic drugs are put aside except for crisis care situations, something miraculous happens. I have seen it happen, and perhaps you have as well – or hopefully soon will. These powerful substances meld seamlessly with the body, be it human or animal. They provide fast results, and restore equilibrium. With repeated use, they support and strengthen the immune system, yielding levels of vitality previously not considered possible.

The Tea Tree Debate

Tea Tree is one of the most popular and well-known essential oils presently being used commercially. It is available everywhere and has quickly become a household name. A bottle can be picked up at just about any health food shop or supermarket. Tea Tree, or *Melaleuca alternifolia,* is frequently recommended for use with all types of animals with no respect for their size or metabolic functions.

Personally, I care very little for Tea Tree. I do use it on occasion, but always an oil of the highest quality in dilution with other oils. It definitely has great therapeutic value, but as with any essential oil, its intensity leaves much room for misuse.

This misuse is readily apparent in various human and animal toxicology reports, most of which detail incidents involving the ingestion of large amounts of Tea Tree. This is seen in an excerpt from *Veterinary and Human Toxicology,* "Toxicity of Melaleuca Oil and Related Essential Oils Applied Topically to Dogs and Cats".

ABSTRACT

Cases of Melaleuca oil toxicosis have been reported by veterinarians to the National Animal Poison Control Center when the oil was applied dermally to dogs and cats. In most cases, the oil was used to treat dermatologic conditions at inappropriate high doses. The typical signs observed were depression, weakness, incoordination and muscle tremors. The active ingredients of commercial Melaleuca oil are predominantly cyclic terpenes.

Melaleuca oil is marketed for use on dogs, cats, ferrets and horses in skin care products for cleaning, healing and relieving itching associated with allergies, insect bites, hotspots, abrasions and other minor rashes and irritations. It also makes claims as a deodorizer, detangler and external parasite repellent. It has proven antibacterial and fungicidal properties, and it is an effective topical treatment for acne in humans when applied in a 5% water-based gel. Other uses of Melaleuca oil are as an expectorant in vaporizers for inhalation, a flavoring and antiseptic agent in denture and mouth washes, and for the treatment of furunculosis and vaginitis. Some pathogens eliminated by Melaleuca-containing solutions include Candida albicans, Epidermophyton floccosum and Trichophyton mentagrophytes, Staphylococcus aureus, Streptococcus spp, and Salmonella typhi. The oil is obtained by steam distillation of the freshly harvested leaves of the Melaleuca alternifolia tree, which yield about 2% oil. The tree is known as Australian Tea Tree and originated from the central coastal of eastern Australia.

CHEMISTRY

Most of the hydrocarbons emitted by plants (predominantly trees) are terpenes. Nearly all the terpenes found in essential oils have carbon skeletons make up of isoprene units joined in a regular head-to-tail fashion. The oil of Melaleuca is a colorless or pale yellow oil, containing 50–60% terpenes (p-cymene, terpinenes and pinene) and 6–8% cineole. The Australian standard for oil of Melaleuca requires that cineole be under 15% and terpinen-4-ol be over 30%. Terpinen-4-ol is the main antimicrobial ingredient of Melaleuca oil. In practice, as oil of 15% cineole and 39% terpinen-4-ol is an inferior oil, with a superior oil having 2.5% and 40–47%, respectively. The poor quality of high-cineole oil is attributed to the potential for cineole to irritate mucous membranes and skin. However, Melaleuca oil products will deteriorate over time through oxidation of terpenes (terpinen-4-ol, pinene, gamma-terpinene, and terpinolene) to the aromatic hydrocarbon p-cymene. The optimal storage condition to prevent aging is a cool, dark and dry environment.

TOXICITY

The most typical clinical signs reported to the National Animal Poison Control Center by veterinarians with adverse reactions in dogs and cats after dermal exposure of Melaleuca oil include ataxia, incoordination, weakness, tremors,

*behavioral disorders and depression. In all these cases the use of Melaleuca oil on
the animals was regarded as inappropriate or erroneous. Except in one instance in
which two kittens were dipped in a cleaning product containing Melaleuca oil and
developed tremors, incoordination and weakness within minutes, the onset of
clinical signs after topical application of different products containing Melaleuca oil
has been between 2–8 hours.*[27]

I feel that Tea Tree is singled out due to its popularity. The more people
who are using a substance, the more documented cases of misuse there will
be. Also, we must take into account the context of the substance – is it
natural or synthetic? We hear very little about the millions of reactions that
occur each year from the misuse, overdose and mismanagement of synthetic
allopathic drugs produced by the pharmaceutical industry, yet when one
remote instance of an adverse reaction shows up involving the use of a
natural substance, it is all over the news, and spreads like wildfire across the
internet. In all truth, the incidence of adverse effects from natural
substances is far less than those from synthesized drugs and medications.
Confusion also arises because too many people perceive things that are
natural as being totally safe, benign and without side effects. This is never
the case, no matter what type of substance you are dealing with.

The mass production of Tea Tree to meet demand has also most surely
met with adulteration and poor quality oils, resulting in more adverse
reactions and irritation. I can't tell you how many bottles of Tea Tree I have
seen on health food store shelves, being sold in clear glass bottles with
insufficient labeling and instructions. The lack of knowledge surrounding
the use of any substance will surely lead to errors in use, especially when
advertising charms you into believing that a natural substance is a veritable
cure-all for ailments of every type for family members ranging from the baby
to the pet bird.

My advice? Don't bother with Tea Tree oil. Use its gentler relative
Niaouli (MQV) instead, or opt for an essential oil with a similar range of
action such as Sweet Marjoram or Ravensare aromatica.

Canine Aromatherapy Remedies and Recipes

I have compiled many years worth of research and recipes in this section,
creating numerous safe, effective and simple aromatic potions that you can
use with your dogs. The guesswork and intimidation of using these powerful
aromatic substances has been removed from the equation for you. All you
need to supply are high quality essential oils, a dose of accuracy in

measuring the ingredients, and a dose of tender loving care while you create them.

Recipes are given in both imperial and metric measures. The metric measures are an approximate conversion based on 1 oz = 30 ml. For the purpose of accuracy I will always refer to all essential oils in terms of number of drops. A table of weights and measures and conversion tables have been included in Appendix 1.

You will need some basic tools for the creation of your own canine blends. I recommend the following to start:

- Measuring pipettes (plastic)

- Beaker which measures in milliliters (I own 10 and 50 ml beakers)

- Cobalt, amber or green glass bottles in ¹/₂, 1, 2 and 4 oz (15, 30, 60, 120 ml) sizes

- Glass beaker or Pyrex measuring cup

- Small scale for measuring dry ingredients

- Measuring cups for dry ingredients

- Bowls of various sizes for mixing

- Paper fragrance blotter strips

- Wooden sticks for stirring

- Grain alcohol or vodka for cleaning utensils and disinfecting bottles

- Various essential oils, base oils and botanical ingredients as needed

Some Things to Consider When Creating the Recipes in This Book

- Follow all recipes exactly as indicated. Recipes can be cut in half, doubled or tripled for convenience.

- Never use the essential oils undiluted. Always dilute in base oils or suggested botanicals.

- When dispensing drops to a dog use a pipette for accuracy.

- Remember, the number of drops administered (dosage) is dependent on the size of the dog. Smaller dogs get fewer drops. Large dogs get more drops.

- Never use more than the recommended number of drops.

- All essential oil/water/hydrosol combinations (usually referred to as misters or spritz sprays) need to be shaken well before each use. Essential oils and water do not mix.

- Keep bottles of neat (undiluted) essential oils out of reach of your pets and small children. It is safest to use essential oils that have orifice reducers inside their caps. This also makes accidental spills less likely to happen. If you knock over a bottle with an orifice reducer in place, you may lose a drop or two. Without one, you may lose half the bottle!

- Store all of your essential oils and essential oil blends in glass bottles. Rubber dropper tops are fine, but they will degrade within 9–12 months. It is fine to store spritzers or shampoos in plastic, but PET plastic is preferable.

Grooming Shampoos and Soaps

All-natural aromatherapy grooming begins with the addition of essential oils to an all-natural soap or shampoo base. The key here is that the ingredients be all natural. As we have discussed, it is futile to add high quality essential oils to a synthetic chemical soup and bathe your dog with it. Take the time to find a truly all-natural soap or shampoo, or create your own using the following recipe.

RECIPE FOR ALL-NATURAL DECYL POLYGLUCOSE SHAMPOO BASE

This exceedingly gentle, generously foaming soap shampoo base is the perfect natural solution for all of your dog grooming needs.

This recipe makes 8 oz (240 ml) of unscented shampoo base, to which you can add your essential oils. I recommend infusing your water with several herbs to increase therapeutic value. I presently use herbs such as coltsfoot, chickweed, nettles, horsetail, slippery elm, marshmallow root, comfrey root, calendula blossoms, chamomile flowers or oatstraw in the water phase of my shampoos.

4.5 oz (135 ml) Distilled Water
3.2 oz (95 ml) Decyl Polyglucose
$^1/_2$ tsp Xanthan Gum Powder
$^1/_2$ tsp Cider Vinegar
1 ml Grapefruit Seed Extract (GSE)
1 ml Rosemary Antioxidant Extract

These ingredients are simple to combine into an all-natural shampoo base for your dog. You can even use this base recipe to create shampoos for yourself.

Since I normally infuse my water phase with herbs, I always start off with hot water. After my herbs are infused, I add the cider vinegar, GSE, Rosemary antioxidant and decyl polyglucose and mix completely. I use a stick blender for all blending, as it is the most efficient and uniform way to blend your ingredients together. While the mixture is still very warm, add the xanthan gum powder and blend until uniform. Let cool, add essential oils and you now have your own all-natural shampoo ready for use with your dog.

ESSENTIAL OIL BLENDS TO ADD TO 8 OZ (240 ML) OF SHAMPOO BASE

You can create a variety of different aromatic shampoos for your dog using the decyl polyglucose shampoo base recipe. As a rule, I never add more than 15–20 drops of essential oils to the standard 8 oz (240 ml) recipe. If you are using more or less of the shampoo base, then remember to reduce or increase your drops of essential oils.

SKIN SOOTHING SHAMPOO – FOR DOGS WITH ITCHY SKIN AND ALLERGIES

Add the following essential oils to 8 oz (240 ml) of all-natural shampoo base:

2 drops Geranium, *Pelargonium graveolens*, essential oil
6 drops Rosewood, *Aniba roseadora*, essential oil
6 drops Lavender, *Lavandula angustifolia*, essential oil
1 drop Roman Chamomile, *Anthemis nobilis*, essential oil
2 drops Carrot Seed, *Daucus carota*, essential oil

A tablespoon of finely ground oatmeal can be blended in to provide further relief.

HEALING SHAMPOO – FOR DOGS WITH SKIN INFECTIONS AND SMALL WOUNDS, SUCH AS MINOR SCRAPES, NICKS AND INSECT BITES

Add the following essential oils to 8 oz (240 ml) of all-natural shampoo base:

4 drops Ravensare, *Ravensare aromatica*, essential oil
2 drops Labdunum, *Cistus ladaniferus*, essential oil

1 drop Helichrysum, *Helichrysum italicum*, essential oil
3 drops Lavender, *Lavandula angustifolia*, essential oil

Calming Shampoo – for Dogs That Need to Relax When They Are Bathed

Add the following essential oils to 8 oz (240 ml) of all-natural shampoo base:

3 drops Valerian, *Valeriana officinalis*, essential oil
2 drops Vetiver, *Vetivera zizanoides*, essential oil
4 drops Petitgrain, *Citrus aurantium*, essential oil
3 drops Sweet Marjoram, *Origanum marjorana*, essential oil
2 drops Sweet Orange, *Citrus sinensis*, essential oil

Flea and Insect Repelling Shampoo

Add the following essential oils to 8 oz (240 ml) of all-natural shampoo base:

4 drops Clary Sage, *Salvia sclarea*, essential oil
2 drops Citronella, *Cymbopogon nardus*, essential oil
8 drops Peppermint, *Mentha piperita*, essential oil
4 drops Lemon, *Citrus limon*, essential oil

Tick Repelling Shampoo

Add the following essential oils to 8 oz (240 ml) of all-natural shampoo base:

2 drops Geranium, *Pelargonium graveolens*, essential oil
2 drops Rosewood, *Aniba roseadora*, essential oil
3 drops Lavender, *Lavandula angustifolia*, essential oil
2 drops Myrhh, *Commiphora myrrha*, essential oil
2 drops Opoponax, *Commiphora erythraea*, essential oil
1 drop Bay Leaf, *Pimenta racemosa*, essential oil

Puppy Shampoo

Add the following essential oils to 8 oz (240 ml) of all-natural shampoo base:

2 drops Rose, *Rosa damascena*, essential oil
2 drops Ylang Ylang, *Cananga odorata*, essential oil
5 drops Geranium, *Pelargonium graveolens*, essential oil
2 drops Roman Chamomile, *Anthemis nobilis*, essential oil
5 drops Petitgrain, *Citrus aurantium*, essential oil

SPICY DEODORIZING SHAMPOO

Add the following essential oils to 8 oz (240 ml) of all-natural shampoo base:

> 5 drops Cinnamon Leaf, *Cinnamonum zeylanicum*, essential oil
> 5 drops Caraway, *Carum carvi*, essential oil
> 3 drops Black Pepper, *Piper nigrum*, essential oil
> 3 drops Bay Leaf, *Pimenta racemosa*, essential oil

WOODSY CONDITIONING SHAMPOO

Add the following essential oils to 8 oz (240 ml) of all-natural shampoo base:

> 6 drops Atlas Cedarwood, *Cedrus atlantica*, essential oil
> 4 drops Rosemary, *Rosmarinus officinalis*, essential oil
> 2 drops Patchouli, *Pogostemon cablin*, essential oil
> 3 drops Vetiver, *Vetivera zizanoides*, essential oil

REFRESHING CITRUS SHAMPOO

Add the following essential oils to 8 oz (240 ml) of all-natural shampoo base:

> 3 drops Sweet Orange, *Citrus sinensis*, essential oil
> 3 drops Lemon, *Citrus limon*, essential oil
> 3 drops Lime, *Citrus aurantifolia*, essential oil
> 3 drops Grapefruit, *Citrus paradisi*, essential oil
> 3 drops Mandarin, *Citrus reticulata*, essential oil

DELICATE FLORAL SHAMPOO

Add the following essential oils to 8 oz (240 ml) of all-natural shampoo base:

> 4 drops Lavender, *Lavandula angustifolia*, essential oil
> 2 drops Ylang Ylang, *Cananga odorata*, essential oil
> 4 drops Rose, *Rosa damascena*, essential oil
> 6 drops Petitgrain, *Citrus aurantium*, essential oil

FRESH HERBAL SHAMPOO

Add the following essential oils to 8 oz (240 ml) of all-natural shampoo base:

> 4 drops Sweet Basil, *Ocimum basilicum*, essential oil
> 4 drops Lavender, *Lavandula angustifolia*, essential oil
> 4 drops Clary Sage, *Salvia sclarea*, essential oil
> 4 drops Coriander Seed, *Coriandrum sativum*, essential oil

Herbal Aromatherapy Canine Glycerin Shampoo Bars

Many people enjoy using a bar of soap instead of a liquid shampoo with their dogs. This works especially well for short-coated dogs that do not have dry or sensitive skin. Soap strips more of the natural fats and oils from the skin and coat than a natural shampoo such as the decyl polyglucose soap base. On the positive side, natural glycerin and cold process soaps are more gentle and moisturizing than synthetic cleansers such as sodium or ammonium laurel sulfate.

The key is finding the most natural glycerin soap base that you can find. In Section 2, the different soap making processes (cold process soap and glycerin, or "melt and pour", soap) are described in detail. For the purpose of creating shampoo bars for dogs, I will keep it simple and refer only to glycerin, "melt and pour", soaps. As previously discussed, it is very difficult to find an all-natural glycerin soap base. I have done quite a bit of my own research on the subject, because making soap is a truly enjoyable hobby.

Here is an example of the type of glycerin soap base you want to stay away from, because it is full of synthetic chemicals that act as foaming agents, water softeners and remelting solvents. The only natural ingredients in this soap are indicated in **bold** type:

> Cocamide DEA, **Deionized Water**, Propylene Glycol**,
> Sodium Cocoate (coconut oil soap)**, Sodium Laureth
> Sulfate, **Sodium Oleate (olive oil, or "castile" soap)**,
> **Sodium Stearate (palm oil soap)**, Sorbitol,
> Triethanolamine Laurel Sulfate, Triethanolamine,
> **Vegetable Glycerin**

Here is an example of a soap base that is much healthier for you, your dog and the environment. While this soap base is not all natural, it is the closest you can get to all natural without making cold process soap. The natural ingredients in this soap base are once again, indicated in **bold:**

> **Olive Oil, Palm Oil, Castor Oil, Safflower Oil, Vegetable
> Glycerin, Purified Water, Sodium Hydroxide,** Sorbitol
> Sorbitan Oleate, **Soy Bean Protein,** EDTA (water softener)

It is fun and easy to make melt and pour glycerin soaps. All you need to do is melt the soap base, then add herbs and essential oils. You can pour your soaps into molds, or simply use a round plastic container as a mold. I find that a round bar, approximately sized to the palm of your hand, makes a convenient way to wash the dog. Often the addition of certain herbs will give your bar an exfoliating quality, which helps to slough away dry skin and release hairs ready to be shed.

Here are some ideas for creating glycerin soaps for your dog. As you can see, many things can be added to glycerin soap – herbs and flowers, clays and oils, milk powders and oatmeal and essential oils. Just use your imagination and knowledge of essential oils, and have fun creating:

FRESH MINT AND COFFEE SOAP

This bar is very deodorizing and exfoliating, due to the presence of ground coffee. I use decaf coffee in all of my soaps containing coffee. This bar is not appropriate for use on white dogs, as it may yellow their coat. To every 8 oz (240 ml) of soap base, add 8 drops of Peppermint, *Mentha piperita*, essential oil, and a heaping tablespoon of ground coffee.

GENTLE CHAMOMILE AND CALENDULA SOAP

This bar is very gentle and very simple to make. To every 8 oz (240 ml) of soap base, add a small handful of chamomile flowers and calendula petals, and 8 drops of Roman, *Anthemis nobilis*, or German Chamomile, *Matricaria recutita*, (or both) essential oils.

LAVENDER AND OATMEAL SOAP

Add a heaping tablespoon of finely ground oatmeal, 4 drops of Lavender, *Lavandula angustifolia*, essential oil and 4 drops of Geranium, *Pelargonium graveolens*, essential oil to every 8 oz (240 ml) of soap base to make this skin-soothing soap.

MINT AND CITRUS SOAP

Add a small handful of ground orange peel, 6 drops of Sweet Orange, *Citrus sinensis*, essential oil and 2 drops of Peppermint, *Mentha piperita*, essential oil to create a fresh and clean scented soap which helps to repel fleas. The above amounts are to make 8 oz (240 ml) of soap.

GERANIUM ROSEBUD SOAP

Add a small handful of rosebuds and petals to 8 oz (240 ml) of soap base. 8 drops of Geranium, *Pelargonium graveolens*, or 4 drops Geranium and 4 drops of Rose, *Rosa damascena*, *to* make a sweet, floral scented soap.

FRANKINCENSE AND MYRRH SOAP

This precious soap is excellent for dogs with dry, flaky skin. Add a teaspoon of Frankincense powder, *Boswellia carterii*, a teaspoon of Myrhh powder, *Commiphora myrrha*, 4 drops of Frankincense essential oil and 4 drops of Myrrh essential oil to 8 oz (240 ml) of soap base.

CARROT SOAP

Carrot Seed essential oil is excellent for dry or irritated skin. It has a distinctive earthy, sweet aroma. I like to create a soothing soap by adding a tablespoon of powdered carrot and 8 drops of Carrot Seed, *Daucus carota*, essential oil to 8 oz (240 ml) of soap base.

AUSTRALIAN GREEN CLAY SOAP

This is a perfect soap for dogs with oily skin and coat, and over-active sebum production. Add a heaping tablespoon of green clay, 4 drops of Niaouli, *Melaleuca quinquenervia viridiflora*, and 4 drops of Eucalyptus radiata to 8 oz (240 ml) of soap base.

GENTLE BUTTERMILK SOAP

A tablespoon of buttermilk (whole milk powder or goat's milk powder will also work), 4 drops of Lavender, *Lavandula angustifolia*, and 4 drops of German Chamomile, *Matricara recutita*, to create a gentle, moisturizing bar.

Aromatic Grooming Sprays

Before we get into the more "serious" holistic recipes for dogs, it's always a pleasure to point out some of the ways that you can have fun with aromatherapy. That's why I began this chapter with shampoos, soaps and grooming sprays. Essential oils smell wonderful – there is no denying. And dogs don't always smell so great. This makes them a perfect combination. There are a variety of aromatic deodorizing sprays that you can make to use on your dog and home while avoiding the commercially available synthetic grooming sprays which are based on fragrance oils and other petrochemicals.

I like to keep a bottle of good-smelling spritz on hand for those wet or stinky dog days. They are perfect when you don't bathe your dog much, as many of us have larger dogs that are more difficult to bathe. And the fact of the matter is that dogs don't need to be bathed as much as some people think. My little dog, Blossom, gets bathed about every two to three weeks because she is white, has fluffy fur and is close to the ground. My big dog, Nigel, probably hasn't had a bath in six months, thanks to his short, wiry fur, dense coat and color (he's black). Every dog is different, but for those in-between times, aromatherapy is a great way to "clear the air". Especially if you have houseguests arriving!

I have included recipes for the six major categories of scents: minty, citrusy, spicy, woodsy, herbal and floral. Eventually, you can begin to mix and match your own groups of fragrances to create more complex scents. The recipes below offer you a basic palette to start from.

AROMATIC GROOMING SPRAY BASE

Makes 8 oz (240 ml). Store in a dark or opaque mister bottle and shake well before using, as essential oils and water do not mix.

> 1 teaspoon Vegetable Glycerin
> $^1/_2$ oz (15 ml) Grain Alcohol or Vodka
> 1 teaspoon Sulfated Castor Oil
> 1 oz (30 ml) Aloe Vera
> 10 drops Grapefruit Seed Extract
> 6 oz (180 ml) Distilled or Spring Water

Add one of the following aromatic blends of your choice to put the finishing touches on your spritz.

MINTY BLEND

> 6 drops Spearmint, *Mentha spicata*, essential oil
> 6 drops Peppermint, *Mentha piperita*, essential oil

CITRUS BLEND

> 3 drops Sweet Orange, *Citrus sinensis*, essential oil
> 3 drops Lemon, *Citrus limon*, essential oil
> 3 drops Lime, *Citrus aurantifolia*, essential oil
> 3 drops Grapefruit, *Citrus paradisi*, essential oil
> 3 drops Mandarin, *Citrus reticulata*, essential oil

SPICY BLEND

4 drops Cinnamon Leaf, *Cinnamonum zeylanicum,* essential oil
3 drops Caraway, *Carum carvi,* essential oil
3 drops Black Pepper, *Piper nigrum,* essential oil
5 drops Bay Leaf, *Pimento racemosa,* essential oil

HERBAL BLEND

4 drops Sweet Basil, *Ocimum basilicum,* essential oil
4 drops Lavender, *Lavandula angustifolia,* essential oil
4 drops Clary Sage, *Salvia sclarea,* essential oil
4 drops Coriander Seed, *Coriandrum sativum,* essential oil

FLORAL BLEND

4 drops Lavender, *Lavandula angustifolia,* essential oil
2 drops Ylang Ylang, *Cananga odorata,* essential oil
4 drops Rose, *Rosa damascena,* essential oil
6 drops Petitgrain, *Citrus aurantium,* essential oil

WOODSY BLEND

6 drops Atlas Cedarwood, *Cedrus atlantica,* essential oil
4 drops Rosemary, *Rosmarinus officinalis,* essential oil
2 drops Patchouli, *Pogostemon cablin,* essential oil
3 drops Vetiver, *Vetivera zizanoides,* essential oil

A Therapeutic Environment – The Diffusion of Essential Oils via Nebulization

A nebulizing diffuser is one tool that no aromatherapy-prone home should be without. Especially one that houses pets! While aromatherapy candles and oil burners are fine for enjoying the aesthetics of fragrance, they are not considered to be capable of providing a therapeutic dose of essential oils. There are numerous reasons for this. The main reason is heat. Candles and oil burners use heat to cause essential oils to evaporate. We have learned that any given essential oil is composed of a myriad of chemical components. These various components all have different volatility, meaning that some are heavier than others. Some evaporate faster than others, especially when heat is introduced. You may recall from our discussion of steam distillation in Section 2 that essential oils that are hastily distilled at high temperatures for a short period of time yield an incomplete oil, whereas carefully controlled temperature and distillation time yields a chemically complete oil. The same principle applies to diffusion of the oils. The process simply works best when heat is not involved.

A nebulizing diffuser is best suited for this purpose. A nebulizing diffuser consists of a glass bulb (which looks surprisingly like some sort of drug paraphernalia) attached to a small air pump, often identical to those used with aquariums. The diffuser works by virtue of a small current of air, paired with the speedy vibration of the pump which actually ionizes complete particles of essential oil, yielding the suspension of the "complete" oil into the air.

Many essential oils can be nebulized. The technique is especially useful for cleaning room air (via the use of antimicrobial essential oils), creating a calming environment (it's perfect to use a nebulizer on a timer for a dog with separation anxiety throughout the day), deodorizing (a big plus for any home that houses a dog), and helping clear up and prevent illnesses, such as colds and flu.

Neat, or undiluted, essential oils must be used in a nebulizing diffuser. Any of the blends in this book can be used provided that they do not contain thick and viscous essential oils such as Vetiver or resinous essential oils such as Myrrh or Frankincense. The instructions provided with your nebulizer will most often go into greater detail as to what will clog your diffuser, necessitating the use of rubbing alcohol to unclog it. As a rule, I use only clear or light-colored essential oils that are very thin in texture in my diffuser. This usually prevents most clogs.

Canine First Aid

The antibacterial, analgesic, anti-inflammatory and skin regenerating properties of essential oils make them ideal for any type of first aid application. Some large or deep wounds will always require the immediate attention of a veterinarian. Do not use essential oils on puncture wounds until the threat of infection has passed and the healing process is under way, as the action of the essential oils may heal the surface of the wound, sealing bacteria inside and leading to a painful abscess.

Boo Boo Wipes – First Aid Cleanser

These pre-moistened wipes are convenient to have on hand for immediate wound care. This recipe calls for 30 cotton pads (round or square) or small pre-cut squares of heavy-duty paper towel. You can use a large-mouth jar or simply a plastic container to store the wipes. Keep them refrigerated for the longest shelf life and also a cooling, soothing effect when used.

Moisten the pads with the following solution:

> 1 teaspoon Vegetable Glycerin
> 1 teaspoon Grain Alcohol or Vodka
> 1 teaspoon Sulfated Castor Oil
> 8 drops Grapefruit Seed Extract
> 1 oz (30 ml) Witch Hazel Hydrosol, *Hamamaelis virginiana*
> 1 oz (30 ml) Distilled or Spring Water
> 6 drops Ravensare, *Ravensare aromatica*, essential oil
> 3 drops Labdunum, *Cistus ladaniferus*, essential oil
> 2 drop Helichrysum, *Helichrysum italicum*, essential oil
> 5 drops Lavender, *Lavandula angustifolia,* essential oil

The above solution can also be added to spray bottle and used as a mist.

Boo Boo Essential Oil Blend – First Aid Treatment

> $^1/_2$ oz (15 ml) base oil (I use hazelnut or sweet almond)
> 4 drops Ravensare, *Ravensare aromatica*, essential oil
> 2 drops Labdunum, *Cistus ladaniferus*, essential oil
> 1 drop Helichrysum, *Helichrysum italicum*, essential oil
> 3 drops Lavender, *Lavandula angustifolia,* essential oil

Combine all ingredients, shake and store in a dark glass bottle.

Apply a small amount directly to minor cuts, wounds, scrapes, irritations, insect bites, burns, bruises and post-operative incisions.

Boo Boo Healing Salve

Makes approximately 4 oz (120 ml) of salve. Add to a mixing bowl:

> 1 oz (30 ml) Sweet Almond Oil
> 1 oz (30 ml) Hazelnut Oil
> 1 oz (30 ml) Sunflower Oil
> 1 oz (30 ml) Olive Oil
> $^1/_2$ oz (14 g) Beeswax

Gently heat base oils and beeswax over low heat (a double boiler set-up is ideal) until beeswax is thoroughly melted. Add 20 drops of Vitamin E oil, a natural antioxidant preservative.

Allow to cool for 3–5 minutes, then add the following essential oils and stir thoroughly:

> 6 drops Ravensare, *Ravensare aromatica*, essential oil
> 3 drops Labdunum, *Cistus ladaniferus*, essential oil
> 2 drops Helichrysum, *Helichrysum italicum*, essential oil
> 5 drops Lavender, *Lavandula angustifolia*, essential oil
> 5 drops Geranium, *Pelargonium graveolens*, essential oil
> 5 drops Rosewood , *Aniba roseadora*, essential oil
> 5 drops Thyme thujanol, *Thymus vulgaris ch. thujanol*, essential oil

Pour into a dark (cobalt or amber) glass jar. Allow to cool completely before putting on lid.

Boo Boo Healing Salve is a wonderful all-purpose first aid ointment for all sorts of wounds and irritations. Excellent for paw care.

To increase therapeutic value, the base oils can be infused with a variety of skin-soothing herbs. I often use calendula petals, rose petals, chamomile flowers and lavender flowers.

Canine Ear Cleaning Formulations

Dirty, waxy or infected ears can be greatly helped with essential oils and hydrosols. I have seen dogs who had become resistant to conventional veterinary otic cleansers and antibacterial or antifungal ointments turn around to have pink and healthy ears with the addition of aromatherapy ear cleansers and a change in diet. An overproduction of ear wax is often indicative of an allergy, and dogs are frequently allergic to certain ingredients in their food.

I recommend that dogs be fed a natural diet – whether it be the BARF (Bones and Raw Food) diet, Pitcairn diet, Schultze diet, Billinghurst diet or a high quality, human-grade kibble (For more information on various canine diets and lists of high quality foods, see Appendix 2: Holistic Resource Guide starting on page 212).

The antibacterial, antifungal, anti-inflammatory, antipruritic and skin-regenerating properties of essential oils once again make them the top choice for both preventing and clearing up infections.

CANINE OTIC CLEANSER

Makes 8 oz (240 ml). Store formulation in a dark or opaque bottle. A spritz bottle is most convenient, as the mixture can be sprayed directly in the ear (if your dog will allow) or on a cotton ball or pad. Shake well before use.

> 1 teaspoon Vegetable Glycerin
> $^1/_2$ oz (15 ml) Grain Alcohol or Vodka
> 1 teaspoon Sulfated Castor Oil
> $^1/_2$ oz (15 ml) Aloe Vera
> $^1/_2$ oz (15 ml) Cider Vinegar (Organic preferred)
> $^1/_2$ oz (15 ml) Witch Hazel Hydrosol, *Hamamaelis virginiana*
> 10 drops Grapefruit Seed Extract
> 5 oz (150 ml) Distilled or Spring Water
> 4 drops Lavender, *Lavandula angustifolia,* essential oil
> 7 drops Bergamot, *Citrus bergamia,* essential oil
> 3 drops Niaouli (MQV), *Melaleuca quinquenervia viridiflora,* essential oil
> 2 drops Roman Chamomile, *Anthemis nobilis,* essential oil

Hydrosols of Lavender, Roman Chamomile, German Chamomile, Rose or Cornflower can be added in place of the water in this mixture to increase therapeutic value.

Use this formula to cleanse the ears, removing surface dirt and wax. Remember, you should never stick your fingers or cotton swabs, balls or pads down into your dog's ear canal!

CONVENIENT CANINE EAR WIPES

Moisten cotton pads on small squares of heavy-duty paper towel with Canine Otic Cleanser. Store in a large-mouth jar or plastic container in the refrigerator – for a cooling and soothing ear treatment.

CANINE OTIC ESSENTIAL OIL BLEND – AN EAR TREATMENT

This formula is meant to be used after a thorough ear cleansing. Drop 2–4 drops of the blend into the ear canal and massage in by externally massaging the outside of the ear. The natural base oils in the formula will help to break down ear wax and dirt and bring it up out of the ear canal where it can be easily wiped away. Most dogs will shake their heads after the oil drops are massaged in, facilitating the removal of the dirt and wax.

Cleaner ears result in fewer infections, and in turn a happier, healthier dog!

$^1/_2$ oz (15 ml) base oil (I use hazelnut or sweet almond)
4 drops Lavender, *Lavandula angustifolia*, essential oil
7 drops Bergamot, *Citrus bergamia*, essential oil
3 drops Niaouli (MQV), *Melaleuca quinquenervia viridiflora*, essential oil
2 drops Roman Chamomile, *Anthemis nobilis*, essential oil

Combine all ingredients, shake and store in a dark glass bottle.

Potions for Itchy Skin, and Other Skin Problems

Essential oils win yet another award due to their innate abilities to calm and soothe inflamed skin conditions, reduce itching, act as analgesics and even provide antihistaminic effects.

As with chronic or recurrent ear problems, skin infections and rashes are one of the most common ways in which an allergic dog will manifest the condition. Common culprits are diet, cleaning products used in the home and seasonal, airborne allergies such as pollens and molds.

Dogs afflicted with skin conditions will often frantically bite at themselves, chew or gnaw on the paws or limbs, or lick certain areas obsessively. All of this behavior results in sore, inflamed and irritated skin that is prone to infection, and often, large areas of hair loss.

SOOTHING SKIN SPRAY

Makes 8 oz (240 ml). Store formulation in a dark or opaque bottle. A spritz bottle is most convenient, as the mixture can be sprayed directly to treat large affected areas, particularly itchy bellies!

1 teaspoon Vegetable Glycerin
$^1/_2$ oz (15 ml) Grain Alcohol or Vodka
1 teaspoon Sulfated Castor Oil
$^1/_2$ oz (15 ml) Aloe Vera
$^1/_2$ oz (15 ml) German Chamomile Hydrosol, *Matricaria recutita*
$^1/_2$ oz (15 ml) Lavender Hydrosol, *Lavandula angustifolia*
10 drops Grapefruit Seed Extract
5 oz (150 ml) Distilled or Spring Water
2 drops Geranium, *Pelargonium graveolens*, essential oil
6 drops Rosewood, *Aniba roseadora*, essential oil
6 drops Lavender, *Lavandula angustifolia*, essential oil
1 drop Roman Chamomile, *Anthemis nobilis*, essential oil
2 drops Carrot Seed, *Daucus carota*, essential oil

Shake well before use. Apply as needed to itchy, reddened or irritated skin to help ease symptoms and speed healing process.

This formulation can also be added to cotton pads or small squares of heavy-duty paper towels stored in a jar or plastic container and kept in the refrigerator to create a cooling skin-soothing treatment.

Soothing Skin Essential Oil Blend

$^1/_2$ oz (15 ml) base oil (I use hazelnut or sweet almond)
2 drops Geranium, *Pelargonium graveolens*, essential oil
6 drops Rosewood, *Aniba roseadora*, essential oil
6 drops Lavender, *Lavandula angustifolia*, essential oil
1 drop Roman Chamomile, *Anthemis nobilis*, essential oil
2 drops Carrot Seed, *Daucus carota*, essential oil

Combine all ingredients, shake and store in a dark glass bottle.
Use 2–4 drops of this blend to spot treat smaller areas of affected skin.

Soothing Skin Herbal Rinse

This is an herbal and oat-based rinse that can be used after shampooing as a finishing rinse to increase the therapeutic value of an anti-itch bath. Grind all herbs and oats and seal into a large heat sealable tea bag or muslin tea bag. Infuse into hot water for 5–10 minutes then allow to cool to a reasonable temperature for rinsing your dog.

1 oz (28 g) Witch Hazel Herb, *Hamamaelis virginiana*
1 oz (28 g) Calendula Petals, *Calendula officinalis*
1 oz (28 g) Chamomile Flowers, *Anthemis nobilis* or *Matricaria recutita*
1 oz (28 g) Lavender Flowers, *Lavandula angustifolia*
1 oz (28 g) ground oats, *Avena sativa*
1 oz (28 g) Rose petals, *Rosa damascena*
1 oz (28 g) Slippery Elm, *Ulmus fulva*

Hot Spot Healer (Moist Acute Pyoderma)

$^1/_2$ oz (15 ml) base oil (I use hazelnut or sweet almond)
3 drops Sage, *Salvia officinalis*, essential oil
7 drops Lavender, *Lavandula angustifolia*, essential oil
15 drops Clove Bud, *Eugenia carophyllata*, infusion (NOTE: This is not Clove Bud essential oil!)

Store in a dark glass bottle.

The Clove Bud infusion in this recipe is used rather than Clove Bud essential oil, which is dermocaustic. With aromatherapy for dogs, we will avoid the use of the essential oil. You can create an oil infusion with clove buds simply by adding $^1/_2$ cup of Clove Buds to 1 cup of Sweet Almond Oil. I simmer the buds and oil together over very low heat, for two days, then strain the oil out and store in a dark glass bottle. This infusion provides some of the analgesic and anti-inflammatory effects of the Clove Buds without the risk of irritation.

This blend is designed to stop hot spots in their tracks. Hot spots, technically known as moist acute pyoderma, can quickly spread from the size of a dime to the size of a pancake overnight. They are painful, itchy and accompanied by a moist and weeping open wound with loss of fur around the area. I recommend the use of 2–4 drops of Hot Spot Healer several times a day to the affected area. I normally avoid the use of ketone-containing essential oils, such as Sage. While Sage contains only a moderate level of ketones, their drying and mucolytic properties are important in helping to heal a weeping wound. Note that I use the Sage essential oil in a very small amount, just enough to provide a beneficial effect.

Once the hot spot stops weeping and begins to heal, you can begin using the Boo Boo Healing Salve or Boo Boo Essential Oil Blend on the area.

MANGE TREATMENT BLEND

$^1/_2$ oz (15 ml) base oil (I use hazelnut or sweet almond)
5 drops Lavender, *Lavandula angustifolia*, essential oil
7 drops Niaouli (MQV), *Melaleuca quinquenervia viridiflora*, essential oil
1 drop Helichrysum, *Helichrysum italicum*, essential oil
2 drops Sweet Marjoram, *Origanum marjorana*, essential oil

Store in a dark glass bottle.

I have previously used this blend to treat both demodetic and sarcoptic mange. Before use, I recommend bathing the dog with a 100% natural shampoo that contains the same essential oil blend as the mange treatment – 15 drops of essential oil per 8 oz (240 ml) of shampoo base (that is 5 drops Lavender, 7 Niaouli, 1 Helichrysum and 2 Sweet Marjoram per 8 oz (240 ml) of shampoo base).

Then 2–4 drops of the Mange Treatment Blend should be applied topically to affected areas, twice a day for at least two weeks. Observe the area for a week afterwards and repeat if necessary. If applicable, try to prevent the dog from licking the affected area for as long as possible.

Sometimes I recommend the use of a T-shirt, bandanna or even a pair of socks to delay dogs from "getting at" essential oil applications for at last 30 minutes.

TICK BITE TREATMENT – ESSENTIAL OIL BLEND

$^1/_2$ oz (15 ml) base oil (I use hazelnut or sweet almond)
5 drops Thyme thujanol, *Thymus vulgaris ch thujanol*, essential oil
3 drops Hyssop decumbens, *Hyssop off. ch decumbens*, essential oil
8 drops Lavender, *Lavandula angustifolia*, essential oil

Store in a dark glass bottle.

This blend is intended for use on tick bites or immediately after a tick is removed to help prevent infection, reduce redness and inflammation and possibly prevent Lyme's disease. I was inspired to formulate this blend after a day of taking a master's aromatherapy course with Dr. Kurt Schnaubelt. Schnaubelt suggested that Thyme thujanol and Hyssop decumbens be used to help in the prevention of Lyme's disease from tick bites. I presently have many clients using this blend for their dogs, particularly those who live in areas with high tick populations, and so far, so good – no known instances of Lyme's disease. Whenever there is a chance that a dog is exposed to ticks or a tick bite is found, the animal should always be carefully watched for any signs of Lyme's disease. It is a debilitating illness that should not be taken lightly. If you suspect that your dog may have contracted Lyme's disease, see your vet immediately. (Symptoms of Lyme's disease include fever, lameness and soreness, listlessness, loss of appetite, swollen glands and joints.)

Tooth and Mouth Care

Essential oils possess natural antibacterial effects in addition to minty and fresh aromas that are ideal for clearing up a case of stinky breath. Preventative care is the best way to prevent bad breath and the need for frequent teeth cleanings. Many of my clients find that feeding a natural BARF (Bones and Raw Food) diet, or giving weekly beef marrow bones in combination with weekly teeth cleanings is especially effective for keeping teeth clean and white, plaque to a minimum and breath freshened.

The use of essential oils of culinary origin is safe in small and diluted amounts. These oils are regarded as safe for use with humans due to their high prevalence of use in the pharmaceutical and food industries.

FRESH BREATH SPRITZ

Makes 8 oz (240 ml). Package in a cobalt, amber, green or opaque spritzer bottle.

> 1 teaspoon Vegetable Glycerin
> $^1/_2$ oz (approx 30 ml) Grain Alcohol or Vodka
> 1 teaspoon Sulfated Castor Oil
> 10 drops Grapefruit Seed Extract
> 7 oz Distilled or Spring Water
> 6 drops Cardamom, *Elletaria cardamomum*, essential oil
> 4 drops Coriander Seed, *Coriandrum sativum*, essential oil
> 6 drops Peppermint, *Mentha piperita*, essential oil

Shake well before use. Spritz 1–2 times inside the dog's mouth up to 4 times a day to aid in alleviating mouth odor. Most dogs will not enjoy having anything sprayed in their mouths, so don't be surprised if your dog starts smacking his lips and drooling when you use this formulation. It's perfectly normal.

TEETH CLEANING WIPES

Fresh Breath Spritz added to cotton pads or small squares of heavy duty paper towel and stored in a jar or plastic container can be used for cleaning your dog's teeth. These wipes will not remove hardened plaque deposits, but rather help in preventing the formation of plaque, when used along with diet and raw bones for teeth cleaning.

Teeth Cleaning Wipes are ideal to begin using regularly after a veterinary dental cleaning has occurred and the teeth are plaque free. Prevention is the best medicine!

FRESH BREATH ESSENTIAL OIL BLEND

> $^1/_2$ oz (15 ml) base oil (I use hazelnut or sweet almond)
> 6 drops Cardamom, *Elletaria cardamomum*, essential oil
> 4 drops Coriander Seed, *Coriandrum sativum*, essential oil
> 6 drops Peppermint, *Mentha piperita*, essential oil

I prefer to package this blend in a glass bottle with a dropper top. The dropper makes it much easier to dispense 1–3 drops inside of the dog's mouth. However, any dark glass bottle will do; just use a pipette to measure the drops administered.

PUPPY TEETHING PAIN POTION

$^1/_2$ oz (15 ml) base oil (I use hazelnut or sweet almond)
6 drops Myrrh, *Commiphora myrrha*, essential oil
4 drops Roman Chamomile, *Anthemis nobilis*, essential oil
15 drops Clove Bud, *Eugenia carophyllata*, infusion (NOTE: this is
    not the essential oil! To create the infusion, follow the simple
    instructions in the "Hot Spot Healer" recipe on page 145.)

Store in a dark glass bottle. Apply 1–4 drops of the blend directly to the
teething pup's gums to help relieve teething pain. I also like to add several
drops of this blend to a frozen rope toy for puppy to chew on.

Calming Essential Oil Formulas for Dogs

I have had great success with the use of essential oils for calming dogs in
numerous situations: dogs with separation anxiety; training or show nerves;
hyperactivity; hypersexuality; fear of people, places or things; fear of loud
noises; essential oil blends have been ideal in all these stressful situations.
    Blends for these purposes are best applied topically for inhalation. This
is the fastest method in which essential oils work, for the large size of a
dog's nasal cavities leaves plenty of surface area for the vascular absorption
of essential oil molecules, which are quickly carried into the bloodstream,
upon which the central nervous system experiences gentle sedation.

CALM CANINE ESSENTIAL OIL BLEND

$^1/_2$ oz (15 ml) base oil (I use hazelnut or sweet almond)
3 drops Valerian, *Valeriana officinalis*, essential oil
2 drops Vetiver, *Vetivera zizanoides*, essential oil
4 drops Petitgrain, *Citrus aurantium*, essential oil
3 drops Sweet Marjoram, *Origanum marjorana*, essential oil
2 drops Sweet Orange, *Citrus sinensis*, essential oil

Store in a dark glass bottle.
Calm Canine Essential Oil Blend is my standard calming blend, which
has had a very impressive track record for dogs in numerous situations. The
calming effect ranges from "taking the edge off" to soothing a dog to the
point where it gets very mellow and takes a nap. You can adjust the number
of drops used to get the desired effect, anywhere from 1–6 drops depending
on the size of the dog.

I frequently donate bottles of this blend to rescue organizations across the country, as groups find that it is particularly helpful for use with dogs that have been abandoned or abused, when combined with massage and Tellington Touch (T Touch)™ methods.

QUICK AND SIMPLE CANINE CALMING BLEND

$^1/_2$ oz (15 ml) base oil (I use hazelnut or sweet almond)
3 drops Lavender, *Lavandula angustifolia,* essential oil
3 drops Sweet Marjoram, *Origanum marjorana,* essential oil
3 drops Roman Chamomile, *Anthemis nobilis,* essential oil
3 drops Neroli, *Citrus aurantium,* or Sweet Orange, *Citrus sinensis,* essential oil

Store in a dark glass bottle.

CALM DOG MIST WITH FLOWER AND GEMSTONE ESSENCES

Makes 8 oz (240 ml). Package in a cobalt, amber, green or opaque spritzer bottle. Shake well before use.

1 teaspoon Vegetable Glycerin
$^1/_2$ oz (15 ml) Grain Alcohol or Vodka
1 teaspoon Sulfated Castor Oil
10 drops Grapefruit Seed Extract
7 oz Distilled or Spring Water
3 drops Valerian root, *Valeriana officinalis,* essential oil
2 drops Vetiver, *Vetivera zizanoides,* essential oil
4 drops Petitgrain, *Citrus aurantium,* (leaves/twigs) essential oil
3 drops Sweet Marjoram, *Origanum marjorana,* essential oil
2 drops Sweet Orange, *Citrus sinensis,* essential oil

To increase the calming and balancing qualities of this formula, I like to add several drops of flower essences Star of Bethlehem, Rock Rose, Clematis, Impatiens and Cherry Plum, and gemstone essences of Amethyst (calms a hyperactive or overly stressed animal), Rose Quartz (helps to restore the feeling of trust and security) and Quartz (the master healer crystal which amplifies the effects of other crystals in its presence).

Calm Dog Mist can be spritzed into your hands and massaged into the neck and chest of the dog, sprayed on bedding or misted in the air.

Hypsersexuality Essential Oil Blend

Several years ago, I sold quite a few bottles of this blend to a group who trained guide dogs for the blind. Apparently, it worked very well for them in helping their energetic, intact male dogs concentrate during their training sessions, even when around female dogs in heat. Traditionally, those who had to live a chaste lifestyle, particularly monks, used Marjoram. It is believed to be a powerful anaphrodisiac. After learning this, I thought it would be interesting to try it with dogs and see what effects it had on them. Time and time again, my clients tell me how well it works for their "problem boys".

$^{1}/_{2}$ oz (15 ml) base oil (I use hazelnut or sweet almond)
10 drops Sweet Marjoram, *Origanum marjorana*, essential oil
2 drops Lavender, *Lavandula angustifolia*, essential oil
2 drops Lemongrass, *Cymbopogon martini*, essential oil
Store in a dark glass bottle. Apply 2–4 drops as needed, up to 4
times daily.

Essential Oil Blend for Fear or Separation Anxiety

$^{1}/_{2}$ oz (15 ml) base oil (I use hazelnut or sweet almond)
1 drop Neroli, *Citrus aurantium*, essential oil
2 drops Sweet Basil, *Ocimum basilicum*, essential oil
4 drops Bergamot, *Citrus bergamia*, essential oil
6 drops Petitgrain, *Citrus aurantium*, essential oil
1 drop Ylang Ylang, *Cananga odorata*, essential oil

Separation anxiety is a common problem, especially considering the number of dogs who are left home alone all day while their owners are at work, as well as the incomprehensible number of dogs who are turned over to shelters when their owners decide they can no longer "handle" them because they have behavioral problems which could easily be remedied with time and training.

I have seen the positive effects of combining aromatherapy with massage and gentle human touch, with my own rescue dog, Nigel (See Nigel's Story, page 12). Some of my clients who have dogs with very severe cases of separation anxiety have found the greatest relief by using both the Essential Oil Blend for Fear or Separation Anxiety and the Calm Canine Essential Oil Blend.

Pesticide-Free Flea and Tick Preparations

The aromatic aspect of essential oils is what makes them so effective against fleas and ticks. Because pests are repelled by scent, the essential oils must be frequently reapplied in order to remain effective. They are not as convenient to use as the once-a-month pesticide treatments, but the benefits far outweigh any inconvenience. For starters, you are not exposing your dog, your family or yourself to potentially dangerous pesticides that once on your dog, will rub off onto hands, furniture and floors. You may have to use these essential oil formulations frequently, but that gives you more quality time with your dog, and these formulas smell attractive as opposed to the harsh, chemical smell of synthetic pesticides.

It is important to note that essential oils do not kill fleas and ticks – they repel them. There are many things you can do to holistically supplement the process of flea and tick-repelling. Holistic veterinarians have found that the healthier a dog is, the less appealing he is to pests. The health of your dog dictates how often you'll need to use aromatherapy repellents. I only need to use the repellents once per week, and sometimes I forget. I feed my dogs a natural diet, which includes herbal, vitamin and mineral supplements. You'll need to determine your frequency of use with a little trial and error.

Essential oils are a common ingredient in many flea or tick repellents labeled as being "natural". It is important to note that many of these products contain essential oils of unknown quality, potentially dangerous or irritating essential oils such as Pennyroyal, Rue, Wormwood or Thuja, and often contain much larger amounts of essential oils than necessary for adequate and effective pest repelling. Even more frightening, many of these powerful blends are recommended for young puppies and cats. My main goal in formulating flea and tick preparations for dogs using essential oils is to choose the gentlest essential oils possible, in the smallest dilution necessary to still be effective. So far, I have had excellent results with the blends which follow. I hope that you experience the same results and find it unnecessary to return to the use of synthetic pesticides.

You may be wondering why I have two separate formulas for flea and tick repelling and not a single all-purpose formula. There are definite reasons for this. Fleas and ticks are most effectively repelled by different essential oils, and a combination of these oils does not smell all that great! I have always opted to create two separate blends. If you find that you need to repel both fleas and ticks, then I suggest that you apply one blend in the morning and one in the afternoon, as this practice avoids over-application.

FLEA-FREE ESSENTIAL OIL BLEND

$^1/_2$ oz (15 ml) base oil (I use hazelnut or sweet almond)
4 drops Clary Sage, *Salvia sclarea*, essential oil
1 drop Citronella, *Cymbopogon nardus*, essential oil
7 drops Peppermint, *Mentha piperita*, essential oil
3 drops Lemon, *Citrus limon*, essential oil

Store in dark glass bottle. Apply 2–4 drops topically to the neck, chest, legs and tail base of the dog. You can also add the drops to a bandanna or cotton collar.

FLEA-FREE SPRITZ

Makes 8 oz (240 ml). Store in a dark or opaque glass or plastic spritz bottle. Shake well before use.

1 teaspoon Vegetable Glycerin
$^1/_2$ oz (15 ml) Grain Alcohol or Vodka
1 teaspoon Sulfated Castor Oil
10 drops Grapefruit Seed Extract
7 oz Distilled or Spring Water
4 drops Clary Sage, *Salvia sclarea*, essential oil
1 drop Citronella, *Cymbopogon nardus*, essential oil
7 drops Peppermint, *Mentha piperita*, essential oil
3 drops Lemon, *Citrus limon*, essential oil

A spritz makes it easy to apply the repellent to a larger dog, and also convenient when you don't want to get any product on your hands. Some dogs do not like the sound of the spritz bottle, however. In these situations, applying the formula with your hands is the most effective method.

GOODBYE TICKS ESSENTIAL OIL BLEND

$^1/_2$ oz (15 ml) base oil (I use hazelnut or sweet almond)
2 drops Geranium, *Pelargonium graveolens*, essential oil
2 drops Rosewood, *Aniba roseadora*, essential oil
3 drops Lavender, *Lavandula angustifolia*, essential oil
2 drops Myrhh, *Commiphora myrrha*, essential oil
2 drops Opoponax, *Commiphora erythraea*, essential oil
1 drops Bay Leaf, *Pimento racemosa*, essential oil

Apply 2–4 drops topically to the neck, chest, legs and tail base of the dog. You can also add the drops to a bandanna or cotton collar.

GOODBYE TICKS SPRITZ

Makes 8 oz (240 ml). Store in a dark or opaque glass or plastic spritz bottle. Shake well before use.

> 1 teaspoon Vegetable Glycerin
> ¹/₂ oz (15 ml) Grain Alcohol or Vodka
> 1 teaspoon Sulfated Castor Oil
> 10 drops Grapefruit Seed Extract
> 7 oz Distilled or Spring Water
> 2 drops Geranium, *Pelargonium graveolens*, essential oil
> 2 drops Rosewood, *Aniba roseadora*, essential oil
> 3 drops Lavender, *Lavandula angustifolia*, essential oil
> 2 drops Myrhh, *Commiphora myrrha*, essential oil
> 2 drops Opoponax, *Commiphora erythraea*, essential oil
> 1 drop Bay Leaf, *Pimento racemosa*, essential oil

Aromatherapy for Increasing the Appetite

Very old or sick dogs often lose their appetites for stretches of time. Unfortunately, this often occurs at inopportune times when nourishment would provide a boost to their immune systems and energy levels. The citrus oils in this blend, predominantly monoterpene hydrocarbons, gently stimulate the entire system. This principle is also seen in the use of citrus oils with anorexics, to stimulate their appetites.

I recommend the creation of a topical massage blend for this purpose.

> ¹/₂ oz (15 ml) base oil (I use hazelnut or sweet almond)
> 2 drops Sweet Orange, *Citrus sinensis*, essential oil
> 2 drops Lemon, *Citrus limon*, essential oil
> 2 drops Grapefruit, *Citrus paradisi*, essential oil
> 2 drops Lime, *Citrus aurantifolia*, essential oil
> 2 drops Bergamot, *Citrus bergamia*, essential oil

Combine all ingredients, shake and store in a dark glass bottle.

Apply 2–6 drops of the final blend to the neck and chest of the dog via gentle massage. This blend is also revitalizing for fatigued animals, refreshing and bright in fragrance, and uplifting.

Can be repeated as needed, up to 6 times a day.

Blends for Boosting the Immune System

One of the most wonderful things about essential oils is their ability to boost the immune system while acting as antibacterial, antifungal and antiviral agents. I follow very specific vaccination protocols with my dogs. After my Golden Retriever died as a result of fibrosarcoma (a type of cancer commonly found in cats which is believed to be caused by vaccinations), I gave serious thought to the yearly vaccinations that most animals receive. This is a controversial subject, but there is an assortment of excellent holistic vets who provide excellent, reliable information on the topic. Marina Zacharias, DVM, hosts the website Natural Rearing (www.naturalrearing.com), and a vast amount of useful information can be found there.

Essential oils for this purpose should be used on a daily basis in highly dilute amounts. In many cases, when you begin using various aromatherapy formulas on a daily basis, this same positive immuno-supportive benefit will be experienced. For the specific purpose of providing complementary support to a dog which you are not vaccinating or with which you are using a reduced vaccination schedule, you can use the following blend. This blend will not interfere with the use of nosodes. (Nosodes are homeopathic remedies used as oral vaccines.) It is a broad spectrum blend, composed of a variety of essential oils. I usually limit my blends to four or five oils, but this one contains seven.

Immune-Boosting Essential Oil Blend

$^{1}/_{2}$ oz (15 ml) base oil (I use hazelnut or sweet almond)
2 drops Bay Laurel, *Laurus nobilis*, essential oil
2 drops Ravensare, *Ravensare aromatica* essential oil
2 drops Palmarosa, *Cymbopogon martini*, essential oil
2 drops Eucalyptus radiata essential oil
2 drops Niaouli, *Melaleuca quinquenervia viridiflora*, essential oil
2 drops Coriander Seed, *Coriandrum sativum*, essential oil
2 drops Thyme thujanol, *Thymus vulgaris ch. thujanol*, essential oil

Apply 2–4 drops daily via massage to the neck and chest daily.

IMMUNE-BOOSTING SPRITZ

Makes 8 oz (240 ml). Store in a dark or opaque glass or plastic spritz bottle. Shake well before use.

> 1 teaspoon Vegetable Glycerin
> $^1/_2$ oz (15 ml) Grain Alcohol or Vodka
> 1 teaspoon Sulfated Castor Oil
> 10 drops Grapefruit Seed Extract
> 7 oz Distilled or Spring Water
> 2 drops Bay Laurel, *Laurus nobilis*, essential oil
> 2 drops Ravensare, *Ravensare aromatica*, essential oil
> 2 drops Palmarosa, *Cymbopogon martini*, essential oil
> 2 drops Eucalyptus radiata essential oil
> 2 drops Niaouli, *Melaleuca quinquenervia viridiflora*, essential oil
> 2 drops Coriander Seed, *Coriandrum sativum*, essential oil
> 2 drops Thyme thujanol, *Thymus vulgaris ch. thujanol*, essential oil

This spritz can be used directly on the animal (1–4 spritzes per day massaged in to the fur of the neck and chest). It can also be sprayed on puppy's paws after walks to eliminate possible microbes that may have been picked up while outdoors. Another use is to spray on bedding, or in the dog's environment. This is a gentle blend of oils, but as with any aromatherapy formula, it should be used in moderation!

Essential Oil Blends for Colds and Congestion

This blend for relieving nasal congestion or cold symptoms in dogs can be used in several ways. Several drops can be massaged into the fur of the dog's neck and chest, or placed on a cloth bandanna. The blend can also be added to the animal's bedding. Another possible use is for the dog owner to bring the animal into the bathroom when they are showering and allow the dog to lay on the floor. The owner would then drop 6–10 drops of the blend onto the floor of the shower. The combination of the steam and vaporized oils is greatly helpful for clearing sinus congestion.

The blend can also be created without the base oils and used in a nebulizing diffuser, 5 minutes at a time up to several times a day.

> $^1/_2$ oz (15 ml) base oil (I use hazelnut or sweet almond)
> 5 drops Eucalyptus radiata essential oil
> 5 drops Myrhh, *Commiphora myrrha*, essential oil
> 5 drops Ravensare, *Ravensare aromatica*, essential oil

Store in a dark glass bottle.

Fatigue Essential Oil Blend

This blend is balancing and revitalizing for dogs that are suffering from fatigue and malaise. It was blended for use with dogs that are old or suffering from a chronic illness, but can be used for temporary fatigue from overactivity as well.

> ¹/₂ oz (15 ml) base oil (I use hazelnut or sweet almond)
> 7 drops Rosemary, *Rosmarinus officinalis*, essential oil
> 6 drops Tangerine, *Citrus reticulata*, essential oil
> 3 drops Ylang Ylang, *Cananga odorata*, essential oil

Use 2–4 drops as needed. Store in a dark glass bottle. Use Rosemary essential oil with caution with dogs that are prone to seizures.

Flatulence Essential Oil Blend

This is one of those common yet annoying canine problems, quite simply caused by excess gas. It always seems to hit home when you have guests over, doesn't it? A simple blend of essential oils can help to greatly alleviate the problem. I recommend that 1–2 drops be placed on your dog's food, and then 1–2 drops be given after eating. Many dogs enjoy the taste of this spicy blend and will simply lick it off your hand. The spice oils in this blend are commonly found in a variety of food flavorings and pharmaceutical preparations, hence ingestion is commonly regarded as safe. Of course, always use the highest quality essential oils when ingestion is involved.

> ¹/₂ oz (15 ml) base oil (I use hazelnut or sweet almond)
> 3 drops Caraway, *Carum carvi*, essential oil
> 3 drops Cardamom, *Elletaria cardamomum*, essential oil
> 3 drops Cinnamon Leaf, *Cinnamonum zeylanicum*, essential oil
> 3 drops Nutmeg, *Myristica fragrans*, essential oil
> 3 drops Tangerine, *Citrus reticulata*, essential oil
> Store in a dark glass bottle.

Joint Rub Essential Oil Massage Blend

This is an ideal blend to partner with a gentle massage. Excellent for animals with muscle soreness, arthritis, hip dysplasia or sprains. This blend, combined with simple massage techniques will help to stimulate circulation to the injured area, greatly speeding the healing process. I have plenty of clients who also use this blend on themselves (one who is an avid runner who applies the blend to her shin splints). When using this blend, use 2–4 drops and try to get the blend as close to the animal's skin as possible. This can be tricky when your dog has a dense coat, but do your best. I recommend that a patch test be done with this blend, as it can potentially cause slight skin irritation. To do a patch test, take 1 drop of the blend and apply it to the sparsely coated area under your dog's "armpit". Check 24 hours later for any signs of redness or irritation. I have yet to see irritation in any dog, but it can never hurt to err on the side of safety.

> $^1/_2$ oz (15 ml) base oil (I use hazelnut or sweet almond)
> 3 drops Black Pepper, *Piper nigrum,* essential oil
> 4 drops Peppermint, *Mentha piperita,* essential oil
> 3 drops Spearmint, *Mentha spicata,* essential oil
> 4 drops Juniper Berry, *Juniperus communis,* essential oil

Store in a dark glass bottle.

Motion Sickness

If your dog is prone to motion sickness, you've probably tried numerous remedies… from ginger snaps and anti-static pads, to newspapers under the dog, acupressure bands, Dramamine™, herbal tablets or even Benadryl™ or tranquilizers. Motion sickness can put a real damper on any trip – even a short one!

Many dogs with motion sickness truly do have motion sickness and intense nausea. Others experience intense fear and anxiety over being in the car and going somewhere. Most dogs have a combination of the two.

There are numerous techniques that can help to reduce your dog's motion sickness. My dog Nigel, a rescue, was a particularly tough case. I'd like to share his story and how behavioral modification and essential oils have made our car rides drool and vomit free.

NIGEL – A CAR-SICK RESCUE DOG

When I adopted Nigel from a local humane society, I knew within minutes that he had an intense fear of the car. He did not want to get in! It took three of us to get him into the cage in the back of my Jeep for the five minute ride home. He whined the entire time and vomited numerous times. I knew that I had a problem on my hands.

Nigel experienced extreme anxiety over going in the car, so my first task was to get him used to the car and to realize that it was not anything to be scared of. Initially, Nigel would not even go near the car without "putting on the brakes", pulling on the leash and then rolling over and beginning to urinate. I coaxed him closer and closer to the car, using various excuses. Many times, I simply would get something out of the car or open the door and sit and pet him or talk to him in a soothing voice. I soon combined a blend of essential oils for fear and anxiety and began to incorporate this into our training sessions with a gentle massage. We got closer and closer to the car, and soon Nigel was retrieving toys and treats off the car seat, and approaching me while I sat in the car, to get a head rub or a kiss.

Once I got him to jump into the back of the car on his own accord, I spent time talking to him, giving him treats and belly rubs. We were soon ready for short trips around the block. At first, Nigel still exhibited signs of extreme anxiety once the car was moving, such as constant drooling, panting and crying. We began to take longer car rides, calming much of his anxiety with training and essential oils, but he still experienced the nausea and would vomit after ten minutes in the car.

At this point, I began to incorporate the use of an essential oil blend for motion sickness, composed of essential oils of Ginger, Zingiber officinale, and Peppermint, Mentha piperita. I gave Nigel 3 drops in his mouth and also applied 2 drops to a tissue and lodged it in the car's fresh air vent to help circulate it throughout the car. This combination of essential oils greatly eased Nigel's nausea. We have traveled up to three hours at a time uneventfully. I have discovered that Nigel does best when allowed to look straight ahead in the car. When he looks out the back window, he begins to get sick again.

The use of essential oils has greatly helped Nigel. He by no means loves going in the car, but he will jump in on his own, allow me to buckle him in, and immediately assume his facing forward position. A far cry from his anxiety-stricken days when he would vomit multiple times in just a few minutes!

MOTION SICKNESS ESSENTIAL OIL BLEND

$^1/_2$ oz (15 ml) base oil (I use hazelnut or sweet almond)
7 drops Ginger, *Zingiber officinale*, essential oil
8 drops Peppermint, *Mentha piperita*, essential oil

Store in a dark glass bottle.

Labor Ease Essential Oil Blend

This is an intense calming and balancing blend for use with the female dog in labor. It can be applied to the fur of the neck and chest, or 1–4 drops can be rubbed into the belly. Diffusion for 5 minutes at a time is also effective. Clients have found this blend is especially helpful for use with first-time mothers who may be restless and experiencing anxiety over the onset of labor.

This blend's calming powers can also be used with any dog in need of relaxation… or even with dog owners!

$^1/_2$ oz (15 ml) base oil (I use hazelnut or sweet almond)
6 drops Clary Sage, *Salvia sclarea*, essential oil
1 drop Neroli, *Citrus aurantium*, essential oil
5 drops Petitgrain, *Citrus aurantium*, essential oil
2 drops Lavender, *Lavandula angustifolia*, essential oil
1 drop Roman Chamomile, *Anthemis nobilis*, essential oil

Store in a dark glass bottle.

SECTION 5

AROMATHERAPY FOR CATS – SENSITIVE AND MYSTERIOUS CREATURES

Not long after I first became mesmerized by aromatherapy, I got a kitten. I named her "Champaca" upon receipt of my first bottle of Champaca absolute from a mail order aromatherapy company. One sniff of the warm and spicy oil, and I knew that the name just fit perfectly with my fiery tabby cat. But I quickly noticed that while I loved essential oils and absolutes, Champaca didn't. When I came home from my day job and began blending my special potions, she would disappear, only to turn up later that night in the open window of the attic, as far away from me as she could possibly get. In contrast, Dublin, my Golden Retriever, would lie at my feet, eager for any application of the oils.

It didn't take long for me to figure out that cats and essential oils are not compatible, and that my smart little cat was simply protecting herself by retreating to the rafters. Somehow, she knew that the essential oils permeating the air inside the house were not good for her. Champaca had a way out. Not all cats do. And that is why this chapter is so incredibly important, for it is here that we will learn why you should generally avoid the use of essential oils with cats, and why hydrosols, the watery byproduct of essential oil distillation, are your safest option.

So What Is the Deal with Cats?

When the father of modern aromatherapy, Rene Gattefossé, did his initial essential oil testing on dogs and horses, you have to wonder… why didn't he also test with cats? Perhaps there weren't that many around, or he had some idea of just how sensitive cats are and how different their metabolic processes are from those of other animals. Either way, I have always felt sorry for felines in that for the most part, they cannot partake safely of nature's purest and most incredible gifts – essential oils.

Cats and essential oils are a potentially dangerous combination for several reasons. Cats differ greatly from dogs in how they metabolize and excrete certain substances from their bodies. Veterinarians take great precautions in prescribing medications to cats, for even something as simple as aspirin can be toxic.

Dr. Susan Wynn, DVM, devotes great attention to the sensitivity of cats in an article written for the *Nutrition Science News*, "Pet Metabolism Dictates Dosage: Natural Treatments for Animals Should Reflect Bioindividuality", as well as in her book *Complementary and Alternative Veterinary Medicine: Principles and Practice*. Most of her article on pet metabolism is given to cats due to the high sensitivity to certain substances which cats have demonstrated. According to the article, cats have the following "metabolic idiosyncrasies":[28]

■ *Cats do not convert beta-carotene to Vitamin A, so systemic beta carotene supplementation is not particularly effective in cats.*

■ *They also have a B6 vitamin requirement that is four times that of a dog's.*

■ *Cats detoxify drugs such as coumarin, morphine, certain sulfanomides and salicylic acid much more slowly than humans, causing significant problems in dose and administration.*

■ *Feline hemoglobin, the molecule in the blood that carries oxygen, is extremely sensitive to drugs such as acetaminophen and allyl propyl disulfide (found in foods like onions). The end result is severe anemia and possibly death.*

■ *Cats have completely different reactions to certain drugs because of their species bioindividuality. Morphine, for example, causes excitation in cats.*

- *Cats are uniquely sensitive to phenolics and other compounds containing benzene rings. Compounds preserved in benzyl alcohol are toxic to cats. Exercise caution when administering phenol-containing essential oils such as Thyme (Thymus vulgaris or T. serpyllum), Cinnamon (Cinnamomum zeylanicum) and Tea Tree (also Melaleuca, Melaleuca alternifolia)*

The reason for this sensitivity can be found in their liver. Cats do not have the necessary enzymes to break down certain substances and effectively excrete them. This leads to the buildup of toxins in their bodies. Dr. Safdar Khan, DVM, a Veterinary Toxicologist with the National Animal Poison Control Center, tells us that "Cats are known to be deficient in their ability to eliminate compounds through hepatic glucuronidation (they lack enzyme glucuronyl tranferases). Glucuronidation is an important detoxification mechanism present in most animals except cats. Lack of this important detoxification mechanism in cats may result in slower elimination of certain compounds and thus build up of the toxic metabolites in the body causing toxicity."[29] This buildup of toxic metabolites can be the result of numerous substances cats may be exposed to, be they traditional allopathic medications (such as aspirin), herbs, or essential oils.

This toxin buildup does not always manifest itself immediately in cats. Depending on the cat and what it has been exposed to, it can show up in hours, days, weeks, months or even years. What is even more frightening, is that your cat can't tell you how it feels or what is going on. If you were to develop symptoms of toxicity from overexposure to essential oils, you would feel lightheaded, nauseous, clumsy, tired, headachy and generally lousy. You might experience vomiting, diarrhea, sluggish and uncoordinated movement, slurred speech or confusion, depending on how much and which essential oil you were exposed to. Veterinarians see many cases of what they call "mystery poisoning" in cats. The owner arrives at the vet's office with a pet who is despondent, clumsy and uncoordinated, sometimes partially paralyzed, vomiting, drooling and in a daze. The cat is treated for poisoning, given ample fluids, and kept under supervision for several days before being released. But not all cats are released. Some die. And sometimes, essential oils are to blame. A simple run of bloodwork on a cat showing such symptoms of toxicity almost always reveals highly elevated liver enzymes. Unfortunately, cats inability to fully excrete the toxins from their bodies means that they stay there, resulting in permanently elevated enzyme levels and varying degrees of impaired liver function.

Cats also have very delicate and thin skin and don't like strong odors. These two aspects pale in comparison to the life-threatening and impairing possibilities associated with the repeated use of certain essential oils. In the past ten years, I have come across numerous instances of essential oil toxicity in cats.

Just One Drop of Peppermint Oil Was All It Took

In fall of 1999, I received a frantic call from a new client. She had recently discovered aromatherapy and was using peppermint oil to help combat her nervous stomach and symptoms of irritable bowel syndrome.

Noticing that her cat was vomiting hairballs, she thought that "Tyco" also had an upset stomach, and just like any mother would, she set out to make it all better. She applied a single drop of undiluted peppermint oil, Mentha piperita, to Tyco's belly and massaged it in. Several hours later, she found Tyco lying listless in the hallway, unable to walk or crawl. Tyco was taken to the vet immediately, where it was determined that he was perfectly healthy except for some hairballs and what appeared to be a mysterious case of poisoning.

Tyco received fluids and returned home 2 days later. He is now healthy and happy, and his owner now takes great care to not expose him to any essential oils. It is amazing to imagine that just a single drop of essential oil could have such a powerful effect. Perhaps this case sounds like an extreme isolated incident, but it is certainly worth noting.

A Fatal Case of Citronella Poisoning

The following report was contributed by Gillian Willis, a pharmacist and toxicologist from Vancouver, British Columbia. Gillian is extremely concerned with the potential dangers of using essential oils with birds, but in the course of her research in toxicology frequently comes across information involving cats.

"I have one report on file of a cat that was bathed in Citronella oil. On presentation to the veterinary clinic 24 hours after exposure, the cat was distressed, mewing, disorientated and hypothermic. It had severe irritation and swelling to the skin and was unable to stand.

The cat was bathed, and started on IV fluids. It went into shock and exhibited 'abnormal movements.' The temperature rose to 39° C. Because the prognosis was poor, the cat was euthanized at the request of the owners."

Groomer's Worst Nightmare

The following story is provided by Sue Martin, an aromatherapist certified by the Australasian Aromatherapy Institute, who maintains a website about cat essential oil and hydrosol safety called "The Lavender Cat" at www.thelavendercat.com. While we don't have specifics as to how grossly

...continued

overdosed with essential oils these cats were, this story shows that the lack of knowledge about cats and essential oils and the public's presumption that 100% natural equals 100% safe can prove to be fatal.

"*The following is a true case of Australian tea tree, Melaleuca alternifoila, oil poisoning in three cats: A breeder shaved three Angora cats as they were severely infested with fleas. No nicks caused by shaving were visible on the cats, only numerous fleabites.*

The breeder then used a product labeled for use as a spot treatment for skin lesions, but a catalog advertised that it would repel fleas when diluted and used as a dip. The product contained oil of Melaleuca alternifolia and 60 ml (2 oz) of oil was diluted as per recommendation and applied directly to the skin of all three cats.

Within five hours of treatment, cat #1 was taken to the veterinarian. It was hypothermic, uncoordinated and unable to stand but was alert. Cats #2 and #3 were admitted later in the day. Cat #2 was comatose with severe hypothermia and dehydration. Cat #3 was alert, nervous, trembling and slightly ataxic (failure of muscular coordination). All cats had a strong odor similar to that of the Tea Tree oil product.

The cats were bathed in warm water and mild detergent to remove any remaining oil from the skin. They were treated for any possible oral consumption of oil, re-hydrated with isotonic saline solution and body temperatures raised using heat lamps and warm water bottles.

Gas chromatography – mass spectroscopy testing of urine and Tea Tree samples results: Tea Tree oil contained 42% terpinen-4-ol, which is consistent with M. alternifoila oil and the cat urine also contained terpinen-4-ol and unidentified metabolites.

Cat #3 recovered within 24 hours of being admitted to the veterinary hospital, and cat #1 recovered after 48 hours. Both cats were sent home to the cattery and no problems have been reported since. Cat #2 improved over days 2 and 3 but remained uncoordinated and dull. Although cat #2 was being treated with aggressive fluid therapy, it remained dehydrated. On day 3, it began regulating its own body temperature, but was found dead late that evening."

(*Note from the author: the fact that the terpinen-4-ol was found in the cats' urine reveals that it was excreted by the cat and not left in the cats' body to cause toxicity. Terpinen-4-ol is a monoterpene alcohol, a member of one of the gentlest of essential oil components. Tea Tree oil is composed of primarily 50% monoterpene alcohols. It also contains monoterpene hydrocarbons such as pinene, myrcene, paracymene, limonene and terpinolene. Monoterpene oxides include 1,4 cineole and 1,8 cineole. Various sesquiterpenes are also present in small percentages. It is reasonable to believe that any of the unidentified metabolites in the cats' urine were from essential oil components other than the terpinen 4-ol. Due to the known sensitivity of cats to pinene and limonene (both terpene hydrocarbons), it is reasonable to believe that these compounds, in addition to other compounds in the other essential oils found in this grooming preparation, are suspect.*)

A Litter Box as Fresh as a Pine Forest

"Marlee's" owner thought that she was making for one happy cat when she placed 10 drops of Pine essential oil, Pinus sylvestris, into her cat's enclosed litter box. Marlee was a fastidious cat who would mess in the corner if she found the scent of her box to be less than heaven-scented.

Marlee did use the litterbox on occasion after the Pine oil was added. But she also developed symptoms of toxicity within in a week and was taken to the vet where once again, "mystery poisoning" was the final ruling. Marlee's owner stopped using the Pine essential oil, and all essential oils, and the problem has never returned.

Essential Oil Use and Elevated Liver Enzymes – a Case Study

Sue Martin of the Lavender Cat is both a cat lover and an aromatherapist. Because of this, her cats have been exposed to quite a high level of essential oils. It is only within the last few years with the growing popularity of essential oils and aromatherapy that toxicology cases involving cats and essential oils have surfaced. Sue was able to put her own cat, "Tashan", to the test and show that removing essential oils from Tashan's daily routine drastically lowered his liver enzymes.

Tashan's Experience Part 1

My Bengal cat, Tashan, underwent extensive veterinary testing last week as I recently noticed subtle changes in his behavior and a decrease in his energy. He was examined and evaluated as being in perfect health with one exception: his liver enzyme was elevated to the very high end of normal.

I shared the information from veterinary toxicologist Dr. Khan, with my veterinarian who also believes my long-term daily use of essential oil diffusion may be the culprit of Tashan's liver problem (I never use essential oils or hydrosols on my cats).

The treatment plan is to forego all uses of essential oils for two months and then retest Tashan. If the liver enzyme value goes down, that should be conclusive that the essential oils were the culprit.

Tashan's Follow-up – Two Months Later

Two months later the follow-up liver profile rated a decrease in enzyme values. For two months, no other changes were made in household routine, or in Tashan's diet, only that I did not use aromatherapy. Nothing else was different, so it seems that was the probable culprit.

We are going to re-introduce aromatherapy into the home, but instead of daily diffusion, it will be periodic applications (when I need to use it for myself). I hope that with moderate use, it will not re-elevate Tashan's liver enzymes. If it does, then I will have to stop altogether, but only time will tell. At any rate, now, he is a healthy Bengal cat. With aromatherapy limited to periodic diffusion, the veterinarian will re-test Tashan's enzymes in six months.

Cats Are Particularly Sensitive to Certain Essential Oil Components

While these examples all show cats that have been severely affected by essential oil use, there are most likely just as many that appear to have no problems. While some of this has to do with the variable amounts of time in which toxicity appears, it also has to do with the specific essential oils which the cats have been exposed to. Cats are not equally sensitive to all essential oils. Neither are all essential oils of the same quality: many are adulterated with foreign synthetic substances. These are equally important variables to consider as we determine the true safety threshold of essential oil use with cats.

Essential oils, with their myriad of chemical constituents are all highly individual. Cats are adversely affected by certain essential oil components known as phenols and ketones, just as we humans and our canine companions are. But veterinarians have also determined through toxicology reports that cats are most sensitive to a specific group of essential oil constituents which other mammals are not – monoterpene hydrocarbons. Specifically, the monoterpene hydrocarbons pinene and limonene have been discovered to cause the most adverse effects. These two substances, found most commonly in citrus and pine essential oils, are common ingredients in natural flea and tick repellents and shampoos, as well as natural citrus and pine cleaners. The popularity of such natural products obviously increases the chances that cats exposed to them may develop toxicity from their use. Most people would never imagine that something as seemingly harmless as a natural citrus cleaner could wreak havoc on a cat's liver detoxification mechanisms, but it can.

Market research of natural pest repellents for cats shows many brands manufacturing shampoos, sprays, herbal dips, powders, collars and even aromatherapy cat litter for cats, most of which contain citrus or pine oils, or synthesized pinene and limonene. Both natural and pseudo-natural cleaning supplies are used to clean floors and household surfaces, leaving behind a residue. When such a product is used, cats inhale aromatic molecules of the cleaning product. They walk on counters, floors and other surfaces on which the supplies are used, and later lick their feet. Cats and other animals, simply due to the fact that they are closer to the ground and groom themselves, are far more prone to poisoning with environmental toxins than humans are. We should be cautious about the use of any cleaning products in homes that house animals, especially cats.

I have heard many a vet and layperson say, "Cats are sensitive to terpenes". Yes, they have shown a high level of sensitivity to monoterpene hydrocarbons. We know that cats are also highly sensitive to compounds containing benzene ring structures, such as those essential oils containing phenols (mainly, monoterpene phenols). However, essential oils contain a variety of different types of monoterpenes. There are monoterpene hydrocarbons, monoterpene alcohols, monoterpene ketones, monoterpene aldehydes, monoterpene phenols, monoterpene oxides and monoterpene esters. There are also diterpenes and sesquiterpenes, such as sesquiterpene hydrocarbons, sesquiterpene alcohols and sesquiterpene lactones. These chemicals all have very different molecular structure and effects on the body.

The term "terpene" relates to the fact that the molecule contains ten carbon atoms. Whether or not the molecule is an alcohol, ketone, aldehyde, ester, oxide or phenol is dependent on the functional group that is attached to the basic terpene molecule, which consists of ten carbon atoms. Oxygen, nitrogen and hydrogen atoms bonded to the basic terpene structure produce compounds of varying chemical reactivity and chemical structure. This variance produces vastly different physiological effects. Monoterpene hydrocarbons (found in Orange and Pine oils) are stimulating; the ketone group (Pennyroyal, Sage, Hyssop, Yarrow) is mucolytic; aldehydes (Citronella, Lemongrass, Melissa) are calming; esters (Lavender, Clary Sage, Sweet Marjoram) are antispasmodic; monoterpene alcohols (Geranium, Coriander, Thyme linalol, Rose) are natural tonics; phenols (Oregano, Savory, Thyme vulgaris) are stimulating and irritating; and the oxides act as expectorants, as seen in Tea Tree and Eucalyptus oils.

On this basis, it is quite unfair to say that cats are sensitive to all terpenes, and that all terpenes have the potential to cause adverse effects or, at worst, death. If this were the case, holistic veterinarians would not use any type of essential oils whatsoever with cats. In certain clinical settings, essential oils can be used by veterinarians, and have shown themselves to have marked effects. The important issue is which oils are used, the quality of those oils, the dilution of those oils, and what the achieved effect is. For this reason, you won't find any recipes for cats in this book containing essential oils, and I discourage their use amongst laypeople. There are too many risk factors involved – many of which have nothing to do with the cat owner, and more to do with the unknowns involved in sourcing high quality, pure and unadulterated essential oils.

For these reasons, this book will only present recipes for cats that are based on hydrosols.

Monoterpene Alcohols – the Gentlest Components

Monoterpene alcohols make up a high percentage of most essential oils and are amongst the gentlest components. Essential oils that are high in monoterpene alcohols are suitable for daily and repeat use with humans and dogs, and are easily metabolized and excreted by the body due to their highly hydrophilic, or "water-loving" nature. For this reason, we can assume to a certain extent that their benign and tolerable natural also makes them safe to use with cats. The presence of the monoterpene alcohol terpinen-4-ol and its metabolites in the urine of three cats inadvertently poisoned with Tea Tree oil shows that this particular essential oil component is in fact excreted from cats' bodies and does not appear to be a compound which builds up in their bodies leading to toxicity. However, no extensive testing has been done. This activity must be approached with extreme care and watchful observation. We can safely assume, however, that if certain essential oil components and their metabolites are found in a cat's urine, this points towards the fact that those substances were either metabolized or safely passed from the body – and do not remain in the body where they would contribute to a buildup of toxins and potential permanent changes in liver function.

The reason that terpene alcohols are so gentle within the body is due to their affinity to water. The molecules actually attach themselves to a molecule of water due to the presence of a hydroxide radical (-OH). In this fashion, they are efficiently and quickly excreted from the body, unlike many other essential oil components that take longer, such as monoterpene ketones, which can irritate the liver due to their extended presence there. For this reason, dosing of essential oils containing monoterpene ketones is a delicate subject even with humans. It is one I avoid almost altogether with dogs, and definitely with cats. Terpene alcohols are an important essential oil component to examine, because they are the most common essential oil constituent found in "hydrosols"- the byproduct of the steam distillation of essential oils.

Essential Oils High in Monoterpene Hydrocarbons (50–90% total)		Essential Oils High in Phenols
Lemon, Citrus limon	Citrus paradisi	Oregano, Origanum vulgare
Orange, Citrus sinensis	Lime, Citrus aurantifolia	Thyme, Thymus vulgaris
Tangerine, Citrus reticulata	Bergamot, Citrus bergamia	Clove, Eugenia caryophyllata
Mandarin, Citrus reticulata	Pine, Pinus sylvestris	Summer Savory, Satureja hortensis
Grapefruit,	Spruce, Picea mariana	Winter Savory, Satureja montana
	Fir, Abies balsamica	Cassia, Cinnamomum cassia

Hydrosols – the Safe Way to Enjoy Aromatherapy with Your Cat

Also known as hydrolats, hydrolates and floral waters, hydrosols are the water-based byproduct of the steam distillation of essential oils. Hydrosols contain minute amounts of certain essential oil components, mainly monoterpene alcohols. Hydrosols also contain the water-soluble portions of the plant – something which essential oils, being lipophilic, do not contain. This gives hydrosols a unique range of action. They are extraordinarily gentle substances, and I often describe them as being similar to herbal teas. Their very subtle fragrances make them tolerable and well accepted by cats, and their highly diluted nature makes using and dosing hydrosols safe and simple. Whereas essential oils must be dosed with extreme care for dogs, hydrosols have a much greater amount of room for error. In fact, it would be quite difficult to make a mistake in giving hydrosols to a cat. These aromatic waters are so gentle that a human baby could be bathed in a tubful. But not just any hydrosol – authentic, properly distilled and stored, non-contaminated hydrosol.

The Not So Great Hydrosol Debate

There is currently a great deal of debate over the safety of hydrosol use with cats, and I blame the viral nature of the internet for this misconception. When I first began offering aromatherapy products and consultations on my website in 1998, I actually received a good deal of negative feedback in response to my strongly expressed opinion on the dangers of essential oil use with cats. Many aromatherapists and cat owners were using essential oil and essential oil-containing products on their cats, and thought that my viewpoint was simply absurd. However, the growing popularity of aromatherapy provided numerous opportunities for the potential dangers of essential oil use with cats to come to light, and it very soon became an undisputed fact. Certain essential oils, particularly pine and citrus oils, were toxic to cats.

Three years later, I find myself at the center of another debate – the use of hydrosols with cats. Hydrosols contain minute amounts of certain essential oil components, mainly monoterpene alcohols. Despite the fact that many types of terpenes exist, some aromatherapists, veterinarians and other individuals loosely group all terpenes into one group with a common range of action – that they all can harm cats. Our earlier analysis of terpene chemistry and action reveals this to be a very difficult point to prove. While the hydrocarbon terpenes are lipophilic and polar, the alcohol terpenes are hydrophilic and non-polar. Differences abound, and these cannot be disputed. Certain essential oils contain both types of terpenes. But the fact of the matter is that the extremely gentle, water-like monoterpene alcohol components left in trace amounts in hydrosol waters can hardly be held responsible for the toxic reactions caused by repeated exposure to varying levels of pure and undiluted essential oils with limonene and pinene as their predominant components.

There are no documented cases of hydrosols causing any symptoms of toxicity, skin irritations or poisoning with cats. There is no documentation that reveals that hydrosols impair liver function or increase liver enzyme levels in cats. There is no evidence to indicate that cats cannot metabolize monoterpene alcohols. In fact, veterinary toxicology reports show that these substances and their metabolites are found in the urine of cats exposed to essential oils containing monoterpene alcohols and other essential oil components. Hydrosols are a relative newcomer to aromatherapy. Hence, the best way to learn more about them would be from an expert who has dedicated herself to these gentle waters.

Suzanne Catty and Her Holy Waters

Suzanne Catty has forged a unique path in the present state of aromatherapy. She is the first aromatherapist to fully research and dedicate herself to the pursuit of hydrosols as a form of phytotherapy as complex and powerful as the use of aromatherapy's essential oils. Catty recently authored *Hydrosols: The Next Aromatherapy* and is one of the first to analyze the chemical composition of numerous hydrosols. It is her research that revealed just which essential oil constituents are left after the distillation process is complete. She also has made evident a variety of concerns that must be taken into account when purchasing, storing and using hydrosols to maintain the therapeutic nature of these water-based substances (See Section 2).

Catty's analysis of the chemical makeup of hydrosols has been instrumental in determining the safety of these substances for use with cats. This safety is limited to the use of true, properly stored and fresh hydrosols – not fakes or synthetics. Catty regularly uses and recommends hydrosols for pet care, cats included.

Aromatherapy for cats involving the use of hydrosols is very new territory. When I introduced a line of simple feline hydrosol products several years ago to be sold alongside my Aromaleigh canine aromatherapy essential oil remedies, I never imagined that the safety and gentle nature of these aromatic substances would fall under such adamant interrogation in such a short amount of time. In order to lend credence to these substances, Suzanne Catty recently provided me with a statement of her opinion on the safety of hydrosols with cats for me to post to my website, www.aromaleigh.com.

A STATEMENT FROM SUZANNE CATTY

Contamination of hydrosols is not really a major problem, more problematic are the fakes and synthetic products sold as hydrosols, the real hydrosols with preservatives and/or stabilizers added, or the real hydrosols improperly collected at distillation resulting in virtually non-therapeutic, unstable and only slightly aromatic waters. True hydrosols, true therapeutic hydrosols free of preservatives, alcohol, stabilizers and properly handled are a healing boon for animals of all kinds and are virtually the only choice of aromatic substances to use on cats. Their low odor intensity and non-volatile nature means they are not overpowering to animals, especially cats with their acute sense of smell. Their water solubility means they can be diluted to infinitesimal amounts, as in homeopathic dilutions, and their chemical analysis shows they are more therapeutic than many commercial herbal preparations, tinctures and teas currently in the market. Using sustainably wildcrafted and/or certified organic hydrosols also means that you do not have the issue of contamination from agricultural chemicals, fertilizers, pesticides and herbicides commonly used in herb growing and production all over the world.

If anyone has used a flower remedy on their cats they are using grain alcohol or brandy, and as these seem widely accepted by many for use on cats, I can't see why anyone would object to the use of hydrosols that contain no alcohol. Also, hydrosols contain only a small range of the chemical constituents found in essential oils, and in fact the very gentle functional group of alcohols (linalool, etc) is one of the most common along with the acids which is what gives hydrosols their very specific and rather large pH ranges; this in turn contributes as directly to their functions as the chemical constituents do. In fact with hydrosols the pH dictates the best mode of application in quite a few instances. I am working with four chemists around the world in furthering the research on chemical analysis of hydrosols, all of which are collected according to my established parameters developed in conjunction with two chemists and several distillers. The Canadian government is also undertaking a two-year research project on hydrosols based on my research. Some of this project will look at the veterinary application for things ranging from fleas and ticks to foot and mouth disease.

Hydrosols are absolutely safe for cats, no question; some are more appropriate than others; some work better for some cats; some work more appropriately for some conditions; but they are not a health hazard to felines.

Trace Essential Oil Content in Herbs, Teas and Plants

While hydrosols contain trace amounts of essential oil components, notably monoterpene alcohols, we must also consider the essential oil content of other treatments our cats might be exposed to.

Cats love catnip. The dried herb, which induces drug-like states in cats for the amusement of owners and the treatment of kitty boredom, inevitably contains trace amounts of essential oil, just as all dried herbs do. Any dried herbs given to a cat will contain minute amounts of essential oil components. Any herbal teas made from dry or fresh herbs will also contain the same.

This is one of the many arguments I have in support of the use of hydrosols for cats. Numerous cat owners who wish to use aromatherapy with their cats already practice other sorts of holistic supplementation with their cats. Already, they are exposing them to minute amounts of essential oil components. Amounts that we cannot allow ourselves to get up in arms about.

Your cat's drinking water, diet, the air quality in your home, the cleaning supplies you use and the grooming products you own all have effects on your cat's health in ways which are exponentially more crucial than the giving of dried herbs, teas or hydrosols.

One could argue for hours against the use of hydrosols with cats, but this is fruitless for numerous reasons. We can hardly control every single substance with which our pets, or even we ourselves, come into contact. We can merely hope to minimize exposure, be it to synthetic ingredients or essential oils.

If we have a choice between taking an allergy-ridden cat to the vet and receiving a standard treatment of prednisone shots or pills, we would be much better off to use hydrosols and holistic supplements to manage the symptoms. It is not only safer, it is smarter. We're strengthening the cat in this manner, not detracting from its state of health with the introduction of immunosuppressive steroids. How then can hydrosols be dangerous? True, quality hydrosols are not. It is the impostors, fakes, synthetically preserved, contaminated and irresponsibly distilled hydrosols that we must be concerned with.

Until more valid veterinary research is conducted (which is unlikely to happen) concerning the metabolization of essential oil components by cats, we can only watch and learn as we have from our earliest history. We once foraged through fields and forests to gather herbs and plants. We did not always know what these plants were and what they were good for. We determined this by trial and error. The use of hydrosols with pets is somewhat of a similar quest, but one with many advantages. We know certain substances which cats cannot tolerate (terpene hydrocarbons, terpene oxides, phenols and ketones), and we also know that these components do not appear in hydrosols. We also know that the use of a genuine hydrosol is imperative. With this in mind, we can move forward.

Your Use of Essential Oils Counts Too!

If you love aromatherapy, you most surely use the oils in a variety of ways in your home, on yourself and family members. You bathe with them, spray or diffuse them in the air, apply natural perfumes, lotions and hair products. If these contain essential oils, then they are contributing to your cat's exposure. While you can't eliminate your use of essential-oil-containing products completely, you can minimize exposure. After all, it would be silly to forgo the use of essential-oil-containing products and return to the use of synthetic detergents, cleaning supplies and toiletry items made with petrochemicals and fragrance oils. The best choice for your health – and the wellness of the planet – is obvious: natural products containing essential oils. Just make sure to respect your cat when you use them. If you diffuse essential oils, don't keep your cat enclosed in the room with the diffuser. Open a window and provide ventilation. If you apply oils to your dogs, keep the cats away for at least an hour. (The same goes for you.) You can't eliminate exposure, but you can responsibly minimize it, thus decreasing the chance that any level of essential oils will quickly build up in your cat's system.

Cats are Low Maintenance Pets

When's the last time you took Fifi to the Vet? Probably a long time ago, if you are like most cat owners. But the dog? He went twice last week, didn't he? There's no way around it. Dogs just have more things go wrong with them than cats do! Cats seem to be autonomous and immune. They just don't have the daily common ailments plaguing them which dogs do. But they have their share. And hydrosols are an excellent way to supplement your feline's holistic care.

Many cat owners, lovers and professionals are beginning to incorporate hydrosols into their professional and daily lives. Here are a few examples.

How Hydrosols Are Currently Being Used

DR. KAREN BECKER, DVM – NATURAL PET ANIMAL HOSPITAL, TINLEY PARK, ILLINOIS

Dr. Karen Becker uses hydrosols with her feline patients in a variety of ways. While Becker does occasionally use essential oils for cats, she does so very selectively, and only for acute cases where the benefits outweigh the possible risks. For daily use, hydrosols are most appropriate. Chamomile hydrosol is kept in spray bottles in exam rooms to help calm nervous and frightened cats. Hydrosols are also used for cleaning and deodorizing feline areas, in lieu of essential oils.

CELESTE O'MALLEY, OWNER – THE HANDSOME HOUND DOG & CAT GROOMING, BENNINGTON, VERMONT

Ruby is a Flame Point Himalayan cat that I started to groom five years ago. She had just recovered from a serious ulcerated eye infection and had been a difficult cat to groom from the beginning. She was very shy around her head and face because of the eye, and other groomers refused to groom her. I found that if I groomed her right away and got her home as soon as possible she was all right. But as the years passed by she became more difficult. I eventually found myself to the point of sending Ruby to the vet to be shaved down under anesthesia.

As a last chance effort, I tried a combination of Rose, Lavender, Geranium and Neroli hydrosols misted in the air and gently massaged on Ruby's body. What a difference it has made! Ruby's owners have begun using the hydrosols on her before leaving home, and I am able to brush her out and bath her as soon as she gets in. After her bath I re-apply the hydrosols before putting her under the hair dryer, and I am actually able to finish her grooming. I really didn't think I was going to be able to continue to groom this cat. Thank goodness for aromatherapy and hydrosols, they truly made a difference with this problem cat.

CHRISTIE KEITH, BREEDER –CABER FEIDH SCOTTISH DEERHOUNDS, CAZADERO, CALIFORNIA

Recently, I cared for some rescued cats and kittens and was extremely happy with the results of using hydrosols to clean their ears, teeth, and also to help keep fleas off the very dirty, neglected kittens while we nursed them back to health with good diet.

The kittens were severely infested with fleas, and essential oils were not a safe option. After bathing them in a mild, all-natural shampoo, I applied a blend of hydrosols of Lavender, Lemon Verbena and Rosemary to the kittens twice daily. Within three days, I could not find any more fleas or flea dirt on the kittens, and the hydrosols appeared to have greatly helped reduce the inflammation caused by the scratching of the existing flea bites. I also use this blend of hydrosols as an effective and gentle insect repellent on myself as I am allergic to Peppermint oil – a common ingredient in aromatherapy insect repellents.

Hydrosols Are the Perfect Partner to Other Holistic Remedies

Hydrosols can be used safely in conjunction with a variety of other holistic remedies, with no known problems or reason to fear that any would potentially arise. This isn't a case of one pill interacting with another, and then interacting with food or drink. Nature provides us with plenty of methods with which to care naturally for our cats. We can use one, or we can use several. The synergistic layering of a variety of holistic remedies can do only one thing: strengthen the effect.

FLOWER ESSENCES

Hydrosols work in harmony with flower essences, a form of energy healing commonly used by holistic vets to treat all types of emotional disturbances in pets. Cats, being very sensitive animals, respond remarkably well to the subtle, vibrational nature of flower essences. Hydrosols work in a very similar manner, as the dilute soul essence of the plant. Hydrosols can be combined with flower essences with safe and remarkable results. You may be familiar with the famous product known as Bach Rescue Remedy™. This is a blend of five flower essences that is often used to treat emotional and fear-based situations as well as the trauma caused by injury and accidents. This and other flower essences can be combined with hydrosols for improved results.

HERBS

If you are already treating your cat with herbal remedies, you can safely continue to do so and also use hydrosols. In describing hydrosols to people, I often say, "They are similar to herbal teas – watery, diluted and subtly aromatic". People then immediately understand. Hydrosols contain much of the water-soluble portions of the plants from which they were distilled, just as herb teas do; herbs are the plant, after all.

GEMSTONE ESSENCES

Similar to flower essences, gemstone essences are a form of vibrational energy healing. Instead of being made with flowers, they are made with various gemstones, such as Quartz, Amethyst, Citrine, Moonstone and Rose Quartz. Hydrosols can be mixed with a few drops of gemstone essence and applied to a cat. For instance, Rose Quartz gemstone essence, which is said to impart a more loving nature, is perfect to use in a calming hydrosol blend for a cat that was abused or is frightened.

MASSAGE

Animals love massage, even autonomous creatures such as cats. A few drops of hydrosol can be used to rub into your cat's ears, neck or shoulders as you give them their much-anticipated rub-down. Professional animal masseuses can also use hydrosols in their treatments. In many cases, a calming blend of hydrosols can help an animal relax and be more receptive to treatment. The Tellington Touch (T-Touch)™ massage technique works well with cats and can also be partnered with hydrosols.

Reiki

Yes, there are Reiki practitioners for animals as well as humans! Reiki is a Japanese form of energy healing, in which the Reiki master places their hands on various parts of the body, usually corresponding to the chakras, to affect the flow and blockage of the body's energy pathways. The use of hydrosols before and after a Reiki treatment can clear the energy in the room and help to relax the "patient". Since Reiki does not involve the direct massage of the body, animals often can resist sitting or laying still for a treatment and hydrosols can help with this problem.

Acupressure/Acupuncture

These two forms of Eastern healing, which aim to clear the blockage of energy (chi) within the body, consist of applying manual pressure to the pre-defined energy meridians of the body, or inserting thin needles into those points to release blocked energy. Because of their high vibrational energy, hydrosols can be used with both acupressure and acupuncture to create a positive atmosphere.

Natural Diet

A natural diet is most important in the overall health of your cat. In the course of my consultations with pet owners, I frequently recommend a change in diet as part of all treatments. Hydrosols can help a variety of common ailments in cats and other pets, but many problems are of an internal source, and nutrition should first and foremost be given strict attention. Many cat owners choose to let their cats hunt and naturally feed themselves, but indoor cats don't have this option. Some cat owners feed their cats a BARF (Bones and Raw Food) diet, while others home cook meals according to the strict dietary guidelines offered in books such as *The Ultimate Diet* by Kymberly Schultze or *Natural Health for Dogs and Cats* by Richard Pitcairn (See Recommended Reading, Appendix 3). If you must feed your cat a dry kibble, choose wisely. There are many small companies making wonderful, human-grade, all-natural kibbles for cats. Consider premium foods by companies such as Innova, Wysong, Bil Jac, Solid Gold and Flint River Ranch before buying a bag of food in your grocery store. The health benefits are surely worth the additional cost!

Hydrosols – Not Contraindicated

As of my writing this chapter, there are no known contraindications involving the use of hydrosols with conventional veterinary treatments. Nor are there any for the use of essential oils. Hydrosols can safely and effectively be used in conjunction with a variety of other holistic remedies and treatments, strengthening the results through a synergistic effect. Just as all elements of nature work together to provide health to plants in the wild (and on your windowsill, with your help), holistic remedies work together as well. Nature provides wind, water and light. You hold the elements of nature in your hands as you meld holistic remedies together to achieve the most profound effects. This is synergy, or, quite simply, the principle that the sum of the whole is greater than that of the parts.

But allopathic (Western) medications, although often initially derived from natural sources (such as aspirin from Salycylic acid, or Valium from Valerian), are not always compatible with our bodies or our pets'. Always remember, that the plants came first. Whether you believe in the theory of evolution or that God created the earth in seven days there were the plants, and then there was us. From the basic metabolic processes of plants, larger and more complex molecules are derived, such as those necessary for our existence. For this reason, we are bound to the earth and to nature. It is obvious that a natural remedy would be gentler on our bodies and infinitely more effective in the long run than a synthetic medication. But many times, we have let our bodies, and our pets become so unhealthy that we need to treat the illness with a large explosion instead of a tiny flame.

During these times, allopathic medications and treatments are useful, perhaps even required, when life is threatened by disease, limbs broken or cancer is taking over. But it is never too late to begin to heal the wounds that society has caused in us and our pets. It is never too late to return back to mother earth and let her restore health and vibrancy. One of the joys of using essential oils and hydrosols is that they do this in a profound but rapid manner. Your love affair with aromatherapy harks a speedy return to what you know best, but may have forgotten. The beauty and energy of being close to what is perfect – nature. Even in times of great illness when your pet is suffering and being treated with drugs, you can administer hydrosols to calm and soothe, help with healing, repair damaged tissue, and act as healing and balancing tonics to the body. You can do this with no fear of interfering with the allopathic medications and the recovery process they bring. Hydrosols do not interfere with the protocols that commonly prescribed anti-inflammatory steroids, antibiotics or chemotherapy follow.

They are your first step to restoring your pet to health and learning how important it is to heal from within – the holistic way. For that is what holistic healing is – the bringing about of the wellbeing of an entire organism, not just a part of it. Allopathic medicines are a Band-Aid covering a greater problem – that of internal imbalance.

Common Feline Ailments Helped by Hydrosols

Hydrosols have numerous uses in natural cat care. Of course, we know that this section will be much smaller than the same section devoted to essential oil recipes for dogs. There is a limit to what hydrosols can do, and cats do require less maintenance than dogs. Here are simple recipes that you can make to care for your cat's common ailments and for grooming and for boosting health and immunity. I have limited all of the hydrosols used in these recipes to ten different hydrosols, since hydrosols are more difficult to source and purchase than essential oils. Only a few select companies will carry more than ten hydrosols at most. More advanced applications for hydrosols involve giving them internally. This book focuses primarily on the topical use of hydrosols. If you choose to give hydrosols internally, it is crucial to use only hydrosols of the highest quality.

Feline Flea and Tick Repellents

A spritz or two a day can help to keep the fleas and ticks away. I always recommend a backup method of flea and tick control when using hydrosols for pest control. Due to the subtle aromatic nature of the hydrosols, this is necessary. I suggest herbal collars with no added essential oils. You can easily make your own. Dried peppermint, lemon or orange peel, rosemary and lavender can be ground or powdered, then placed in a fabric tube that ties around the cat's neck. This type of collar will be "energized" when it gets misted with flea- and tick-repelling hydrosol spritzes such as Rosemary, Lavender, Geranium and Lemon Verbena.

FELINE FLEA SPRAY
Makes 8 oz (240 ml)
>   1 oz (30 ml) Lavender, *Lavandula angustifolia*, hydrosol
>   1 oz (30 ml) Lemon verbena, *Lippia citriadora*, hydrosol
>   1 oz (30 ml) Rosemary, *Rosmarinus officinalis*, hydrosol
>   1 oz (30 ml) Vodka (or 1/2 oz (15 ml) Grain Alcohol)
>   4 oz (120 ml) Spring or Distilled Water

Shake well and store in an opaque, amber, green or cobalt blue bottle. Your cat should be misted daily, either directly or by misting your hands and massaging the hydrosols into the cat's fur.

FELINE TICK SPRAY

Once again, consider a backup method of pest control, such as the homemade collar described earlier. Makes 8 oz (240ml)

> 2 oz (60 ml) Lavender, *Lavandula angustifolia*, hydrosol
> 1 oz (30 ml) Geranium, *Pelargonium graveolens*, hydrosol
> 1 oz (30 ml) Vodka (or ½ oz (15 ml) Grain Alcohol)
> 4 oz (120 ml) Spring or Distilled Water

Shake well and store in an opaque, amber, green or cobalt blue bottle. Your cat should be misted daily, either directly or by misting your hands and massaging the hydrosols into the cat's fur.

CALMING YOUR FELINE

The calming properties of hydrosols are amongst their most useful qualities when it comes to caring for cats. Here is a recipe for a very effective feline calming blend.

> 1 oz (30 ml) Lavender, *Lavandula angustifolia*, hydrosol
> 1 oz (30 ml) Rose, *Rosa damascena*, hydrosol
> 1 oz (30 ml) Orange Blossom, *Citrus aurantium*, hydrosol
> 1 oz (30 ml) Geranium, *Pelargonium graveolens*, hydrosol
> 1 oz (30 ml) Vodka (or ½ oz (15 ml) Grain Alcohol)
> 4 oz (120 ml) Spring or Distilled Water

Shake well before use. Spritz your environment, or spray into your hands and massage your cat. Flower or gemstone essences can be added to this spritz for additional calming effects. I suggest the addition of the popular Bach Rescue Remedy™ or mimulus flower essence for fear. For strength after surgery, moving, or a change such as new animals in the house, try Oak or Olive flower essences.

Feline Hydrosol Shampoos

It's not very often that you need to bathe a cat… they naturally take care of it themselves. However, some long-haired breeds or cats that are shown competitively, receive frequent baths. In any of these circumstances, an all-natural, gentle shampoo combined with hydrosols is extremely important. Many commercially available shampoos contain essential oils or synthetic fragrance oils, as well as a host of synthetic foaming agents, chemicals and preservatives. Be wary of shampoos that claim to be "natural" or "all natural" but which don't list the ingredients or have a list of long, scary chemical names as ingredients. In my rulebook, it you can't even begin to pronounce it, it usually is not natural! Of course there are exceptions to this rule. But it works quite well most of the time. I suggest that you make your own shampoo for your cat, using the decyl polyglucose shampoo recipe found on page 131 in the canine section of this book.

Gentle Hydrosol Shampoo
Makes 8 oz (240 ml)

> 4 oz (120 ml) of all-natural unscented shampoo or liquid castile soap
> 4 oz (120 ml) of your hydrosol of choice or of a hydrosol blend

This will be a watery shampoo. But consistency has little to do with shampoo effectiveness. Most commercial shampoos are thick because sodium chloride (salt) is added as a thickener. This can be drying, and is unnecessary.

Some Hydrosols to Consider for Use in Feline Shampoos

Calming Shampoo:	Hydrosols of Lavender and Rose
Anxiety Shampoo:	Hydrosols of Neroli and Roman Chamomile
Revitalizing Shampoo	Hydrosols of Rosemary and Lemon Verbena
Troubled Skin Shampoo	Hydrosols of Witch Hazel and German Chamomile
Itchy Cat Shampoo	Hydrosols of German Chamomile and Lavender. Finely ground oatmeal can also be added for skin-soothing and anti-inflammatory purposes.

FLEA-REPELLING SHAMPOO   Hydrosols of Lavender, Rosemary and Lemon Verbena

TICK-REPELLING SHAMPOO   Hydrosols of Lavender and Geranium

Feline Hydrosol Coat Conditioners and Rinses

Hydrosols can be added to your favorite all-natural cream coat conditioner or added to aloe vera gel or juice (refrain from using aloe vera gels or juices that are loaded with synthetic preservatives to maintain shelf life). After the cat has been shampooed with your home-made hydrosol shampoo, use the coat-conditioning rinse and then rinse with warm water. A small amount can also be used as a leave-in conditioner. This is especially helpful when grooming long-haired cats.

COAT CONDITIONING RINSE BASE

Makes 8 oz (240 ml)

> 4 oz (120 ml) of the conditioning agent
> 4 oz (120 ml) of hydrosol

Shake well. This mixture will be runny and in many cases will work better as an after-shampoo rinse or leave-in conditioner. Flower or gemstone essences can be added for a variety of beneficial effects.

Consider adding any of the hydrosol combinations mentioned with the shampoo recipe in your conditioner. You can simply choose a hydrosol for the shampoo for aesthetic reasons, as well. If you love the delicate scent of Neroli hydrosol, then by all means, try it out!

FELINE HYDROSOL EAR CLEANSER

While dogs are prone to yeasty ear infections, cats are more likely to just have dirty ears or ear mites. This recipe is not for getting rid of ear mites but will surely aid in preventing them, along with feeding a natural diet which will in turn boost you cat's immune system and make him less appealing to mites and other parasites.

Makes 8 oz (240 ml)

> 1 oz (30 ml) Witch hazel, *Hammamaelis virginiana,* hydrosol
> 1 oz (30 ml) Rose, *Rosa damascena,* hydrosol
> 1 oz (30 ml) Lavender, *Lavandula angustifolia,* hydrosol

1 oz (30 ml) Aloe Vera Gel or Juice (no preservatives)
1 oz (30 ml) Vodka or $^1/_2$ oz (15 ml) Grain Alcohol
1 teaspoon Vegetable Glycerin
$^1/_2$ oz (15 ml) Cider Vinegar (organic is best!)
3 oz (90 ml) Spring or Distilled Water

Shake well before use. Most cats don't like having things sprayed on them, so spritz on a cotton pad first!

Feline First Aid and Wound Care with Hydrosols

Hydrosols work best for wounds, bites, scratches and incisions when used straight (undiluted). Most hydrosols have soothing and anti-inflammative properties due to the presence of carboxylic acids and other water-soluble materials from the plant they were distilled from. Witch Hazel hydrosol provides anti-inflammatory effects that are equally as effective as some topical steroids, and without the immunosuppressive effects. This would explain why for over 100 years, Witch Hazel water has been the main ingredient in tonics and astringents made by well-known apothecaries such as Dickinson's and Thayer's. Hydrosols also have gentle antiseptic properties that are important for wound care.

For general first aid and wound care, I recommend the following hydrosols, or a blend of several:

- Witch Hazel, *Hamamaelis virginiana*
- Lavender, *Lavandula angustifolia*
- Rose, *Rosa damascena*
- Geranium, *Pelargonium graveolens*
- German Chamomile, *Matricaria recutita*
- Roman Chamomile, *Anthemis nobilis*

More difficult to find hydrosols such as Helichrysum, *Helichrysum italicum*, and Cistus (Labdunum or Rock Rose), *Cistus ladaniferus*, are also excellent for wound care.

They can be spritzed, poured or dabbed on with a cotton ball. When treating wounds, it is imperative that you are using an authentic, high quality hydrosol that has been properly distilled and stored and does not have bacterial contamination. After all, what sense does it make to jeopardize the wound's healing process by adding bacterial contaminants?

Feline Itchy Skin Spritz

Animals, just like we humans, get dry and itchy skin from airborne pollens and molds, cleaning agents, insect bites, allergic reactions and dry air. Cats, especially, have very thin and delicate skin. Their skin also has fewer layers than that of a dog or a human. When using hydrosols for this purpose, it is often easiest to spray the hydrosol blend on a soft bristle brush or your hands and try to work it in to the skin as closely as possible. You can also make a hydrosol rinse and drench your cat with it, massaging it gently into the skin.
  Makes 8 oz (240 ml)

> 1 oz (30 ml) Witch Hazel, *Hamamaelis virginiana*, hydrosol
> 1 oz (30 ml) Rose, *Rosa damascena*, hydrosol
> 1 oz (30 ml) Lavender, *Lavandula angustifolia*, hydrosol
> 1 oz (30 ml) German Chamomile, *Matricaria recutita*, hydrosol
> 1 oz (30 ml) Aloe Vera Gel or Juice (no preservatives)
> 1 oz (30 ml) Vodka or $^1/_2$ oz (15 ml) Grain Alcohol
> 2 oz (60 ml) Spring or Distilled Water

Shake well and store in an opaque, amber, green or cobalt blue bottle. I recommend storing this in the refrigerator when not in use. To make a hydrosol rinse, combine this recipe with a gallon of spring or distilled water.

Deodorizing and Cleaning

Hydrosols can be used on your cat or in your cat's environment for cleaning, deodorizing and freshening. Any blend of hydrosols combined with an equal amount of water can be spritzed on your cat, a brush or your hands and worked into the coat. They can be sprayed on bedding and furniture or used to clean floors and countertops. I find hydrosols of Lavender and Orange Blossom to be most delightful when used for this purpose. Keep a bottle of diluted hydrosol wherever your cat's litter box is and use this instead of synthetic room sprays or essential oils to freshen things up.
  Here are some ideas for refreshing and deodorizing hydrosol blends for cleaning:

ZESTY CLEANING BLEND	Hydrosols of Peppermint and Rosemary
SUMMER FLOWERS CLEANING BLEND	Hydrosols of Lavender and Rose
FRESH CLEANING BLEND	Hydrosols of Neroli and Lemon Verbena

You can add grain alcohol or vodka to your cleaning blends to increase their antiseptic properties.

Paw Care

Outdoor cats are more prone to cracked or wounded paws than the indoor variety, but in either case, wounded paws can be soaked in a small dish filled with hydrosol to cleanse the wound and help to relieve pain, itching and inflammation. I recommend Witch Hazel, German Chamomile or Lavender hydrosol for this purpose.

Repeat as often as necessary, and gently pat dry after soaking. More serious wounds may need stitches or wrappings. Always consult your veterinarian if you are unsure.

Many cats get dry or cracked paws, especially if they are outdoor cats. Here is my recipe for an herb-infused ointment that is perfect for the paws and also for dry skin and first-aid purposes. It contains no essential oils or hydrosols.

Feline Healing Salve

Makes approximately 4 oz (120 ml) of salve. Add to a mixing bowl:

> 1 oz (30 ml) Sweet Almond Oil (herb infused)
> 1 oz (30 ml) Hazelnut Oil (herb infused)
> 1 oz (30 ml) Sunflower Oil (herb infused)
> 1 oz (30 ml) Olive Oil (herb infused)
> $^1/_2$ oz (14 g) Shea Butter
> $^1/_2$ oz (14 g)Beeswax

Gently heat base oils, shea butter and beeswax over low heat (a double boiler set-up is ideal) until beeswax is thoroughly melted. Add 20 drops of Vitamin E oil, a natural antioxidant preservative.

Pour into a dark (cobalt or amber) glass jar. Allow to cool completely before putting on lid.

To increase therapeutic value, the base oils can be infused with a variety of skin-soothing herbs. I often use Calendula Petals, Chamomile, Rose Petals and Lavender flowers.

INFUSION DIRECTIONS:

To infuse the herbs into the base oils, add a handful of various dried herbs to your base oils and simmer them on your stove (or place in a large glass jar left outside in the direct sunlight) for several days. Strain the herbs out with a coffee filter, and you are left with an herb-infused oil with excellent therapeutic benefits!

Section 6

Aromatherapy for Birds and Other Small Pets

Birds and small pets such as rabbits, guinea pigs, ferrets, hamsters, mice, rats and gerbils have special needs when it comes to aromatherapy, just as cats do. Their small size makes careful consideration of the utmost importance. Dr. Susan Wynn, DVM, who earlier reminded us of the importance of dosage being geared towards the bioavailability of different species, reminds us in "Pet Metabolism Dictates Dosage: Natural Treatments for Animals Should Reflect Bioindividuality" that "The most obvious difference in treating animals is the size of the patient. The size of an animal also corresponds to its metabolic rate – smaller mammals and birds have much higher metabolic rates than larger mammals or reptiles. A mouse or bird requires proportionately more herb or drug to maintain therapeutic levels in the blood." Wynn goes on to detail the various metabolic differences which a variety of animals have, and when presented with the exact determination of doses of certain substances, explains that "It is not possible to catalog all the different dosages. The pharmacology of many herbs and vitamins is not completely understood and species differences greatly affect dosing considerations."[30]

When using widely varied and concentrated substances such as essential oils with small mammals or birds with such differences in metabolism, the potential for disaster is quite clear. With so many unknowns, and so much potential for error and mis-dosing, the most responsible thing to do is to avoid essential oils altogether. It is for this reason, as with cats, that hydrosols are the safest way to use aromatherapy with small companion animals.

Aromatherapy for Birds

A high level of caution should be observed when it comes to the use of any aromatic materials around birds. Numerous instances of birds falling dead off their perches after exposure to fragranced candles, Teflon™ pans on the stovetop, room-freshening sprays and even essential oils exist.

Dr. Peter S. Sakes, DVM, Director of the Niles Animal Hospital in Niles, Illinois, provides valuable information for the bird owner regarding the bird's high level of sensitivity in an article entitled "Making A Safe Home for Your Bird", which is featured on the DuPont corporate website, the makers of Teflon™ coating that is deadly to birds.[31]

Other compounds that have been reported to be toxic to birds include: agricultural gardening chemicals, insecticide sprays, mothballs, disinfectants such as phenols and creosols (if used in high concentrations), denture cleansing solutions, salt (in large amounts), and cigarette butts.

Household fumes can be hazardous to birds because birds are small in size and have very sensitive respiratory systems. You've probably heard stories of old-time miners who used canaries in the mines to detect dangerous gases because birds would show the effects of gas much sooner than humans. Some potentially harmful household substances include: aerosol sprays, nonstick sprays for coating cooking utensils, carbon monoxide from car exhaust or furnaces, paint fumes, cigarette smoke, cooking gas, fumes from self-cleaning ovens, or any material that emits fumes. If you notice a strange smell or fumes, remove your bird to an area with good ventilation.

Fumes from everyday cooking can be harmful to your bird – particularly smoke from burning foods. Overheated cooking oil, fats, margarine, and butter may create dangerous fumes. Scorched plastic handles can contaminate the air. Nonstick cookware, with polytetrafluoroethylene (PTFE) coating, can also emit fumes harmful to birds, if cookware is accidentally heated to high temperatures, exceeding approximately 500°F (260°C) – well above the temperatures needed for frying or baking. In addition, PTFE coated drip pans should be avoided because even in normal use they reach extremely high temperatures and can emit fumes that are hazardous to birds. A simple rule of thumb is: never keep your pet bird in the kitchen.

The fragrance intensity and varied chemical makeup of essential oils puts them in a high-risk category for use on or around birds. In fact, given the extreme sensitivity that birds exhibit, I feel that even hydrosols should be used with the greatest amount of care with birds – perhaps only being administered in highly dilute amounts in the bird's water, thus basically being used in a homeopathic manner for their vibrational, energetic qualities.

Birds have shown extreme sensitivity to essential oils. Once again, Tea Tree is a culprit, most likely due to its high level of popularity.

Gillian Willis is a pharmacist and toxicologist from Vancouver, British Columbia. An avid bird lover, she maintains an informational page at www.exoticbird.com, detailing the many potential household hazards for birds. As a toxicologist, Gillian has access to both human and veterinary toxicology reports. Amongst numerous reports of Tea Tree poisoning with cats, Gillian has found reports of avian poisoning:

The owner of a lovebird applied 1 drop of Tea Tree oil to a bleeding blood feather of her lovebird. Within ten minutes the bird collapsed and was on the bottom of the cage. The bird was rushed to the vet. Fortunately, with intensive care treatment, the bird recovered uneventfully.

A cockatiel had a minor abrasion on its foot and the owner applied full strength Tea Tree oil. The cockatiel became very depressed (was fluffed up) and it developed respiratory distress. Despite aggressive intensive care therapy at an avian vets, the cockatiel died approximately 24 hours later of respiratory failure.

The obvious lesson to be learned from this material is that the use of any aromatic or air-borne substance on or around a bird could prove to be very risky. In many cases, the benefits of attempting treatment certainly do not outweigh the risks. In "Essential Oils for Veterinary Medicine", an article written for *Scentsitivity: The Quarterly Journal for the National Association of Holistic Aromatherapy*, author Nelly Grosjean recommends essential treatments for birds by diffusion. Grosjean explains that "the birds most important function is breathing. You could describe it as a 'flying lung'. Use an electric diffuser several times a day, near the cage, for periods of five minutes each."[32] This article was published in *Scentsitivity* in 1999, but is based on information from Grosjean's 1994 book, *Veterinary Aromatherapy*. In the eight years since the publication, with the increasing popularity of aromatherapy, instances of essential oil poisoning and numerous household poisonings have come to light. Despite the fact that when released, Veterinary Aromatherapy was a ground-breaking work – the first book to ever be written on aromatherapy for pets – I feel that the last 8 years have greatly changed the landscape of the aromatic arts, and some of the suggestions indicated in this book should be carefully reconsidered.

Suzanne Catty, whom we have referred to numerous times throughout the course of this book, is a leading authority on hydrosols. In her book, *Hydrosols: The Next Aromatherapy*, Suzanne outlines some safe hydrosol treatments for birds that involve adding very small amounts of various hydrosols to their water.

According to Catty, "Birds love water, so hydrosols are a natural choice here. Leave a birdbath out for your birds at all times and add no more than 1/8 teaspoon hydrosol to 2 cups (approx 480 ml) of water in the bath."[33]

Catty offers some hydrosol suggestions for common bird ailments. For stress (very common with caged birds, or those who are kept solitary instead of in flocks or pairs, which is most advantageous for birds), Catty recommends adding 3–4 drops of hydrosols of Linden, Neroli, Lavender, Angelica or Roman Chamomile, daily to fresh water in their bowl.

For a bird that is depressed and unresponsive, Catty suggests adding 3–4 drops of hydrosols of Cornflower, Melissa, Lemon Verbena or St. John's Wort to fresh water, daily.

For birds with respiratory problems, Catty suggests 2–3 drops of hydrosol daily in a fresh water bowl. Hydrosols of Inula, Rosemary Verbenon, Green Myrtle or Thyme Linalol are recommended.

Once again, more detailed information about hydrosols and their uses with birds can be found in Suzanne Catty's highly informative work, *Hydrosols: The Next Aromatherapy*.

Aromatherapy for Small Mammals: Rabbits, Guinea Pigs, Rats, Mice, Hamsters, Ferrets, Gerbils and the Like...

The small size and varied metabolic differences of these different small mammals once again calls for extreme caution with the use of essential oils. While none of these mammals appear to exhibit the inability to metabolize certain essential oil components, as with cats, great care still needs to be taken.

With animals so small, dosing gets tricky when using highly concentrated essential oils. One would like to assume that an essential oil is pure, but what if it is not, and the animal being treated is sensitive to the adulterant? With so many unknowns, hydrosols are once again the most responsible way to treat small animals such as these.

Unfortunately, the limited range of action of hydrosols also limits the scope of ailments that can be effectively treated. For the purpose of treating small mammals with aromatherapy hydrosols, please refer to Section 5, Aromatherapy for Cats, for recipes. The recipes in found there must be further diluted for use with smaller mammals, and I recommend cutting back the amount of hydrosols used in the recipes by 50%.

For example, the following feline recipe for **Feline Itchy Skin Spritz:**

> To make 8 oz (240 ml):
> 1 oz (30 ml) Witch Hazel, *Hamamaelis virginiana,* hydrosol
> 1 oz (30 ml) Rose, *Rosa damascena,* hydrosol
> 1 oz (30 ml) Lavender, *Lavandula angustifolia,* hydrosol
> 1 oz (30 ml) German Chamomile, *Matricaria recutita,* hydrosol
> 1 oz (30 ml) Aloe Vera Gel or Juice (no preservatives)
> 1 oz (30 ml) Vodka or $^1/_2$ oz (15 ml) Grain Alcohol
> 2 oz (60 ml) Spring or Distilled Water

Would need to be adjusted in this manner for use with the small mammals we are discussing in this chapter:

> To make 8 oz (240 ml):
> $^1/_2$ oz (15 ml) Witch Hazel hydrosol
> $^1/_2$ oz (15 ml) Rose hydrosol
> $^1/_2$ oz (15 ml) Lavender hydrosol
> $^1/_2$ oz (15 ml) German Chamomile hydrosol
> 1 oz (30 ml) Aloe Vera Gel or Juice (no preservatives)
> 1 oz (30 ml) Vodka or $^1/_2$ oz (15 ml) Grain Alcohol
> 4 oz (120 ml) Spring or Distilled Water

(Hydrosols are cut back 50% and the amount of water is increased to yield the final amount of the recipe, 8 oz (240 ml))

Aromatherapy for Fish and Amphibians

This will undoubtedly be the shortest segment in this book. Because essential oils, hydrosols, fish and amphibians do not mix. Essential oils do not combine with water. This renders them useless for an aquarium. They are also lipophilic and would be attracted to the body of the creature, "sticking" to it and causing an assortment of adverse effects depending on the oil added.

Hydrosols, though water based, are no better option. A very specific pH level must be maintained in an aquarium. The varied pH levels of hydrosols would throw this level off, causing an imbalance in the tank and possible harm to the creatures within. A contaminated or adulterated hydrosol could also introduce bacteria or other foreign substances into the tank, causing any number of potential problems.

On a final note, in *Hydrosols: The Next Aromatherapy*, Suzanne Catty wonders "how a large snake would like a mist bath or scale shine with a fairly neutral hydrosol like Lavender or an exotic from their home country".[34] Catty recommends that if you wish to try anything such as this, you should make sure that the hydrosol is very diluted. Then, check with your vet or a reference material to determine the pH of the snake's skin and do a patch test first, checking back for any adverse effects 24 hours later.

Section 7

Aromatherapy for Horses and Other Large Animals

Aromatherapy can also be used with horses and other large animals for a variety of therapeutic purposes. Equine aromatherapy is extremely popular in the United Kingdom, where licensed essential oil therapists, trained specifically with animals, prescribe protocols of essential oils chosen by the horse via kinesiology.

I personally have not administered any aromatherapy treatments to horses or other large animals. My focus has been primarily on dogs and cats, but I have been approached numerous times in regards to the creation of blends for horses. Horses do not have any known metabolic idiosyncrasies such as cats, although like all animals, they do possess a large nasal cavity and a keen sense of smell. Given that all of my recipes for dogs were formulated for common ailments with utmost respect given to safety concerns such as choice of oils and proper dilution, I felt confident in suggesting various canine recipes for use with horses. As a result, I have a growing number of clients who safely and effectively use the canine formulations (which can be found in this book) on their horses to deal with emotional problems such as nervousness and spooking, skin problems, wound care, grooming and insect repelling.

One would think that due to the sheer size of a large animal, more essential oil can be used. But in reality, this is not the case. Metabolically, a larger animal can process larger amounts of essential oil. However, given that we know that all animals have a more powerful sense of smell than humans, and that they cannot adequately communicate to us how they are feeling, the use of highly diluted essential oils still remains the treatment method of choice.

Equine Aromatherapy

In this section, I will not include any horse-specific recipes. Rather, I suggest that you turn back to the canine and/or feline sections and focus on the safe and effective recipes included there for use with your horses. Like my other clients, I am sure that you will find it necessary to double or even triple some of the recipes to accommodate the large size of your horse (for instance, shampoos or skin rinses).

For those of you who own horses and are curious about aromatherapy, I am including this chapter as a starting point from which you can further your explorations and research into the use of aromatherapy with your horse.

How Aromatherapy Is Being Used With Horses

The use of essential oils is more common and accepted with horses than with any other animal. There are numerous essential oil therapists and companies creating products for horses. If it appears to you that the majority of work with essential oils and horses is being done in the British Isles, your assumption is correct. Aromatherapy for horses is widely accepted in the United Kingdom. I feel that this because aromatherapy is more widely used and understood in the UK, which also has a high percentage of horse owners and many equestrian events. It's only natural that aromatherapy for horses would be so popular!

CATHERINE BIRD, SYDNEY AUSTRALIA

Catherine Bird is an equine aromatherapist based in Sydney Australia. She is one of the world's foremost equine aromatherapists. She is the author of *Horse Scents: Making Sense with Your Horse Using Aromatherapy* and *A Healthy Horse the Natural Way*. Catherine works with horses with topical blends as well as kinesiology techniques. Her articles have been featured in numerous editorial publications, including The Holistic Horse and Natural Horse Magazine.

The following is an excerpt from "Calming Aromatherapy for Fear and Anxiety", an article published in *Natural Horse Magazine*.

One of the most unsettling experiences to deal with when you are handling your horse is an attack of fear or anxiety. Once the incident takes shape of its own then your own emotions come into play and continue the spiral of energy that leads you and your horse down an unpleasant path.

Aromatherapy will not replace good training methods, but it will give you "keys" when you find blocks or resistance to your techniques. Use the essential oils that provide these keys to create a space for the next learning experience and then return to sound training foundations.[35]

For horses in need of soothing, Catherine suggests essential oils of Bergamot and Frankincense as a "first line" of treatment. She also recommends the following oils:

- Juniper – "relieves worries and will also remove from the energy field any debris from past experiences".

- Lavender – "will soothe and nurture a frazzled horse. If the anxiety has gone to the stage of a temper tantrum, you may select [Lavender]".

- Chamomile – "for its deeper relaxation effect".

- Sweet Orange – "provides self-assurance and envelops your horse with a happy hug of warmth".

- Basil, Lemon, Cypress – "provide focus and increase the ability to keep your horse's mind on the task at hand".

- Patchouli – "will provide a solid grounding and keep your horse aware of his feet at all times".

Bird recommends inhalation as the most effective mode of treatment for emotional disorders.

Place a couple of drops neatly into your hand, rub them to warm the essential oils and then hold your cupped hand under your horse's nose. If you have chosen the correct oil, then you will see a response within minutes. In chronic cases, you may decide to apply a blend of diluted essential oils to your horse's neck or chest.[36]

Catherine's Basic Essential Oil Kit for Horses

In "Scented Horses," an article from *Natural Horse magazine*,[37] Bird provides more excellent information regarding the use of essential oils with horses. Many of Catherine's sensible views regarding the use of the oils with horses reflect my own practices with animals, such as the use of diluted essential oils, limited internal application, always seeking the advice of a vet, "less is more" and never using essential oils undiluted on the skin. Bird also suggests complementary holistic remedies as a course of treatment, such as flower essences, herbs and massage, reinforcing how powerful the synergy of holism can be in improving mental and physical health.

Catherine recommends the following essential oils for use with horses:

- Basil
- Bergamot
- Chamomile
- Eucalyptus
- Frankincense
- Geranium
- Lavender
- Lemongrass
- Tea Tree

She tells us that: *Essential oils work two ways with your horse. He may have a physical problem that needs to be addressed or an emotional one. For a physical problem, you can apply the essential oils, diluted in carrier oil or cream, onto the area so the molecules of the essential oil can find their way via the hair follicles into the bloodstream. For an emotional problem, your horse can inhale the molecules of a scent and have it trigger the release of neuro-chemicals in every body cell to help relax or relieve fears.*

It is interesting to note that the use of certain essential oils should be avoided in competitions. Bird mentioned this to me during our correspondence and details it in her article, "Scented Horses":

Care does have to be taken if you are competing at FEI levels where you may be tested for drug use as some essential oils do contain constituents that will test positive. The American Show Horse Association lists Eucalyptus and Peppermint as prohibited. Also, any essential oil with a high camphor content such as Rosemary should be used with care.

Give Your Horse the Final Say

Bird works with essential oils in a manner that directly involves the horse in the healing process. Animals definitely are more sensitive and intuitive than we humans are, but some people feel that horses possess an almost uncanny sense of knowing what is best for them. The following information was provided by Catherine specifically for this book:

If I am unsure which essential oil is needed, I will offer the uncapped bottle to the horse and waft it under his nose. Hold it about six inches away and move slowly back and forth. If he agrees that that is the essential oil he needs, he will lean forward or his nostrils will widen and his breath become more intense, or he will even do the Flehman response where he curls his lip and traps the scent in his nasal cavities. If a horse doesn't agree with my choice, he may appear disinterested or turn away from the bottle.

Sometimes a horse's response may be difficult to gauge, so it is important to get to understand each horse. A young horse often wants to inhale every bottle I offer, an emotionally closed down horse may only show a slight change in respiration initially and then over a period of time open up to become more expressive. Older horses tend to more serious in their assessment.

A recent phenomenon I have heard of concerns me where people were placing essential oils neat (undiluted) on the horse's muzzle. This I consider intrusive, and the horse has difficulty escaping the scent, especially if he does not like it. One example recently was a competitor wanting to calm a horse and placing Lavender essential oil on his muzzle. The scent overpowered the horse and it was not long before he looked stressed and I would presume he had a headache. Horses are entitled to choice.

Mary Ann Simonds, Vancouver, Washington

Simonds, the creator of the video *Herbs and Aromatherapy for Horses* is an avid horse lover, behavioral ecologist and holistic health educator. She founded the Whole Horse Institute for Horse Education in 1995 and specializes in horse behavior. Simonds regularly offers clinics and is available for consultations. Many of her articles on horse behavior appear in the *Natural Horse Magazine* and are available archived on their website. Her 28-minute video can be purchased from a variety of horse-related retailers and is described as "a stroll through pastures and gardens to find out what herbs are good for horses. Learn to make herbal fly sprays and poultices. Stock the 'natural medicine' cabinet. Understand how smells affect your horse."

CAROLINE INGRAHAM, HAY-ON-WYE, UNITED KINGDOM

The author of *Aromatherapy for Horses*, Caroline is a prominent voice in the use of essential oils with animals. She focuses primarily on the use of kinesiology aromatherapy with animals. Caroline provides educational opportunities for those who would like to learn more about the use of kinesiology aromatherapy with animals and is associated with the Guild of Essential Oil Therapists for Animals (GOETA).

Caroline feels that "Animals are very sensitive intuitive creatures and given adequate choice they will usually select the plant medicine that they need. Their nose can smell and identify thousands of different molecules, which are transferred into messages that are sent to various parts of the brain where mood and bodily function can be affected. When treating very stressed animals the aroma alone can sometimes cause them to relax and even fall to sleep within minutes of inhalation; however other animals may need a stronger treatment and choose to take it orally."[38] Caroline is currently working on a more comprehensive book on aromatherapy for animals.

HILTON HERBS, UNITED KINGDOM

Hilton Herbs is a company that specializes in herbal and aromatherapy products for horses and dogs. Their line of aromatherapy remedies for horses can be ordered online and through distributors. The products range from rubs and sprays for sore muscles, wound care and irritated skin to a set of essential oils to address emotional issues. According to Hilton Herbs, "Horses and ponies, even those which live relatively unnatural lives in yards or manicured paddocks, have generally retained their natural instinct to know what is good for them and will, where possible, select beneficial plants from meadow or hedgerow for themselves. However, the opportunities for free browsing and the available plant life are these days largely curtailed for most equines. Consequently, we have to choose for them, and our choices are legion."[39]

NAYANA MORAG, ESSENTIAL ANIMALS, UNITED KINGDOM

Nayana is a qualified essential-oils-for-animals therapist and is a member of GOETA. She works with kinesiology, as Caroline Ingraham does. Nayana also provides educational opportunities and has written articles for several publications, including the *Natural Horse*.

Susan George, Naturally, United Kingdom

"Susan George, the international film star, breeds, rides and exhibits horses and thrives on alternative treatments for herself, her family, her equines and canines. Susan George's interest in alternative therapies began 20 years ago when she turned to homeopathy in favor of traditional medicine. She treats all her own horses with alternative remedies."[40] The Susan George line of equine aromatherapy products was developed in conjunction with a team of veterinarians, pharmacists and aromatherapists. The products are primarily for topical application, ranging from grooming shampoos and sore muscle sprays to wound salve and flower essences for emotional balance.

A web search for "aromatherapy for horses" or "equine aromatherapy" will also turn up thousands of sites and references on the topic. While this may at first glance seem like a gold mine of information, tread carefully and always consider the background, training, philosophy and education of the author of such material. The internet is a wonderful tool, but unfortunately the internet has no editors. Anyone can post anything and indiscriminate use of information gotten from websites and newsgroups should always be carefully examined.

When in doubt, you can always consider the use of hydrosols with your horse instead of essential oils. The many wonderful therapeutic properties of subtly fragrant hydrosols can be beneficial to your horse in a variety of ways, from skin and coat care to wound care, and for calming nervousness, anxiety or spooking. Hydrosols can even be used for massage in a base of aloe vera gel.

Aromatherapy for Large Animals

Essential oils can also be safely used with other large animals, such as cows, sheep, donkeys, pigs, goats and the like. While I realize that most people who own such animals do not see them as "pets", these owners may still have a desire to care for such an animal holistically. Aromatherapy can be employed as a method of complementary care, and I suggest the same protocol for these animals as I do for horses. Just as many of my clients have taken canine recipes and formulations and adapted them for use with horses, this same thing can be done with any blend being made for any of the animals mentioned here.

The regular tenets of high quality oils, highly diluted blends, avoidance of certain oils, limited internal application and methods of application still apply. Some of the possible applications for which you might find yourself using aromatherapy for farm animals include: skin problems, wound care, congestion, calming, and cleaning room air via nebulization.

In short, the many uses which essential oils have for companion animals such as dogs and cats can be passed along to other animals as long as respect is given to basic safety requirements. I would suggest that even if you do not own a dog or cat, if you are considering using essential oils or hydrosols on horses or other large animals that you read both of the chapters devoted to dogs and cats. Besides being highly informative, they give you a very good idea of what aromatherapy is capable of in terms of complementary care.

Aromatherapy at the Zoo?

If you start to get creative, you can see that the uses of aromatherapy with animals are boundless. Many animals are kept caged, penned or restricted against their will. A trip to a pet store, animal shelter – or especially, a zoo – will reveal a myriad of animals out of their natural habitats and homes, most certainly dealing with the stress of captivity.

What could aromatherapy offer animals in these situations? Would a calming blend of essential oils relieve stress for a captive gorilla, bear, elephant, zebra or giraffe? I think that it would. It's all a matter of increasing the level of awareness about this solidly scientific, yet oft misunderstood, holistic modality. It may seem like a silly thought right now, but I have a feeling that in the future, we will be hearing much more about the use of aromatherapy with animals, and who knows? In the future you may even see a story on the news about a captive zoo animal responding well to daily aromatherapy treatments. It's all a matter of perspective, and time…

SECTION 8

BREWING UP YOUR OWN POTIONS: SUPPLIERS, PACKAGING, RESOURCES AND EDUCATION

In this section, you will find resources and references for just about everything you will need for aromatherapy education, including educational resources such as magazines, professional organizations and internet groups (websites were accessed in 2002). You will also find lists of suppliers of essential oils and hydrosols, flower and gemstone essences, packaging and raw botanical materials. Ten years of sourcing materials has provided plenty of time for me to be exposed to not only the best, but also the worst, suppliers. We won't mention any of the worst here, so focus on the positive and best of luck as you begin exploring and learning about aromatherapy and its many wonderful uses for your animals.

Pre-blended Aromatherapy Products for Animals

For those of you who want to use aromatherapy with your animals, but wish to try pre-blended aromatherapy products first, here are some suppliers of high quality, safely blended aromatherapy products for animals.

AROMALEIGH HOLISTIC
AROMATHERAPY
180 St. Paul St. Suite 506
Rochester, NY 14604
Web: www.aromaleigh.com
Contact: Kristen Leigh Bell
Email: kbell@aromaleigh.com
Tel: (585) 454-0042
Fax: (585) 454-7519

HILTON HERBS
Downclose Farm
North Perrot, Crewkerne
Somerset, UK TA18 7SH
Web: www.hiltonherbs.com
Tel: +44 (0) 1460 270700
Fax: +44 (0) 1460 270702

Recommended Essential Oil/Hydrosol Suppliers

It can be a daunting and overwhelming task to find a good supplier. Fortunately, I have been doing aromatherapy for ten years and along the way I have found many excellent suppliers and also met many wonderful people at conferences and seminars that are essential oil and hydrosol suppliers. Here is my list of recommended suppliers whom I myself have used or had recommended to me. All suppliers carry essential oils. Those who also carry hydrosols are indicated as such.

NORTH AMERICAN SUPPLIERS

ACQUA VITA
85 Arundel Avenue
Toronto, ON M4K 3A3 Canada
Web: www.acqua-vita.com
Contact: Suzanne Catty
Email: info@acqua-vita.com
Tel: (416) 405-8855
Fax: (416) 405-8185
Carry hydrosols

AMRITA ESSENTIAL OILS
1900 West Stone
Fairfield, IA 52556
Web: www.amrita.net
Email: info@amrita.net
Tel: (641) 472-9136
Fax: (641) 472-8672

ANATOLIAN TREASURES/
APPALACHIAN VALLEY NATURAL
PRODUCTS
138 Walnut Street, P.O. Box 515
Friendsville, MA 21531
Web: www.av-at.com
Contact: Butch Owen
Email: butchbsi@av-at.com
Tel: (888) 907-6457
          (301) 746-4630
Fax: (301) 746-4633
Carry hydrosols

AROMACEUTICALS
3626 North Hall Street
Dallas, TX 75219
Web: www.aromaceuticals.com
Contact: Kath Koepen
Email: aromaceu@swbell.net
Tel: (214) 522-3666

BASSETT AROMATHERAPY
P.O. Box 176
Cardiff by the Sea, CA 92007-0176
Web: www.aromaworld.com
Contact: JoAnn Bassett
Email: joanne@aromaworld.com
Tel: (858) 794-9759
Fax: (858) 509-0713

CHANGES WITHIN
P.O. Box 326
Freeburg, PA 17827
Web: www.changeswithin.com
Contact: Susan Renkel, RN
Email: changes@sunlink.net
Tel/Fax: (570) 374-6735
Carry hydrosols

ESSENTIAL OIL UNIVERSITY
2676 Charlestown Rd., Suite #3
New Albany, IN 47150
Web: www.essentialoils.org
Contact: Dr. Rob Pappas
Email: Dr.P@essentialoils.org
Tel: (812) 945-5000
Fax: (603) 506-2563
Bulk/wholesale essential oils and absolutes

FRAGRANT EARTH U.S.A.
Web: www.fragrant-earth.com
Contact: Jade Shutes
Email: all-enquiries@
          fragrantearth.com
Tel: 800-260-7401

NATURE'S GIFT
1040 Cheyenne Blvd.
Madison, TN 37115
Web: www.naturesgift.com
Contact: Marge Clark
Email: marge@naturesgift.com
Tel: (615) 612-4270
Fax: (615) 860-9171
Carry hydrosols

ORIGINAL SWISS AROMATICS
P.O. Box 6723
San Rafael, CA 94903
Web: www.pacificinstitute
          ofaromatherapy.com

Contact: Kurt Schnaubelt
Email: aroma@pacbell.net
Tel: (415) 479-9120
Fax: (415) 479-0614
Carry hydrosols

PRIMA FLEUR
1525 East Francisco Blvd. Suite 16
San Rafael, CA 94901
Web: www.primafleur.com
Email: info@primafleur.com
Tel: (415) 455-0957
Fax: (415) 455-0966

SAMARA BOTANE
1811 Queen Anne Ave North # 103
Seattle, WA 98109
Web: www.winged-seed.com
Contact: Marcia Elston
Email: samara@wingedseed.com
Tel: (206) 283-7191

THE AROMATHERAPIST
32432 Alipaz Industrial Park,
Suites N - O, San Juan Capistrano,
CA 92675
Web: www.thearoma
          therapistusa.com
Email: webmaster@
          thearomatherapistusa.com
Tel: (949) 661-7430
Fax: (949) 661-7510

UK AND EUROPEAN SUPPLIERS

FLORIHANA
42 Chemin des aubépines
06130 Grasse, France
Web: www.florihana.com
Contact: info@florihana.com
Tel: 33 (0)4 93 77 88 19
Fax: 33 (0)4 93 77 88 78
Carry hydrosols

FRAGRANT EARTH UK
Web: www.fragrant-earth.com
Contact: all-enquiries@
          fragrantearth.com
Tel: +44 (0) 1458 831216

Essential Oil Testing

Should you have the need to get a sample of an essential oil tested for purity, here are some independent labs which provide services at a reasonable cost.

ANALYTICAL INTELLIGENCE
10 Mount Farm, Junction Road
Churchill, Chipping Norton
Oxon, UK OX7 6NP
Tel: +44 (0)1 608-659522
Fax: +44 (0)1 608-659566

ESSENTIAL OIL UNIVERSITY –
APPLIED ESSENTIAL OIL RESEARCH
2676 Charlestown Rd., Suite #3
New Albany, IN 47150
Web: www.essentialoils.org
Contact: Dr. Rob Pappas
Email: Dr.P@essentialoils.org

Tel: (812) 945-5000
Fax: (603) 506-2563
A variety of testing services, including: GC/MS (Gas Chromatography/Mass spectroscopy), NMR (Nuclear Magnetic Resonance spectroscopy), FTIR (FT Infra-Red spectroscopy, UV-Vis (UltraViolet-Visible spectroscopy), Optical Rotation, Refractive Index, Specific Gravity

Flower and Gemstone Essence Suppliers

NORTH AMERICAN SUPPLIERS

ANIMAL ELEMENTALS – GEMSTONE
ESSENCES
Web: www.animalelementals.com
Email: sales@
          animalelementals.com
Tel: (800) 898-4460
Fax: (603) 429-4694

BACH U.S.A.
100 Research Drive
Wilmington, MA 01887
Web: www.nelsonbach.com
Email: info@nelsonbach.com
Tel: (800) 319-9151
Fax: (978) 988-0233

FLOWER ESSENCE SERVICES
P.O. Box 1769
Nevada City, CA 95959
Web: www.fesflowers.com
Email: fes@fesflowers.com
Tel: (530) 265-0258
Fax: (530) 265-6467

UK SUPPLIERS

THE AROMATHERAPY
ORGANISATIONS COUNCIL
P.O. Box 19834
London, UK SE25 6WF
Web: www.aocuk.net
Email: info@aocuk.net
Tel: +44 (0) 20 8251 7912
Fax: +44 (0) 20 8251 7942

THE DR EDWARD BACH CENTRE
Mount Vernon, Sotwell
Wallingford, Oxon, UK OX10 0PZ

Web: www.bachcentre.com
Email: mail@bachcentre.com
Tel: +44 (0) 1491 834678
Fax: +44 (0) 1491 825022

Findhorn Flower Essences
Cullerne House, Findhorn
Scotland, UK IV36 3YY
Web: www.findhornessences.com
Email: info@findhornessences.com
Tel: +44 (0) 1309 690129
FAX: +44 (0) 1309 691300

Recommended Packaging Suppliers

You'll need a variety of different sizes of bottles, as well as pipettes, beakers and test tubes when you are blending. Here are some of my favorite resources for bottles and packaging. **Mangobutter** is an internet resource for packaging and supplies. It currently allows searching in the US and UK and is an excellent place to begin a search for a supplier in your region: www.mangobutter.com

E.D. LUCE & SON
1600 East 29th Street
Signal Hill, CA 90806
Web: www.essentialsupplies.com
Email: harriett@
          essentialsupplies.com
Tel: (562) 997-9777
Fax: (562) 997-0117

FROM NATURE WITH LOVE
258 Longstreet Avenue
Bronx, NY 10465
Web: www.fromnature
          withlove.com
Email: information@from-nature-
          with-love.com
Tel: (718) 518-8555
Toll Free: 888-376-6695
Fax: (718) 842-6620

LAVENDER LANE
7337 # 1 Roseville Road
Sacramento, CA 95842
Web: www.lavenderlane.com
Email: healthychoices@
          lavenderlane.com
Tel: (916) 334-4400
Toll Free: 888-593-4400
Fax: (916) 339-0842

LIBERTY NATURAL PRODUCTS
8120 SE Stark, Portland, OR 97215
Web: www.libertynatural.com
Toll Free: 800-289-8427

MAJESTIC MOUNTAIN SAGE
881 West 700 North Suite 107
Logan, Utah 84321
Web: www.thesage.com
Tel: (435) 755-0863
Fax: (435) 755-2108

Miron Glass – Dark Violet
Glass Bottle Specialty Supplier
2485 N. Beachwood Drive
Los Angeles, CA 90068
Email: mironusa@aol.com
Tel: (323) 467-0558
Fax: (323) 467-5558

Qosmedix
150-Q Executive Drive
Edgewood, NY 11717
Web: www.qosmedix.com
Tel: (631) 242-3270
Fax: (631) 242-3291

SKS Bottle and Packaging
3 Knabner Road
Mechanicville, NY 12118

Web: www.sks-bottle.com
Email: toiletries@sks-bottle.com
Tel: (518) 899-7488
Fax: 800-810-0440

Specialty Bottle Supply
2730 1st Avenue South
Seattle, WA 98134
Web: www.specialtybottle.com
Tel: (206) 340-0459
Fax: (206) 903-0785

Sunburst Bottle
5710 Auburn Boulevard
Suite 7, Sacramento, CA 95841
Web: www.sunburstbottle.com
Tel: (916) 348-5576

Sources for Botanical Raw Materials

Need base oils, butters, clays, aloe, glycerin or herbs? Here are some suppliers who can help get you started with whatever you may need to create the recipes in this book. www.mangobutter.com is also an excellent place to begin a search for a supplier in your region.

From Nature With Love
258 Longstreet Avenue
Bronx, NY 10465
Web: www.fromnature
          withlove.com
Email: information@from-nature-
          with-love.com
Tel: (718) 518-8555
Toll Free: 888-376-6695
Fax: (718) 842-6620

Frontier Natural Products Co-op
Web: www.frontiercoop.com
Email: customercare@
          frontiercoop.com
Tel: 800-786-1388
Fax: 800-717-4372

Lavender Lane
7337 # 1 Roseville Road
Sacramento, CA 95842
Web: www.lavenderlane.com
Contact: healthychoices@l
          avenderlane.com
Tel: (916) 334-4400
Toll Free: 888-593-4400
Fax: (916) 339-0842

Liberty Natural Products
8120 SE Stark
Portland, OR 97215
Web: www.libertynatural.com
Toll Free: 800-289-8427

MAJESTIC MOUNTAIN SAGE
881 West 700 North Suite 107
Logan, Utah 84321
Web: www.thesage.com
Tel: (435) 755-0863
Fax: (435) 755-2108

RAINBOW MEADOW INC.
P.O. Box 457, Napoleon MI 49261
Web: www.rainbowmeadows.com
Contact: Melody Upham
Email: melody@dmci.net

Tel: (517) 817-0021
Toll Free: 800-207-4047
Fax: (517)817-0025

SUNROSE AROMATICS
P.O. Box 98 Throggs Neck Sta.
Bronx, NY 10465
Web: www.sunrosearomatics.com
Contact: Rosanne Tartaro
Email: sunrose112@aol.com
Tel: (718) 794-0391
Toll Free: 888-382-9451

Soap Suppliers/Decyl Polyglucose Suppliers

Here are the names of a few suppliers for those of you who would like to get creative and create your own glycerin or cold process soaps for animal grooming. Remember, glycerin soaps can never be all natural! Some suppliers formulate soaps that are more natural than others.

BRAMBLEBERRY INC
1208 Bay St, Suite C
Bellingham, WA. 98225
Web: www.brambleberry.com
Tel: (360)734-8278
Fax: (360)752-0992
One of the most natural glycerin soap bases available.

CHERYL'S HERBS- PRE-MADE DECYL
POLYGLUCOSE SOAP BASE
836 Hanley Industrial Court
St. Louis, MO 63144

Web: www.cherylsherbs.com
Email: info@cherylsherbs.com
Tel: 800-231-5971
Fax: (314) 963-4454

SOMERSET COMPANY- DECYL
POLYGLUCOSE
P.O. Box 337, Renton, WA 98058
Web: www.makingcosmetics.com
Email: somerset@
          makingcosmetics.com
Tel: (888) 449-1979
Fax: (425) 271-4629

Aromatherapy Education

It's a great idea to get some formal aromatherapy education, especially since you are using the oils with your animals. Here are some of the best schools available. Please note that very few of these schools will specifically offer information for animals. What you will take away from higher education in aromatherapy is the ability to know essential oils and their chemistry better, thus enabling you to make more sound, safe and educated decisions about which essential oils to use and how to use them.

Acqua Vita – The Aromatic Lyceum
85 Arundel Avenue
Toronto ON M4K 3A3 Canada
Web: www.acqua-vita.com
Contact: Suzanne Catty
Email: info@acqua-vita.com
Tel: (416) 405-8855
Fax: (416) 405-8185

Atlantic Institute of Aromatherapy
16018 Saddlestring Dr.
Tampa, FL 33612
Web: www.atlanticinstitute.com
Contact: Sylla Sheppard-Hangar
Tel: (813) 265-2222

Australasian College of Herbal Studies
530 First Street, P.O. Box 57
Lake Oswego, OR 97034
Web: www.herbed.com/
Tel: (503) 635-6652

Finger Lakes School of Massage
1251 Trumansburg Rd.
Ithaca, NY 14850
Web: www.flsm.com
Email: admissions@flsm.com
Tel: (607) 272-9024

Guild of Essential Oil Therapists for Animals (UK only)
Horsehay Farm, Duns Tew Road
Middle Barton, Oxon, UK OX7 7DQ
Web: www.geota.com
Tel: +44 (0) 1869 349813
Fax: +44 (0) 1869 340969
Predominant focus on kinesiology aromatherapy

Institute of Dynamic Aromatherapy
4925 6th Ave NW.
Marysville, WA 98271
Web: www.theida.com
Tel: (360) 651-9809
Fax: (206) 547-2680

Les Herbes – American Institute for Aromatherapy & Herbal Studies
P.O. Box 490
Centerport, NY 11721
Web: www.aromatherapyinst.com
Contact: Mynou de Mey
Email: info@aromatherapyinst.com
Tel: (631) 269-0016
Fax: (631) 269-0016

Pacific Institute of Aromatherapy
P.O. Box 6723, San Rafael, CA 94903
web: www.pacificinstituteof
          aromatherapy.com
Contact: Kurt Schnaubelt
Email: aroma@pacbell.net
Tel: (415)479- 9120
Fax: (415)479 –0614

Rochester Center for Aromatic Studies
180 St. Paul St. Suite 506
Rochester, NY 14604
web: www.aromaleigh.com
Contact: Kristen Leigh Bell
Email: kbell@aromaleigh.com
Tel: (585) 454-0042
Fax: (585) 454-7519
Animal aromatherapy tele-classes, group seminars

Professional Organizations

Become more involved in aromatherapy. Find a practitioner in your area. Keep up with what's current and on the cutting edge of safety and research.

BRITISH COLUMBIA ASSOCIATION OF PRACTICING AROMATHERAPISTS
#123 25 Maki Road
Nanaimo, British Columbia
Canada V9V 6N3
Web: www.bcapa.org
Contact: info@bcapa.org
Tel: (250) 741-0007

GUILD OF ESSENTIAL OIL THERAPISTS FOR ANIMALS (UK ONLY)
Horsehay Farm, Duns Tew Road
Middle Barton, Oxon, UK OX7 7DQ
Web: www.geota.com
Tel: +44 (0) 1869 349813
Fax: +44 (0) 1869 340969
Predominant focus on kinesiology aromatherapy

HANDCRAFTED SOAPMAKER'S GUILD
P.O. Box 71, Sidney, OH 45365
Web: www.soapguild.org
Email: Info@SoapGuild.org

Tel: 203-267-5522
Toll Free: 866-900-SOAP (7627)
Fax: 203-267-5522

HANDMADE TOILETRIES NETWORK
7613 Old Chapel Drive
Bowie, MD 20715
Web: www.handmade
          toiletries.com
Contact: Donna Maria Coles Johnson
Email: donnamaria@
          handmadetoiletries.com
Tel: (301) 464-4515
Toll Free: 800-934-5611
Fax: (301) 464-2719

NATIONAL ASSOCIATION FOR HOLISTIC AROMATHERAPY (NAHA)
4509 Interlake Ave N., #233
Seattle, WA 98103-6773
Web: www.naha.org
Email: info@naha.org
Tel: (206) 547-2164
Toll Free: 888-ASK-NAHA
Fax: (206) 547-2680

Aromatherapy Publications and Online Resources

Yes, there are aromatherapy magazines and newsletters that you can subscribe to, to learn more about essential oils and hydrosols.

alt.aromatherapy – online aromatherapy newsgroup (groups.google.com, search for alt.aromatherapy)

AROMA MAGAZINE – PACIFIC INSTITUTE OF AROMATHERAPY
P.O. Box 6723, San Rafael, CA 94903
web: www.pacificinstituteof
          aromatherapy.com
Contact: Kurt Schnaubelt

Email   aroma@pacbell.net
Tel: (415) 479-9120
Fax: (415) 479-0614

AROMATHERAPY @ IDMA EMAIL LIST
Web: www.idma.com/aromatherapy

AROMATHERAPYPETS @ YAHOO GROUPS
Kristen Leigh Bell's email discussion group for aromatherapy for pets
http://groups.yahoo.com/group/aromat herapyPETS/

AROMATHERAPY JOURNAL :
NATIONAL ASSOCIATION FOR
HOLISTIC AROMATHERAPY (NAHA)
4509 Interlake Ave N., #233
Seattle, WA 98103-6773
Web: www.naha.org
Email: info@naha.org
Tel: (206) 547-2164
Toll Free: 888-ASK-NAHA
Fax: (206) 547-2680

AROMATHERAPY THYMES MAGAZINE
1235 S. Citrus Avenue
Los Angeles, CA 90019
Web: www.aromatherapy
           thymes.com
Tel: (323) 933-7359
Fax: (323) 933-2313

AROMA WEB
Web: www.aromaweb.com
"Your Online Source for Aromatherapy Information"

INTERNATIONAL JOURNAL OF AROMATHERAPY
Journals Marketing Department
Harcourt Publishers Ltd
32 Jamestown Road
London, UK NW1 7BY
Web: www.harcourt-inter
           national.com/journals/ijar
Email: journals@harcourt.com
Toll Free: 877-839-7126

PERFUMER & FLAVORIST MAGAZINE
362 S. Schmale Road
Carol Stream, IL 60188-2787
Web: www.perfumeflavor.com
Tel: (630) 653-2155, ext. 656
Fax: (630) 665-2699

Appendix 1
Table of Weights and Measures
and Conversion Tables

Weights and Measures		
Teaspoon	=	60 drops
Teaspoon	=	6 milliliters
Cup	=	48 teaspoons
Cup	=	8 (liquid) ounces
Cup	=	236.5 milliliters
Ounce (dry)	=	28.36 grams
Ounce (liquid)	=	29.57 milliliters
Ounce (liquid)	=	6 teaspoons
Ounce (liquid)	=	480 drops
Pound	=	453.59 kilograms
Kilogram	=	2.2 pounds

Conversion Tables
(US and Metric Standard Units of Measurement)

GRAMS (G)		KILOGRAMS (KG)		OUNCES (OZ)		POUNDS (LB)
1.0000	=	0.001	=	0.0353	=	0.0020
28.3495	=	0.028	=	1.0000	=	0.0625
453.5900	=	0.454	=	16.0000	=	1.0000
1,000.0000	=	1.000	=	35.2740	=	2.2046

LITERS (L)		PINTS (PT)		QUARTS (QT)		GALLONS (GAL)
1.000	=	2.113	=	1.057	=	0.264
0.473	=	1.000	=	0.500	=	0.125
0.946	=	2.000	=	1.000	=	0.250
3.785	=	8.000	=	4.000	=	1.000

OUNCES (OZ)		MILLILITERS (ML)		OUNCES (OZ)		MILLILITERS (ML)
0.02	=	0.59	=	1	=	29.57
0.08	=	2.31	=	2	=	59.14
0.12	=	3.69	=	4	=	118.29
0.25	=	7.39	=	8	=	236.58
0.50	=	14.79	=	16	=	476.16

Appendix 2

Holistic Resource Guide

A source listing for aromatherapists, veterinarians, holistic health professionals, alternative health practitioners, trainers, groomers and breeders who use aromatherapy with animals.

Providing you with this information has been important to me, because the scope of holistic aromatherapy is not merely confined to aromatherapy itself. Many other modalities come into play, and the available resources are vast and varied. I've provided a mere cross-section here. Further research will turn up a surprising number of possibilities. (Websites were accessed in 2002.)

Animal Aromatherapists

BELL, KRISTEN LEIGH – CANINE, FELINE
Email: Kbell@aromaleigh.com
Web: www.aromaleigh.com

BIRD, CATHERINE – EQUINE (AUSTRALIA)
Email: happyhorses@ hartingdale.com.au
Web: www.hartingdale. com.au/~happyhorses/

HARRINGTON, SASHA – CANINE
Email: PawsNaturally@ earthlink.net

INGRAHAM, CAROLINE – EQUINE, CANINE (UK)
Email: caroline@ingraham.co.uk
Web: www.ingraham.co.uk

MORAG, NAYANA – EQUINE, CANINE (UK)
Web: www.essentialanimals. bigstep.com
Tel: (44) 1823 680490

WEINHOLD, GINGER–CANINE
Tel: (727) 321-9459

HOLISTIC VETERINARIANS USING AROMATHERAPY

I have included in this list all of the holistic vets who list aromatherapy or essential oils in the AHVMA listing, as well as vets that I know of who are using essential oils or essential oil products with animals.

BECKER, KAREN, DVM /NATURAL
PET ANIMAL HOSPITAL
17236 South Harlem Avenue
Tinley Park, IL 60477
Tel: (708) 342-1111

BITTAN, MARC, DVM
11673 National Blvd.,
Los Angeles, CA 90064
Tel: (310) 231-4415

BLAKE, STEPHEN R, DVM
12436 Grainwood Way
San Diego, CA 92131
Tel: (858) 566-3588

BRANDT, NANCY, DVM
2591 Windmill Pwy #2
Henderson, NV 89014
Tel: (702) 617-3285

BUCHOFF, GERALD, DVM
NORTH BERGEN ANIMAL HOSPITAL
9018 Kennedy Blvd
North Bergen, NJ 07047
Tel: (201) 868-3753

DAVIS, LAUREL M, DVM
3 Webb Cove Rd
Asheville, NC 28804
Tel: (828) 254-2221

HEBBLER, TAMARA, DVM
P.O. Box 501604
San Diego, CA 92150
Tel: (858) 613-1282

JUDAY, CYNTHIA, DVM
INTEGRATIVE MEDICAL CENTER FOR
ANIMALS
3646 Birky Street
Sarasota, FL 34232
Tel: (941) 954-4781

LUCKENBILL, BRAD, DVM
THE PONY EXPRESS VETERINARY
HOSPITAL
893 Lower Bellbrook Road
Xenia, OH 45385
Tel: (937) 376-PONY

MACK, HEATHER K, DVM
78-359 US Highway 111
La Quinta, CA 92253
Tel: (760) 564-1154

MESSONIER, SHAWN, DVM / PAWS
AND CLAWS ANIMAL HOSPITAL
2145 W Park Blvd
Plano, TX 75075
Tel: (972) 867-8800

PARKS, GAEL, L.Ac. D(HOM)MED
WARNER CENTER PET CLINIC
20930 Victory Blvd.
Woodland Hills, CA 91367
Tel: (818) 710 8528

PRIEST, SANDRA, DVM
FOUR WINDS HOLISTIC ANIMAL
SERVICES
600 Bennington Circle
Knoxville, TN 37909
Tel: (865) 584-1588

ROPER, CROSBY, DVM
BAY PARK PET CLINIC
1102 Morena Blvd.
San Diego, CA 92110
Tel: (619) 276-1616

SMITH, S. ANNE, DVM
PROGRESSIVE HEALTH SYSTEMS
San Diego, CA 92117
Tel: (619) 225-2121

WEISETH, PAUL, DVM
ALL ANIMAL VETERINARY HOSPITAL
1811 W Hwy 101
Port Angeles, WA 98363
Tel: (800) 332-4551

WILLIAMS, MARIA L, DVM
Mobile Veterinarian
San Antonio, TX 78240
Tel: (210) 573-3178

WYNN, SUSAN, DVM
GREATER ATLANTA VETERINARY
MEDICAL GROUP
1080 N Cobb Pkwy
Marietta, GA 30062
Tel: (770) 424-6303

HOLISTIC GROOMERS

A holistic groomer is one who uses only all natural products for bathing and grooming. Aromatherapy, herbals, flower essences and even diet may be topics approached in the course of grooming.

THE HANDSOME HOUND – CELESTE
O'MALLEY
1868 Harwood Hill, Bennington, VT
Tel: (802) 442-2333

PRIMPED & POWDERED PET
BOUTIQUE – SUSAN GREGORY
155 State Street, Newburyport, MA
Tel: (978) 499-7712

KOOL DOG KAFE – KERRY KING
1666 S. Pacific Coast Highway,
Redondo Beach, CA
Tel: (310) 944-3232

TWO DOGS AND A GOAT –
CHARLOTTE REED
326 East 34th Street, New York NY
Tel: (212) 631-1157

HOLISTIC HEALTH CONSULTANTS

4 PAWS NATURALLY – SASHA
HARRINGTON
Email: PawsNaturally@earthlink.net
Holistic animal health/nutritional consultant

HOLISTICARE – HEATHER COLBY
5497 Turtle Station, Westerville
OH 43081
Tel: (614) 818-3629
Complimentary care for small animals and horses

LEFEBVRE , BONNIE
Web: www.geocities.com/
            pet_emporium/pet.html
*Certified herbologist, Herbal Healer
Academy*

MOORE, DEBRA, NATUROPATHIC
DOCTOR
Email: RevHerbDoc@
            worldnet.att.net
Tel: (352) 542-7597

NATURAL ANIMAL – BONNIE NOLTE
Tel: (607) 746-9300
*Comprehensive canine and feline
nutritional programs and consultations.*

NO BONES ABOUT IT! PETCARE –
KIMBERLY FISCHER
91 Ballentine Drive
North Haledon, NJ 07508
Tel: (973) 595-1451

PURELY PETS – DARLEEN RUDNICK
Email: darleen@purelypets.com
*Natural holistic care for canines, felines
and other pets*

WULFF-TILFORD, MARY
Email: animals@bitterroot.net
*DiHom (Diploma in Veterinary
Homeopathy), professional herbalist,
American Herbalist's Guild, holistic
animal health care consultant*

TRAINING

APRIL FROST – DOG TRAINING, REIKI
AND AROMATHERAPY
270 Maple Avenue,
Walden VT, 05873
Tel: (802) 563-3381

POSITIVE K9 – MELISSA COCOLA
Rochester, NY
Tel: (585) 727-3647

ENERGY HEALING, FLOWER ESSENCES AND ANIMAL COMMUNICATION

ANAFLORA FLOWER ESSENCES FOR
ANIMALS
Web: www.anaflora.com
Tel: (530) 926-6424

PAWS & REFLECT – BETTY LEWIS
(RVT, DR.A.N.)
Tel: (603) 673-DANE
Animal communication

EARTH CREATIONS – CHERI DYE AND
JANET YOUNG
Email: cdobes985@msn.com
Tel: (630) 378-0462 (Cheri)

Natural Diets

The following is a list of different "types" of holistic canine diets. They are often referred to by the last name of their creator, for instance, "the Pitcairn diet".

- Richard Pitcairn
- Ian Billinghurst
- Kimberly Schultze
- B.A.R.F- Bones and Raw Food

High Quality Commercial Foods and Prepared Diets

Many people find that feeding a natural or home-cooked diet is not possible. When this is the case, feeding the highest quality food possible is the best you can do for your dog's health.

Animal Food Services
Web: www.naturalpetfood.com
Tel: 800-743-0322

Bil Jac
Web: www.biljac.com
Tel: 800-321-1002

California Natural
Web: www.naturapet.com
Tel: 800-532-7261

Canidae
Web: www.canidae.com
Tel: 800-398-1600
        (909) 599-5190

Feed This!
Web: www.feedthis.com
Tel: (707) 887-1122

Flint River Ranch
Web: www.frr.com
Tel: 888-344-4118

Holesome Natural K9 & K9 Kravings
Web: www.holesome.com/naturalk9/
Tel: (604) 826-6242

Innova
Web: www.naturapet.com
Tel: (800) 532-7261

K9 Kitchen, Inc.
Web: www.maxsnacks.com
Tel: 877-259-1825

mORIGINS
Tel: (216) 228-3656

Raw, Naturally!
Calgary, Alberta, Canada
Tel: (403) 285-3745

Solid Gold
Web: www.solidgoldhealth.com
Tel: 800-364 4863

Steve's Real Food
Web: www.stevesrealfood.com
Tel: 888-526-1900
        (541) 683-9950

Wysong
Web: www.wysong.net
Tel: (989) 631-0009

APPENDIX 3

RECOMMENDED READING

AROMATHERAPY

375 Essential Oils and Hydrosols, by Jeanne Rose , Frog Ltd.

Advanced Aromatherapy: The Science of Essential Oil Therapy, by Kurt Schnaubelt, Healing Arts Press

Aromatherapy for Healing the Spirit:Restoring Emotional and Mental Balance with Essential Oils, by Gabriel Mojay, Healing Arts Press

Aromatherapy for Horses, by Caroline Ingraham, Kenilworth Press

Aromatherapy Practitioner Manual, by Sylla Sheppard Hangar, Atlantic Institute of Aromatherapy (self published)

Aromatherapy Workbook, by Marcel Lavabre, Healing Arts Press

Aromatherapy Workbook: Understanding Essential Oils from Plant to Bottle by Shirley Price, Thorsons Publishers

Complete Guide to Aromatherapy, by Salvatore Battaglia

Essential Oil Safety: A Guide for Healthcare Professionals, by Robert Tisserand , Churchill Livingstone Publishers

Gattefossé's Aromatherapy, by Rene-Maurice Gattefossé, C.W. Daniel Company

Horse Scents: Making Sense of Your Horse Using Aromatherapy, by Catherine Bird, The Lyons Press

Hydrosols: The Next Aromatherapy, by Suzanne Catty, Healing Arts Press

The Illustrated Encyclopedia of Essential Oils, by Julia Lawless, Element Books

Medical Aromatherapy, by Kurt Schnaubelt, Frog Ltd.

The Practice of Aromatherapy: A Classic Compendium of Plant Medicines and Their Healing Properties, by Jean Valnet and Robert Tisserand, Inner Traditions Intl. Ltd.

The World of Aromatherapy: An Anthology of Aromatic History, Ideas, Concepts and Case Histories, by Jeanne Rose, et al., Frog Ltd.

Veterinary Aromatherapy, by Nelly Grosjean, C.W. Daniel Company

HOLISTIC PET CARE

All You Ever Wanted to Know about Herbs for Pets, by Mary Wulff-Tilford and Gregory Tilford , Bow Tie Press

Are You Poisoning Your Pets?: A Guidebook to How Our Lifestyles Affect the Health of Our Pets, by Nina Anderson and Howard Peiper

A Healthy Horse the Natural Way: The Horse Owner's Guide to Using Herbs, Massage, Homeopathy, and Other Natural Therapies, by Catherine Bird, The Lyons Press

Cat Care, Naturally: Celeste Yarnall's Complete Guide to Holistic Health Care for Cats, by Celeste Yarnall, Charles E Tuttle Publishers

Complementary and Alternative Veterinary Medicine: Principles and Practice, by Allen M. Schoen (Ed.) and Susan G. Wynn (Ed.), Mosby-Year Book

The Complete Herbal Handbook for the Dog and Cat, by Juliette De Bairacli Levy, Faber & Faber Publishers

Dr. Pitcairn's Complete Guide to Natural Health for Dogs and Cats, by Richard H. Pitcairn DVM, PhD and Susanna Hubble Pitcairn, Rodale Press

Encyclopedia of Natural Pet Care, by C.J. Puotinen, Keats Publishing

Food Pets Die For: Shocking Facts About Pet Food, by Ann Martin and Michael W. Fox, Newsage Press

Give Your Dog a Bone, by Ian Billinghurst

Holistic Guide for a Healthy Dog, by Wendy Volhard and Kerry L. Brown, Hungry Minds Inc.

Natural Dog Care: A Complete Guide to Holistic Health Care for Dogs, by Celeste Yarnall, Book Sales Publishers

Natural Healing for Dogs and Cats A–Z, by Cheryl Schwartz, DVM, Hay
House Publishing

Natural Immunity – Why You Should Not Vaccinate, by Pat McKay, Oscar
Publications

Natural Nutrition for Dogs and Cats: The Ultimate Pet Diet, by Kymythy
Schultze, Hay House Publishing

Natural Remedies for Dogs and Cats, by C.J. Puotinen, McGraw Hill

FLOWER AND GEMSTONE ESSENCES

Bach Flower Remedies for Animals, by Helen Graham and Gregory Vlamis,
Findhorn Press

Bach Flower Remedies for Animals, by Stefan Ball and Judy Howard, CW
Daniel Company

*The Bach Flower Remedies: Including Heal Thyself, the Twelve Healers, Bach
Remedies Repertory,* by Edward Bach, et al., McGraw Hill

Flower Essences and Vibrational Healing, by Gurudas, Cassandra Press

Gem Elixirs and Vibrational Healing, by Gurudas, Cassandra Press

Healing with Flower and Gemstone Essences, by Diane Stein, The Crossing
Press

NATURAL INGREDIENTS/ENVIRONMENTAL TOXINS

*Home Safe Home: Protecting Yourself and Your Family from Everyday Toxins
and Harmful Household Products in the Home,* by Debra Dadd-Redalia,
JP Tarcher

*Living Healthy in a Toxic World: Simple Steps to Protect You and Your Family
from Everyday Chemicals, Poisons, and Pollution,* by David Steinman et
al, Perigee Publishers

*The Safe Shopper's Bible: A Consumer's Guide to Nontoxic Household
Products, Cosmetics and Food,* by David Steinman, MacMillan

END NOTES

1   Weil, Dr. Andrew. 2001. Balanced Living: Health Conditions: Cancer. www.drweil.com

2   Walker, Martin J. 2001. Home Sickness. *The Ecologist Magazine* (April 22).

3   Pottenger, Francis M., Jr. 1983. *Pottenger's Cats: A Study in Nutrition*. La Mesa, California: Price-Pottenger Nutrition Foundation.

4   *Pet Age Magazine*. 2001. (July).

5   Flanigan, Robin L. 2000. Treatment for dogs nothing to sniff at: Aromatherapy for things that plague pooches is a local company's specialty. *Rochester Democrat & Chronicle* (August 30).

6   Gattefossé, Rene Maurice. 1993. *Gattefossé's Aromatherapy*. Saffron Walden, UK: C.W. Daniel Company Limited.

7   Grosjean, Nelly, 1994. *Veterinary Aromatherapy*. Saffron Walden, UK: C.W. Daniel Company Limited.

8   Gattefossé, Rene Maurice. 1993. *Gattefossé's Aromatherapy*. Saffron Walden, UK: C.W. Daniel Company Limited.

9   Klein, Steven B. and Robert R. Mowrer. 1989. *Contemporary Learning Theories: Pavlovian Conditioning and the Status of Traditional Learning Theory*. Lawrence Erlbaum Associates.

10   Schnaubelt, Kurt. 1998. *Medical Aromatherapy: Healing with Essential Oils*. Berkeley, CA: Frog Ltd.

11   Ibid. 161.

12   Ibid. 163.

13   Davis, Patricia. 1991. *Subtle Aromatherapy*. Saffron Walden, UK: C.W. Daniel Company Limited.

14   Leigh, Ixchel Susan and Sharon Starr Walker. 1999. Vibrational Aromatherapy: Pathways for Transformational Healing. *Aromatic Thymes Magazine* 17 (Spring).

15   Lavabre, Marcel. 1990. *Aromatherapy Workbook*. Rochester, VT: Healing Arts Press.

16   Süskind, Patrick. 1986. *Perfume: A Story of a Murderer*. New York: Alfred A. Knopf.

17   Catty, Suzanne. 2001. *Hydrosols: The Next Aromatherapy*. Rochester, VT: Healing Arts Press.

18   Pappas, Dr. Robert S., unpublished personal communication to the author.

19   Catty, Suzanne. 2001. *Hydrosols: The Next Aromatherapy*. Rochester, VT: Healing Arts Press.

20 Lawless, Julia. 1995. *The Illustrated Encyclopedia of Essential Oils*. Rockport, MA: Element Books.

21 Schnaubelt, Kurt. 1998. *Advanced Aromatherapy: The Science of Essential Oil Therapy*. Rochester, VT: Healing Arts Press.

22 Ibid.

23 Catty, Suzanne. 2001. *Hydrosols: The Next Aromatherapy*. Rochester, VT: Healing Arts Press.

24 Wynn, Susan G., DVM. 1997. Pet Metabolism Dictates Dosage: Natural Treatments for Animals Should Reflect Bioindividuality. *Nutrition Science News*. www.nutritionscience.com

25 Grosjean, Nelly, 1994. *Veterinary Aromatherapy*. Saffron Walden, UK: C.W. Daniel Company Limited.

26 Schultze, Kymythy. 1998. *Natural Nutrition for Dogs and Cats: The Ultimate Pet Diet*. Carlsbad, CA: Hay House Publishers.

27 Villar, David, DVM, et al. 1994. Toxicity of Melaleuca Oil and Related Essential Oils Applied Topically to Dogs and Cats. *Veterinary and Human Toxicology* 36 (April).

28 Fooshe, S.K. 1991. The Cat as a Medical Species. In *Consultations in Feline Internal Medicine 1: 6–7, edited by J. August*. Philadelphia, PA: W.B. Sanders.

29 Khan, Safdar, DVM. Interview. The Lavender Cat, www.thelavendercat.com

30 Wynn, Susan G., DVM. 1997. Pet Metabolism Dictates Dosage: Natural Treatments for Animals Should Reflect Bioindividuality. *Nutrition Science News*. www.nutritionsciencenews.com

31 Sakes, Peter S. DVM. Making A Safe Home For Your Bird, DuPont Teflon Website: http://www.dupont.com/teflon/newsroom/bird.html

32 Grosjean, Nelly. 1999. Essential Oil for Veterinary Medicine. *Scentsitivity: The Quarterly Journal for the Natural Association of Holistic Aromatherapy*. Vol 9, Number 4. pp10–11.

33 Catty, Suzanne. 2001. *Hydrosols: The Next Aromatherapy*. Rochester, VT: Healing Arts Press.

34 Ibid

35 Bird, Catherine. 2000. Calming Aromatherapy for Fear and Anxiety. *Natural Horse Magazine 2(4)*.

36 Bird, Catherine. 2000. Scented Horses. *Natural Horse Magazine 2(2)*.

37 Ibid

38 Ingraham, Caroline. Aromatherapy/Kinesiology for People and Animals http://www.ingraham.co.uk

39 Hilton Herbs Website. http://www.hiltonherbs.com

40 George, Susan. Naturally Website. Equine Therapeutic Treatments with Pure Plant Oils. http://www.susangeorgenaturally.com

FINDHORN PRESS

ISBN 978-1-84409-099-0

ISBN 978-1-84409-112-6

ISBN 978-1-899171-72-9

ISBN 978-1-84409-125-6

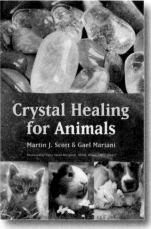

ISBN 978-1-899171-24-8

FINDHORN PRESS

Books, Card Sets,
CDs & DVDs
that inspire and uplift

For a complete catalogue,
please contact:

Findhorn Press Ltd
305a The Park, Findhorn
Forres IV36 3TE
Scotland, UK

Telephone +44-(0)1309-690582
Fax +44-(0)1309-690036
eMail info@findhornpress.com

or consult our catalogue online
(with secure order facility) on
www.findhornpress.com

green press
INITIATIVE

Findhorn Press is committed to preserving ancient forests and natural resources. We elected to print this title on 30% post consumer recycled paper, processed chlorine free. As a result, for this printing, we have saved:

11 Trees (40' tall and 6-8" diameter)
5 Million BTUs of Total Energy
1,120 Pounds of Greenhouse Gases
5,054 Gallons of Wastewater
321 Pounds of Solid Waste

Findhorn Press made this paper choice because our printer, Thomson-Shore, Inc., is a member of Green Press Initiative, a nonprofit program dedicated to supporting authors, publishers, and suppliers in their efforts to reduce their use of fiber obtained from endangered forests.

For more information, visit www.greenpressinitiative.org

Environmental impact estimates were made using the Environmental Defense Paper Calculator. For more information visit: www.papercalculator.org.

FSC
www.fsc.org

MIX
Paper from
responsible sources
FSC® C013483